Japan-ness in Architecture

Japan-ness in Architecture

Arata Isozaki

translated by Sabu Kohso

edited by David B. Stewart

foreword by Toshiko Mori

The MIT Press   Cambridge, Massachusetts   London, England

First MIT Press paperback edition, 2011
© 2006 Massachusetts Institute of Technology

The publisher would like to thank Peter Eisenman, the Institute for Architecture and
Urban Studies, and the former editors of Oppositions Books for their early sponsorship of this book. An earlier version of this text was originally to have appeared as
the fifth book in the Oppositions Books series under the title *The Ruin of Styles:
Selected Writings of Arata Isozaki 1960–1985*.

This book was set in Bembo and Din on 3B2 by Asco Typesetters, Hong Kong, and
was printed and bound in the United States of America.

Library of Congress Cataloging-in-Publication Data

Isozaki, Arata.
Japan-ness in architecture / Arata Isozaki ; translated by Sabu Kohso ; edited by
David B. Stewart
    p.   cm.
Includes index.
"An earlier version of this text was originally to have appeared as the fifth book in
the Oppositions books series under the title: The ruin of styles : selected writings
of Arata Isozaki 1960–1985" — CIP galley.
ISBN-13: 978-0-262-09038-4 (hc.: alk. paper)–978-0-262-51605-1 (pb.: alk. paper)
1. Architecture—Japan. 2. Architecture—Philosophy. I. Stewart, David B. II. Title.
NA1550.I78   2006
720.952—dc22   2006044999

Contents

Unique in Japan, Arata Isozaki is one of a handful of architects anywhere in the world able to develop rigorous architectural theses while engaging in lively comparative discourse on Eastern and Western culture and history. His inquiry is precise, and his broad knowledge of the history of Western architecture offers an enriching perspective for rereading Japanese architectural history. Always in his theoretical writing, as here, he lays a rational and objective basis for far-ranging speculation.

It has taken Isozaki twenty years to complete these essays, during which time he has erected buildings all over the world. His writing project was begun in the early 1980s—at the height of postmodernism—and it has been carried through into the new millennium; architectural tenets, styles, and programs are far different from what they were when he started. Yet these texts boast a timelessness beyond the quotidian struggle of architectural production because, transcending mere theory, they weave a discourse about issues essential to architecture.

Isozaki's field of reference is vast, and what he has to say belies the reductive one-liners that so often claim to represent Japanese cultural style. His essays compel us to view things as more complicated, even confused; his references are not all pleasing, and many are controversial. At the end of the day, Isozaki demolishes our stereotypes by the elaboration and force of his argument, calling into question all unexamined assumptions about "Japan-ness." While retaining buildings as artifacts, Isozaki shrewdly refuses to look only at their physicality—to view them solely as *faits accomplis* of an architectural narrative. Instead he engages us by highlighting the events, personalities, and cultural influences each building embodies. In other words, he approaches each built work as a graph of human ambitions and desire—a rich reflection of rough-and-tumble dealings yielding some of our greatest masterpieces in the most uncertain of times, recalling the political maneuvering of Japanese architects and their sheer will to build.

As a practicing architect, Isozaki is aware of the intense drama that inhabits every building commission. Each project is potentially worthy of an epic; each building might well serve as the protagonist in a novel. His analysis may be seen as a rejoinder to Victor Hugo's famous *mot* "Ceci tuera cela" (The book will kill the cathedral), with reference to the likelihood of written texts overtaking architecture. For Isozaki, buildings are indeed texts that live within the cultural milieu of each era; in leaving myriad questions unanswered, they enable a continuous dialogue between civilization and society. Yet the present book in some ways affirms Hugo: such writing may well last longer even than some of Isozaki's own buildings (all the more so given the rapid rate of construction turnover in Japan). Whatever the case, this volume is certain of an enduring presence among writings on the history and theory of architecture.

It is essential to note that the discipline of architecture (and the profession of architect) scarcely existed at all in Japan until the modern period. Among postwar architects in Japan, Arata Isozaki has been vigorous in positing an activist role for architects while educating the public and nudging the fledgling profession to come to terms with its new leadership position. Thanks in no small measure to such advocacy on his part, architects in Japan have gained recognition as public intellectuals—authoritative voices in contemporary discourse bearing on culture and its social role.

Toshiko Mori

The quartet of essays assembled in this book addresses four separate landmark events in Japanese architectural history; these occurred in the seventh, twelfth, seventeenth, and mid-twentieth centuries. Normally architectural history begins with descriptions and analyses of the buildings themselves. Here, the essays on Ise Shrine (constructed in the late seventh century) and Katsura Imperial Villa (of the early seventeenth century) were originally conceived and written as interpretations of those buildings, so they involve a good deal of objective description. Yet I hope the reader will sense in each essay my conviction that architectural discourse demands that we view buildings as *events* and not simply as inert objects. In a sense this might be equivalent to grasping the buildings as textual spaces. By not only considering the objectness of buildings but also discussing the texts written about them, thus shifting the stance to a metalevel, I believe we can reconstruct the problematic that each building originally internalized.

I shall refer to the three earlier events by nicknames: "Ise," "Chōgen," and "Katsura," corresponding respectively to Ise Jingū, the Southern Gatehouse of Tōdai-ji (directed by the monk Chōgen), and the Katsura Imperial Detached Villa. By this I seek to stress the evolution of each building as a singular event. Buildings involve a space that we can experience directly, but each is also connected to an external context, including the sociohistorical environment. This is why they can be treated as "textual" spaces, capable of introducing plural interpretations vis-à-vis the architectural object. Within such an expanse one signals the domain in which an architectural discourse is engendered and pursued.

My advocacy of buildings as textual space developed as I wrote the earliest essay, "Katsura and Its Space of Ambiguity" in 1983.

Katsura as it exists today consists of pavilions scattered throughout its stroll-style garden. Even aerial photographs cannot give a complete view. The only way to grasp the totality is to experience it by wandering through the building and grounds. One of the most characteristic features of Japanese stroll gardens (which I shall refer to as "touring gardens") is that we experience the garden as an assemblage of fragmentary images received at various designated spots—our views being altered time and again. What is more, each of these fragments is dogged, so to speak, by at least one anecdote or conceit, usually taken from a Chinese or Japanese literary classic (such as *The Tale of Genji*). Triggered by these, multiple interpretations have been created around the architectural ensemble. As a continuation of this practice, I thought of focusing on interpretations by modern architects and problematizing the resultant textual space. The primary moment in this approach was the photography of Katsura by Yasuhiro Ishimoto that was originally published with my essay.[1] These pictures grasp Katsura via a Mondrianesque composition, as it were, and *not* vice versa: perceiving Mondrian-like space in Katsura. In such photographs we view Katsura from our modern experience with Mondrian's composition considered as a template or prototype. Superimposing a hermeneutic reading of the architecture, I sought to read Katsura as a textual space—where visual and verbal language crisscrossed and overlapped.

"Ise—A Mimicry [or Reenactment] of Origin" was written by me in 1995, also as a text to accompany Ishimoto's photographs. Ishimoto made his photos on the occasion of Ise's sixty-third rebuilding/relocation, when photography was allowed only during the few days before the ritual resiting of the precincts was to take place. Thinking of Ise's "architecture" in the context of this unique system of renewing the precincts, called *shikinen-zōkan*, it seemed improper to define it by way of the Western concept of an everlasting materiality. It is thus questionable whether we can call Ise's precinct structures "architecture." On the one hand, we can scarcely escape from the modernist stance that views the architecture of Katsura via the notion of a Mondrianesque grid composition. On the other, we must remove our eyeglasses fitted with the Western concept of "architecture" in order to grasp Ise. Therefore, I was determined to regard the precincts of Ise Shrine as a temporary construction embodying the ritual that takes place every twenty years. In other words, even as undeniable material structures, all elements are also a direct part of this ritualistic event.

It is said that the ritual of rebuilding/relocation reiterates the primary installation of the sacred within the shrine, which includes the entire undertaking—from the invocations to the props to the whole ritualistic procedure. The climax unfolds in darkness and total secrecy. Everything is veiled in this secret ceremony. Buildings such as those of the main precinct and the treasure houses are regularly exposed to the light of day for twenty years, but they are nonetheless surrounded by four layers of hedge, so that no one can see inside. Here the very gesture of hiding creates the mystery. Why has Ise ritual been preserved as a secret ceremony? What can be said with certainty is only that it is a repetition of the identical. It seems to me that there is a certain isomorphism to be found in the Japanese traditional performing arts where mimicry (*modoki*) plays a central role. Ise's repetition, or reenactment, seems a form of this mimicry.

Here one encounters a fundamental question vis-à-vis the notion of *origin* itself—the compulsion to search for origins that has cropped up in every domain of modern sensibility. This obsession of the modern mind has however only led to logical aporias, such as speculations about black holes or the big bang and other theories of universal origin. In the late twentieth century, for instance, people began to talk about Ise freely, in contrast to an earlier time when every subject related even obliquely to the emperor was taboo; most of the essays about the great shrine written since have been queries about origin. But from its earliest beginnings, Ise's origin has never been present, having disappeared forever into the darkness of ancient times. No matter how hard one looks for evidence and speculates on an answer, one can never reach a definite conclusion. As with black holes or the big bang, what awaits us is nothing less than a logical aporia. All in all, the search for origins was born of existential anxiety, nothing more or less than an attempt to ease the pain of modernity. There is thus no answer to the query of Ise's origin. Rather, the very system that reenacts the primary ritual is meant to respond: do not ask about what was before! What was there was simply this: a "beginning" (*not* the origin) of this ritual of rebuilding/relocation. At stake here is a pure gesture of veiling whose purpose is merely to allude to the idea that there *was* something before. Therefore my stance has been to question the *beginning*, albeit countenancing the necessity of alluding to the existence of the absent *origin*.

After publishing the Ise essay in Japan, I heard a conjecture about the Talmud from Israeli friends, namely that page one of the sacred text had been missing since ancient times, and that this fact had itself become a bone of contention. I have been unable to verify this discussion. But what interests me is that on the second page, there are various notes added by rabbis about the presumed contents of the absent first page. Here again, that void of the origin is alluded to. And all that is ascertainable is only that nothing can be known with certainty.

According to my interpretation, the institution of Ise's rebuilding/relocation serves to unknot the riddle concerning origin. It tells us not to query origin, but instead simply to repeat the beginning; and this gesture presents a notion of construction totally at odds with the Western one that relies on an enduring materiality—the only constructive approach corresponding to (and not fighting against) time irreversible.

Both Ise and Katsura were taken up as problematic themes when Bruno Taut first visited Japan, and praised both, in 1933. Fifty years ago when I sought to become a modern architect, it was a matter of course that I studied these two works as a primer. But there was yet another structure that I could scarcely ignore. That was the Great South Gate at Tōdai-ji in Nara. The design, if I do say so, is so rough and ready that it was nearly a failure architecturally. But it still stands—reckless in its limitless and overwhelming power. It has an unusual force that cannot be found anywhere else in the array of Japanese traditional structures. Years later, having visited outstanding buildings around the world, I concede that my faith in the constructive genius of the Great South Gate has only been strengthened.

In the community of architectural and historical scholarship, this building is commonly defined as an example of a Chinese style called *daibutsu-yō*, yet slightly inflected with Japanese taste (*wayō*). This eclectic style evolved in response to the architectonic of the Sung dynasty as the priest Chōgen directed the project of reconstructing the Big Buddha Pavilion (Daibutsu-den) of Tōdai-ji. Thus it came to be called the *daibutsu-yō*. The same style had once been called the *tenjiku-yō*, meaning Indian style. Why so? Perhaps the quite unfamiliar, and so to say spooky, features of the building were associated with a land no one in Japan had seen. There is also a record saying that the master of the original building of Tōdai-ji in the eighth century had been a priest from India. Relying on the achievements of modern architectural history, an architectural scholar, Hirotarō Ōta, reiterates that the style of Tōdai-ji's architecture should indeed be called *daibutsu-yō*, not *tenjiku-yō*, because no such style was known in India. To me this position—which might well be objective and correct—is nonetheless a bit tasteless; I prefer *tenjiku-yō*, for the very reason that the attribution to this imaginary land was owing to the unprecedented image of constructive strength. I believe that the discovery of such structural power is essential to architecture, so it happened that the Great South Gate of Tōdai-ji was the initial work of architecture that I encountered.

In the twelfth century most components of the Tōdai-ji complex were burned down owing to civil disturbances and war at that time. The priest named Chōgen was entrusted with directing the temple's reconstruction. Years after this achievement, however, in the sixteenth century, everything burned down again except for the Great South Gate. Since then, taking this sole remnant as a clue, numerous architects have been enticed to reconstruct the whole Tōdai-ji complex in imaginary fashion. All in all, what has remained clear is that the twelfth century was a time of war: the transitional moment in which power shifted from the aristocracy to the *samurai* class. In this convulsion of nature one could not distinguish friend from foe, nor could one know what would happen next. Yet in such a climate Chōgen realized most of his reconstruction—an incredible achievement.

Sympathetic to Chōgen's innumerable hardships, all have admired his achievement. Yet I am left with one crucial question: what was it in him that motivated this project and empowered its completion? There was one aspect of it that always made me wonder. In the history of Western architecture, pure geometric forms inevitably appear in times of revolutionary change, but they are usually considered anomalous and their radicalism dismissed. Chōgen personifies a rare example of this phenomenon in Japan. Moreover, his project took on an unprecedented scale, since it was "unreal" in all aspects—politically, economically, technically, and aesthetically. I came to believe that his unheard-of *Einbildungs-kraft* (imaginative power) itself drove the project, overcoming all obstacles. In his work the uncanny constructive power is grounded in this incomparable strength of imagination. It was an event peculiar to the revolutionary moment.

For that matter, both Ise and Katsura were likewise constructed amidst turmoil, yet their construction was miraculously achieved though much disturbed by external conditions. Thus we should never treat architecture as mere "object" but rather as event. Only by so doing can the overwhelming power that emanates from architectural objects be grasped.

The times in which these ancient and feudal-period works of Japanese architecture appeared—the late seventh century, the late twelfth century, and the early seventeenth century—had something in common. After civil wars came to an end, new cultural paradigms were established. While absorbing the external pressures that had led to civil war in the first place, such paradigms created a break with the previous age. Though each work exhibits a different formation, one may detect an intentionality common to all. Ise Shrine afforded an antidote to the standard of temple architecture that had recently been imported from the Asian continent. The reconstructed Tōdai-ji took the sturdy architectonic of Sung-style temple architecture as its model but exceeded it in its constructivist tendencies. Katsura Imperial Villa exerted pressure on the orthodox *shoin* style to spawn a new species, a kind of chimera. Though each approach to tradition is different, all these metamorphoses aimed equally at producing something that could be called Japanese.

The central problematic of my book takes form as a hypothesis, namely that the epitome of the creation of this something Japanese is encountered in the twentieth century—with the advent of certain architects who contrived to deal with the external pressures of modern architecture, responding with something unique. My essay "Japan-ness in Architecture" tackles their struggles; it is placed first in the book, but was written last. My aim was to trace their formative stance toward Japan-ness, up to and including my own personal involvement from the late 1960s.[2] The essay is a sort of metacritique of what I had written about Ise, Chōgen, and Katsura and their discursive grounds. It attempted to trace the process through which Japan-ness itself was constructed as a discourse in Japanese modernity.

It has been my contention that the obsessive approaches toward the problematic of Japan-ness are due in the final analysis to

Japan's mentality as an island nation. Its borderline vanishes into the ocean—or is the ocean itself. When means of transport were less advanced, access to and from Japan was only by sea. So when the force of external cultures became too great, it was easy for the Japanese to ward off this pressure by closing the country's ports. What then took place inside was a sophistication and purification of Japan-ness that I dare call Japanesquization. It mostly resulted in restraining, draining off, and removing the energy conceived in each earlier transformative moment—a stylization today considered abroad as emblematic of the Japanese aesthetic. But that aesthetic is far from the embryonic Japan-ness born in such critical moments of an earlier past as are here described.

In Japan since the turn of the present century, it has become harder to create architecture with any real constructive force. Japan has shrunk and once more closed its ports, this time owing to recession. The absence of any external cultural pressure that might provoke a certain critical awareness makes the situation more extreme. Rather today it would seem that the shape of the entire world makes the notion of a borderline that is vanishing into the ocean obsolete, makes it impossible even to close the ports, and divides not only Japan but also the whole world into innumerable archipelagos. If this is indeed the case, the mechanism that drives Japanesquization will be erased, so that even any problematization of Japan-ness will become impossible. I have long sensed this change to be imminent. So it was vital to detect what had entrapped us inside our island nation and bound us to the fictive notions of Japan, Japanese, and Japan-ness, as I have tried to do.

I would like to thank Sabu Kohso who has translated the book into English. The work provides an ideal opportunity: since I believe the gaze of the other to be the primary instance for creating Japan-ness, this book will return that gaze to its source. And, finally, sincere appreciation goes to Etsuko Nomura, Lecturer at the Advanced Research Institute for Science and Engineering at Waseda University in Tokyo, who elaborated her research concerns far beyond my original queries.

Arata Isozaki

Arata Isozaki may be one of the few architects today seriously aware of the destiny of architecture and its forms. He knows that he is a part of the events surrounding his architecture, rather than its author in a romanticist sense; part, in other words, of that wider sociohistorical context where his forms are born, rather than someone who creates forms that engender society and history. *Japan-ness in Architecture* could only have been written thanks to such a critical consciousness. Thus the reader is not simply conducted through Isozaki's theory of architectural form, but is made to scrutinize its background and context—Japan's history and its modernity. Reflecting the nature of this detour, the book is various things: a historical survey, a theoretical-critical analysis and reflection upon Japanese architecture and culture at large, and above all an auto-critical account of the architect Arata Isozaki's own personal trajectory. It is not a work of architectural history in any usual sense, rather Isozaki's own contextual vision is so wide-ranging as to constitute an architectural history of Japan.

The initial approach is by way of a series of hypotheses bearing the prefix "Japan"—Japanese, Japanesque, Japonica, *japonaiserie*—all brought to bear upon Japan-ness in architecture. This Japan-ness, for Isozaki, has nothing of essentialism, however. It comprises all the heterogeneous protagonists of Japanese modernity—a number of foreign names even mix in among the native Japanese. Together their gazes charged with desire crisscross and produce a "Japanese architecture," past as well as present. Japanness is revealed to be nothing less than a problematic configuration constructed from, and owing everything to, a particular geopolitical situation.

Japan was named at the moment the dispersed islands of our archipelago were conceived as an enclosed insular sphere, that is, when Japan emerged as polity. Part I describes the process through which this awareness of islandness arose and then inversely receded, replaced by an impetus toward expansion or incipient globalization. The critical process seems to recur in waves: the era of the Greater East Asia Co-prosperity Sphere in the 1940s or that of the more recent neoliberal globalization in the present century.

The concept *architecture* was first introduced to modern Japan from without, and the Japanese themselves came to recognize that what they had built could rightfully be so called. Therefore, Isozaki must speak here about "Japanese architecture" as unequivocally tied to the discursive formation of modernity. Each problematic of incipient modernity—including those concerning our quintessential "classical" architecture—Ise Shrine, Tōdai-ji, and Katsura Villa—was nurtured. This is the *beginning*, including the ideological production of "tradition" or "origin" itself. Thus Isozaki first introduces the modernist moment—the 1920s and 1930s—and then reviews architectural/cultural events up until the late 1990s.

The space/time configuration of modernity is considered almost as a matrix, as if, by magnifying parts of it, all other space/times would unfold before our eyes. There is no linear beginning or ending, since space and time intertwine to form an expanding and contracting sphere receding in time.

Ise Shrine is bravely analyzed in part II through its original connection with the *tennō* system of Japan's imperial succession. Both posit themselves as primordial origin of Japan's nationhood. Isozaki meticulously traces how such fabrications of origin were constructed: Ise's periodic reconstruction, *shikinen-zōkan*, and the narratives of national mythology, *Kojiki*, are treated as unwitting twins. What is at stake is the mechanism of national culture and language, versus external pressures.

Tōdai-ji in Nara, dealt with in part III, burned to the ground three times over the centuries, and the twelfth-century version designed and built by the monk Chōgen was reputedly gargantuan. Here Isozaki imagines how such a will to construct or "will to form" might have first appeared. He compares Chōgen's situation to Japan's experience after World War II and draws a parallel with his own predicament as a young man at the time of this reconstruction from zero. Not only in the West but also in Japan, revolutionary moments conjure up a radical constructivism and the model/metaphor of primary forms—one of the most fundamental issues for Isozaki.

The first half of the Katsura Villa essay (part IV) was written in the early 1980s. Readers may spot diverse hints of a postmodern aesthetic in the vision of Katsura as a textile of quotation from various decorative modes and especially from early literary sources, such as *The Tale of Genji*. The crux, however, is a praxis drawn from the sophisticated manner of laying out tea utensils, which Isozaki infers to be a gesture of facing contradiction and living out conflicts in a space unapologetically without dialectical synthesis. The juxtaposition of contradictions in Katsura is largely posited as a reflection of the social contradictions of the seventeenth century. Thus Isozaki's image of postmodernity is reoriented from sheer play back to a measure of "living the critical moment."

In these analyses, Isozaki treats architectural form in all of its spatiotemporal complexity. This multiplicity not only surpasses the realization of this or that architect/author's design, but is also in constant becoming, in contradistinction to our supposed being within an eternal present. That is to say, in multiple dimensions, the forms of architecture are inextricably connected to the problematic zone of our social metabolism as it expands and contracts.

In this manner, *Japan-ness in Architecture* entails significant differences from Western architecture: remaining duly within the framework of shared metaphors/models, all in presenting an exotic geopolitical arena where cumbersome, perhaps unintelligible, proper names fight, negotiate, and at times cooperate. It goes without saying that proper names themselves resist the translator's manipulation or the annexation of metaphors/models. May the reader pardon, or may she enjoy, the excess of transcribed exotic sounds that thunder like protagonists throughout this book.

The following are technical points:

1. When I began to translate the essays by Arata Isozaki to be published as a book by the MIT Press, they had not yet been brought together as a book in Japanese. I proceeded with my own translation in New York, while Shinchōsha Press prepared the Japanese version in Tokyo. Isozaki had hoped to publish both books at the same time. In the end, the Japanese version appeared first, but that

is not to say that the Japanese version is "original" to the English version.

I met a number of times with Isozaki to discuss details of the English version in terms of editorial revision necessary to the process of translation. In consequence, significant differences between the Japanese and English versions of the text are to be found. Most notably, the order of the essays is different: the English version starts with the section on modernity to the present and then follows a historical order: from antiquity to the medieval, feudal, and modern ages; the Japanese version inverts the entire historical order: from modernity backward to antiquity.

2. The English version has a glossary of terms related to Japanese architecture and history, many of which appear first in footnotes and are recapitulated in the glossary.

3. Throughout, many Japanese terms appear with phonetically transcribed suffixes; I have tried to be simple and consistent. For instance, for temples and shrines, the suffix *in* or *ji*, as in Byōdō-in or Tōdai-ji, denotes a temple, while *jingū*, as in Ise Jingū, denotes a shrine. "Byōdō Temple" or "Tōdai-ji Temple" would sound strange or redundant to the Japanese ear. A similar problem occurred with *yō*, in descriptions of style as in *daibutsu-yō* (Great Buddha style) or *zenshū-yō* (Zen sect style), and I have generally followed the procedure of retaining the Japanese suffix.

4. Certain repetitions in the book are due to the fact that it is a collection of essays, but I have eliminated these whenever possible.

5. Japanese names are transcribed in a somewhat unconventional manner. In Japan, names are customarily written (and spoken) family-name first and given-name second. Usually in Japanese area studies, this order is retained, while in other fields the order is Westernized. I have chosen a middle path with a break at the Meiji Restoration (1867), following which, Western name order has been adopted.

Sabu Kohso

Japan-ness in Architecture

Part I

Japan-ness in Architecture

From its inception the problematic of "Japan-ness" has belonged to an external gaze, that gaze directed toward Japan from beyond this insular nation. It has not emerged *causa sui*. Were an insular nation merely a closed, self-sufficient community, it would have no need to solicit its proper characteristics or the essence of its culture. Any such query would be halted in a circle of self-referentiality. Only when a gaze from without supervenes has a response to be formulated in an effort of introspection bound to shape aesthetic tastes. Throughout history, the problematic of Japan-ness surfaces whenever an encounter has occurred on the archipelago's perimeter, that is, at the edge of the lapping ocean.

In the mid-nineteenth century the West developed a passion for collecting *japonaiserie*—exotica such as *ukiyo-e* (woodblock prints), *byōbu* (folding screens), *kacchū* (*samurai* helmets and armor), *inrō* (ivory or shagreen medicine boxes), and so on. Much like today's Japanese electronic commodities and cars, though some were already antique, such objects embodied a certain notion of Japanese taste and promoted a new Japanophilia. It is generally understood that this flow of artifacts exerted a vast influence upon impressionism and art nouveau, among other tendencies of proto-modernist art and design. Nonetheless, like the eighteenth-century picturesque's assimilation of *chinoiserie* and cubist reference to African artifacts, all this hardly accounted for more than another shelf in the cabinet of the West's exoticist collection. That is to say that such tastes were fundamentally different from the West's obsession with its own presumed origins in ancient Greece, a passion that has recurred continually in the wake of all its various attempts at self-renewal.

Notwithstanding its comparative marginality in the West, the new taste for *japonaiserie* provoked measures of response within Japan. A connoisseurship evolved whereby items were selected to satisfy the appetites of Western collectors, and skilled craftsmen were on occasion sent abroad. What is notable is that in Japan these objects had not theretofore been considered art, nor the craftsmen artists. The professional appraisal that originated in selecting and judging what would now be called "art" from among everyday utensils was formed by Western-style "Japanese taste." Thus, from the very beginning, the Japan-ness commonly considered as Japanese conformed, in fact, to an external gaze.

Roughly a century has passed since such infatuations began, yet Japanese taste persists, except that the focus seems to have shifted from material objects to the concepts perceived to underlie their production—simplicity, humility, purity, lightness, and *shibusa* (sophisticated austerity). Even nowadays these concepts speak to Japanese taste and continue to guide selection and judgment of Japanese objects. In fact, fragments of these qualities did and do exist, in varying degrees, in many things Japanese. But it is only recently that such qualities came to be markers of "Japanese-ness." With respect to architectural design, in particular, an identification of Japan-ness began in the twentieth century, most intensively at the beginning of the 1930s—the critical juncture of the nation's modernization. It overlapped with the process by which Japan adopted Western modernism in architecture. What occurred, then, was that modernism in architecture was introduced to Japan concurrently with efforts to construct the problematic of Japan-ness. It was in the late 1920s that the United States adopted art deco and in the early 1930s that it began to import the International Style. The Japanese adopted such trends almost simultaneously, but their incorporation entailed a peculiar element, owing to Japan's status as an insular nation in the Far East—namely, the selfsame problematic of Japan-ness.

Contact with an external gaze intensified in the mid-nineteenth century when Japan began its path to modern nation-statehood,[1] characterized by exchange and collaboration between Japan and the West. In the domain of aesthetics Tenshin Okakura (1862–1913),[2] who later lived in Boston, where he contributed to the establishment of an Eastern art section at the Museum of Fine

Arts, had first learned both modern aesthetics and fine art appraisal from Ernest Fenollosa (1853–1908),[3] an American philosopher initially invited to Japan as a teacher by the Meiji government. Okakura became Fenollosa's assistant as the latter researched antique Japanese and Asian artifacts.

Okakura subsequently led a movement to modernize Japanese traditional painting—*nihonga*. In 1906 he wrote the small but celebrated *Book of Tea*, thus elaborating an aesthetic of the tea ceremony, which had previously been dealt with only as an esoteric practice, from a more modern viewpoint. Okakura wrote in English now known to have been influenced by Emerson, a fact illustrating the degree to which he espoused an external gaze. Speaking in New York in 1952, Frank Lloyd Wright gave a talk entitled "The Destruction of the Box"[4] in which he recalled his wonder at reading *The Book of Tea* upon publication. Okakura's explanation of the *chashitsu* (tearoom) and tea utensils was highlighted by an invocation of the Chinese philosopher Lao-tse: "The reality of a room … was to be found in the vacant space enclosed by the roof and walls, not in the roof and walls themselves. The usefulness of a water pitcher dwelt in the emptiness where water might be put in, not in the form of the pitcher or the material of which it was made. Vacuum is all potent because all containing."[5] In calling attention to this Taoist concept of omnipresent emptiness, Okakura stressed his point that the tearoom, as well as the tea utensils, have significance only in terms of this emptiness. But Wright misinterpreted this key issue not as *omnipresent emptiness*, but as a teleologically constructed internal space. Indeed, Wright had begun to theorize his own unique manner of destroying the box or enclosure, so as to stress and thus objectify its "contents." Upon reading Okakura's little book, he was shocked to find his idea of an objectified internal space seemingly confirmed. All too soon, Wright regained his native confidence and maintained that he alone had made internal space an end in itself through the destruction of the box.

Wright's possibly willful misinterpretation created a form of cultural confusion. He collapsed an ontology based upon *nothingness* into the process of designing a specified space. Perhaps this confusion is one that inevitably confronts all architects, conditioned as they are to regard form as both intentional and tactile.

1.1 The Imperial Hotel by Frank Lloyd Wright (1913–1923): entrance façade and porte-cochère, as salvaged and relocated to the Meiji Mura outdoor architectural museum in rural Aichi prefecture ⟨http://www.meijimura.com/⟩. Note specially cast brick enlivened by Wright's *ōya-ishi* detailing.

In any event, this cross-cultural encounter piqued Wright's interest in Japan. Around that time, he began to collect and, later on, even to deal in *ukiyo-e* prints.

In 1922, he was finally commissioned to design the Imperial Hotel in Tokyo (fig. 1.1). Ironically, the work of Wright, the architect so much in love with Japanese things, seems not to have been referred to even once in prewar discourses on Japan-ness, such as in Japan became particularly heated around 1930. To a Westerner, the Imperial Hotel may have appeared Asian or Japanese, but not to the Japanese eye. This may be owing in part to Wright's extensive use of a porous stone from Tochigi prefecture called *ōya-ishi*, rarely if ever used in Japanese traditional architecture for aesthetic ends, and moreover to a lack of that *flatness* particular to much Japanese space, as seen in the lack of perspec-

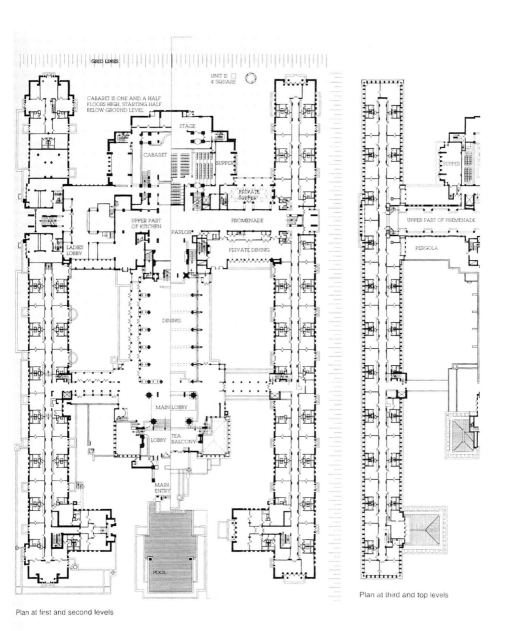

Plan at first and second levels

Plan at third and top levels

Above, composite floor plans of Imperial Hotel, exhibiting mirror-image symmetry of Beaux-Arts planning centered on reflecting pool (shaded, at bottom).

tive in *ukiyo-e*, for example. Wright's design entailed a conventional Beaux-Arts compositional scheme unrelated to the Japanese way of sensing space, in which depth comprises layers of planes without regard to graduated perspective. It was, I think, only natural that Wright should fail to understand the ancient Eastern notion of omnipresent emptiness.

The basic plan of the Imperial Hotel established common facilities such as the lobby, main dining room, and auditorium on a principal axis, and placed bedroom accommodation in trailing left- and right-hand wings. This arrangement had long provided the basic form of Western institutional architecture, as passed down via Palladio. But a similar arrangement is seen at the Hō-ō-dō (Phoenix Hall) of Byōdō-in in Uji, Kyoto (cf. fig. 1.7), about which Wright must have learned from a near replica at the World's Columbian Exposition of 1893 in Chicago that had first provoked his passion for Japan. For this reason, it is rather commonly believed that Wright predicated the layout of the Imperial Hotel on traditional Japanese composition. There was, however, one Japanese architect who protested this interpretation. This was Kikutaro Shimoda (1866–1931), who was active in Chicago and had also submitted a proposal for the hotel project before Wright even became involved. Shimoda claimed that Wright had copied his design, because his proposal was too similar to Shimoda's for the resemblance to have been coincidental. One might argue that the scheme of central axis and wings is a very basic form for which no one can claim authorship. Shimoda, however, had also proposed setting a Japanese-style tiled roof, resembling that of the Hō-ō-dō, over a low masonry building. Wright's design had a gently sloping roof, which must have derived from his Prairie House typology where he had evolved a roof that was almost flat. But Shimoda argued that the manner of placing such a roof on a stone or concrete building was his own invention, and Wright's design, therefore, an appropriation. Naturally, this protest was ignored and Wright's midcareer masterpiece eventually constructed.

Shimoda's idea had been to design the roof as a traditional element over a building constructed with new techniques and materials as a unification of rational structure and traditional symbol, thus affording an emblem simple enough to be widely appreciated. He called it *teikan-heigō-shiki* (crown-topped style) and also promoted the idea in the ongoing competition for the National Diet Building in Tokyo. Afterward he even seems to have persuaded the Diet to encourage his crown-style roof as symbol of the Japanese state. As a structure, it recalls Robert Venturi's much later notion of the "decorated shed," except that Shimoda's crown-style roof was without irony. It expressed a sheer will to represent the state.

Shimoda's challenge to Wright resulted somewhat later in the production of a full-blown neonationalist style of architecture. Beginning in the late 1920s, the Japanese nationalist "decorated shed" became popular as an easy, practical way of representing Japanness. The programs for important competitions from around 1930 onward clearly urged architects to express Japanese taste. Many thought that the *teikan* style was the most direct way of realizing that purpose, and accordingly a number of public buildings of the prewar era showcased such ideology. While it was natural to stress Japanese taste when representing the Japanese nation-state, it should not be forgotten that the same manner delineated a broader "Eastern taste" once Japan was poised to expand into Asia. So it was that the domain of nationalist representation expanded, as a colonial version of Japan-ness was duly applied abroad.

Japan-ness also insinuated itself into the discursive framework of modern architecture via the influence of yet another external gaze, namely that of the German expatriate architect Bruno Taut (1880–1938). Taut came to Japan as a refugee from Nazi Germany in 1933, soon after Hitler seized power. No one knows for sure how much Taut knew about Japanese architecture before he came, but I would suppose almost nothing. He arrived from Russia, via Siberia, and went first to Kyoto. The very next day, Taut was taken to Katsura Imperial Villa, which under the guarded administration of the Imperial Household Agency did not until many years later open to the public. Since Katsura, therefore, was not publicly known, it was almost impossible for anyone to learn about its architecture except by the limited means of photographs then available. The brash idea of showing such a secluded work to Taut belonged to a group of younger Japanese architects from Osaka calling themselves Nihon Intānashonaru Kenchikukai (Japan International Architectural Association).[6] Their leader, Isaburō Ueno (1892–1972), had studied at the Wiener Werkbund. Ueno and the others

1.2 Prime example of *teikan-heigō-shiki* (imperial crown style): Tokyo Imperial Museum by Jun Watanabe (1937) at Ueno, Tokyo.

propounded a new agenda of Japan-ness through a reinterpretation of Japanese "traditional" architecture—then gaining currency in Japan—all in accordance with the principles of modern architecture. This same group protested the aim of the Tokyo Imperial Museum competition to realize "Japanese taste" through promotion of the *teikan* style (fig. 1.2). They sought to mobilize International Style modernists in resistance to the nationalist tendency to adopt this new eclecticism as a symbol. Instead, the group wished to demonstrate that "pure" Japanese elements and rationalist (or, to them, functionalist) modern architecture could coexist under one and the same aegis. They believed that modernism in architecture might replace the elevational eclecticism of the *teikan* style, if only they could isolate the key compositional elements common to traditional Japanese architecture and modern design. They needed, however, an authoritative spokesperson. Taut

1.3 Shien-sō (House of Purple Haze) by Sutemi Horiguchi (1926, demolished).

intuitively understood his role and played it to the hilt, in exchange for being allowed to stay in Japan. This is to say that the discursive device of Japan-ness that once appeared to have been informed mainly by Taut and to have coalesced in the mid-1930s, had in fact been constructed piecemeal over the previous decade—mainly by those Japanese architects privileged to study contemporary modern buildings in Europe.

Such an individual was Sutemi Horiguchi (1895–1984) who, in the mid-1920s, first designed an architecture seeking an interpretation of modern design; he called his approach *hitoshiteki-na-mono* (nonurban elements). The aim of his 1926 design for a residence, Shien-sō (House of Purple Haze) (fig. 1.3), was a straightforward combination of modern design with the Japanese teahouse. Distinct from the imported art deco then in fashion, Horiguchi's work proposed instead to critique the eclectic nationalist architecture officially promoted as authentic. The *sōan* (thatched cottage)-style teahouse is marked by its free composition of rustic materials; there are a number of elements in common with modernism, such as direct exposure of materials, as well as overall simplicity and lightness. By the early 1930s, when nationalism and the discourse on Japan-ness began to flourish in earnest, Horiguchi had become an active participant in the debates. In 1932, he rated historical architecture by its measure of Japan-ness. Rejecting Buddhist styles that had been imported in various waves directly from the continent, he chose architectural types from either native Japanese style or the *wayō* style—an imported manner transformed to accord with Japanese taste and custom.[7] Both types exhibited simplicity of detail. They thus embodied those characteristics of "rationalism" recognized by Japanese architects of the 1930s: exposed materials, elimination of decorative detail, and orthogonal composition with movable partition walls, among other features. Further to this typology arose the custom of opposing the Shintō shrine to the Buddhist temple, and of positing the *minka* (premodern rural dwelling) and the teahouse as everyday spaces versus the feudal castle and mausoleum as symbols of authority.

This historicist trend voiced a protest against the ascendant eclecticism favoring the *teikan* style and strove to express Japanness by way of modernist design. By 1933, the year Taut arrived, this discourse of Japan-ness had become entrenched to a certain extent. Meanwhile, in his diaries, a self-marveling Taut wrote, "I seem to be considered the discoverer of Katsura Imperial Villa."[8] And Taut's impressions of Katsura, published soon after his visit, did create a sensation. The Japanese believed him to be a world-renowned authority on modern architecture. It was dizzying that this globetrotting figure had affirmed the Katsura Imperial Villa, to which Japanese architectural historians had paid scant attention, as a masterpiece according to the measure of modern architecture. In his diaries and other writings, Taut recorded having told his hosts that this architecture should be called "functionalist." This discursive encounter fostered a belief that there existed a set of universal principles of functionalist architecture that went beyond historical and geographical particularities.

Katsura was the first stop. Next was Ise Jingū (Ise Shrine), dedicated to the ancestral gods of the imperial household, and therefore anointed as the national center of religious worship by Japan as a modern nation-state. Taut expressed his awe of Ise

Jingū, noting "that before the nobility of the deity everyone unwittingly bows, and does so repeatedly; that Ise Jingū will become an ultimate destination of architectural pilgrimage, like the Acropolis."[9] In fact, like Katsura, Ise Jingū had been little appreciated in the context of Japanese architectural history. Chūta Itō (1867–1954) was the first scholar to have planted the seed of the Western concept of architecture in any precise sense, but he, too, later turned out a passionate promoter of the *teikan* style. Yet he used his authority to disclaim for Ise Jingū anything of value in relation to architecture; he said it was like the huts of South Sea aboriginals. Thus Ise was acknowledged as an important religious site, but not an object of architectural interest. Taut's intervention overturned all that.

Taut went so far as to introduce the standard whereby soon all Japanese historical architecture would be evaluated in terms of binary oppositions: *honmono* (authentic)—meaning imperial, i.e., Ise and Katsura—versus *ikamono* (kitsch)—represented by the Tokugawa shōgunate and Nikkō Tōshōgū, their cluster of mausolea. *Honmono* and *ikamono* were terms used originally for the appraisal of antiques. Before Taut's intervention, highly valued tea utensils had been subjected to the excessive connoisseurship typical of boom economies; a specific code of aesthetic judgment had been established for their appraisal, and Japanese architects may have imparted this jargon to Taut. Applying such categories to architecture, he identified Katsura as *the* masterpiece of functionalist architecture, at the same time comparing Ise with the Acropolis as one of the points of origin of world architecture. Hence the ideology that the truly important models of Japanese architecture had been produced by imperial fiat, while the Nikkō Tōshōgū represented an excessively decorative style, a sort of Japanese baroque. The latter implied a repetition of the vulgarism of the late Ming and early Qing dynasties in China. Even now this "vulgar" taste represents one aspect of Japan-ness, one that in the past had been exemplified by the brusque *samurai* (warrior) class, who used its popular appeal to confirm their authority. The ideology of Japan-ness backed up by Taut sought to devalue this vulgarism as *ikamono*. One of the reasons that Taut's aesthetic ideology was so successful was its sanction of the historical friction between imperial household and Tokugawa shōgunate existing since the sixteenth century. The basis of such opposition was rearticulated in the mid-nineteenth century and influenced the course of Japan's history during the period of its consolidation as a modern nation-state. There was a simmering contradiction between the actual sovereign power of the shōgunate and the symbolic sovereignty of *tennō* (the emperor, literally, the king of heaven), that is, until shōgunal power was brought to an end by the Meiji Restoration of a nominal imperial sovereignty. In the 1930s the image of a *tennō*-ruled nation-state persisted, and even intensified. When Taut made his unfortunate pronouncements, just at the time Japan was about to expand into Asia, the ramifications of admiring things imperial were incalculable.

We have also to remember that because of its internationalist associations, modern architecture was oppressed and persecuted in Japan during the 1930s. At the time the Axis was established between Japan, Germany, and Italy, and the nonaggression pact signed between Japan and the Soviet Union, international modern architecture was being similarly oppressed by the totalitarian regimes of Hitler and Stalin. It is easy to surmise that Taut could well have been forced to leave Japan for another place of refuge had he not understood the discursive necessity of Japan-ness in which he played a formative part, with its net effect of inverting the discursive climate. On one hand, political protection was assured him by the safeguard inherent in Taut's appreciation of imperial architecture from the standpoint of modernist principles of functionality and rationality. On the other, his intervention allowed avant-garde modernists to criticize openly the authoritarian *teikan* style as eclecticist—even though placed under the sign of *tennō*. It proved, indeed, a bizarre struggle for the survival of the International Style under the flag of imperial Japan-ness. The crux of the matter lay with neither Ise nor Katsura per se, nor in any direct importation of the style of the Bauhaus or Le Corbusier, then beginning to receive public attention, but in the new task of synthesizing what was modern and what was Japanese. Nonetheless, against the background discourse of Japanese expansionism, the new tendency was increasingly spoken of as a victory of Japan-ness over the modern.

In the late 1930s, Japan began its invasion of Asia—an attempt to expand its politico-economic influence under a pretext of liberating Asia from Western domination. The goal was to construct a supra-Asian community—the so-called Greater East Asia Co-prosperity Sphere[10]—under Japanese sponsorship. As this intensified aggression sorely strained national resources, new construction in Japan greatly diminished. Steel was earmarked for military purposes, and the only possible new construction had to make use of wood. At the same time as the insertion of Japan-ness into architectural discourse, then, the opportunity to realize large projects was gradually lost. But even in such a climate, Hideto Kishida (1899–1965) was nonetheless able to promote the idea of Japanese design. He first published a collection of architectural photographs, *Kako no Kōsei* (Composition of the Past), in 1929.[11] It was a pioneering work praised in the photographic field as "Japanese beauty of composition." Kishida pioneered a method by which to enframe past architectural artifacts through capture by a modernist gaze, suppressing, in other words, all temporal distance. As professor at Tokyo Imperial University, Kishida was in the privileged position of planning state-sponsored projects and judging a number of important competitions, subverting many eclecticist architects of the previous generation. He was thus well placed to promote his goal of realizing a transparent space for Shintōism—a ritualistic space originating in Shintō that is austere and reductionist and one in certain ways compatible with modern design. He sought out the characteristics of this transparency among the ritualistic implements used in religious ceremonies as well as in the space of daily life. He not only composed his image—as the title of the book indicates—but also looked to develop a new architecture from it. But until the end of World War II, almost no buildings were realized, only plans. It was his student Kenzō Tange (1913–2005) who eventually responded most effectively to Kishida's directive, making his debut as a polemicist for Japan-ness.

Tange won in succession three important competitions for which Kishida was a juror: Daitōa Kinen Eizōbutsu, 1942 (Greater East Asia Memorial Building; fig. 1.4), Nittai Bunka Kaikan, 1943 (Japan Cultural Center, Bangkok, based on the design of the Imperial Palace in Kyoto, a building also praised by Taut; fig. 1.5), and Hiroshima Genbaku Kinen Kōen, 1950 (Atomic Bomb Memorial Park, Hiroshima). The two former competitions were held near the end of the war but never built, while the latter was

1.4 Rendering of unbuilt, premiated submission for Daitōa Kinen Eizōbutsu, 1942 (Greater East Asia Memorial Building competition) by Kenzō Tange, from *Kenchiku Zasshi* (Architecture Journal), September 1942.

1.5 Rendering of unbuilt, premiated submission for Nittai Bunka Kaikan, 1943 (Japan Cultural Center competition in Bangkok), by Kenzō Tange, published in *Kenchiku Zasshi* (Architecture Journal), January 1944.

realized as the first large-scale, postwar public architectural project in Japan. The Greater East Asia Memorial Building was to have symbolized Japan's "gathering the whole of Asia under one roof"; it was planned to be built near the base of Mt. Fuji—like *tennō*, a quintessential symbol of Japan. The Japan Cultural Center was to represent Japanese culture in Bangkok, at the time virtually occupied by imperial Japan. The Atomic Bomb Memorial Park has become the world-renowned memorial to peace erected in Hiroshima, that city reduced to rubble by the atomic attack that for Japan ended the war. All three projects were thought of as significant expressions of the Japanese nation-state, albeit reflecting various ideological phases of the war effort and its conclusion. These varied messages—Japan's unification of Asia, cultural domination of colonies by Japan, and the commemoration of an ultimate though self-inflicted disaster—all nevertheless represented prime themes of the state.

Each design by Tange took a Japanese work of historical architecture as model: Ise Jingū, the Kyoto Imperial Palace, and Katsura Imperial Villa, the selfsame places Taut had nominated as authentically imperial. As Kunio Maekawa (1905–1986), a slightly older architect whose designs were runners-up in all three competitions, had remarked in 1942, "speaking positively, [such] modeling proved the architect's talent, but negatively speaking, it proved his shrewdness."[12] All in all, Kishida's project had succeeded well enough. The Memorial Peace Center at Hiroshima (as finally realized within its park; fig. 1.6) was smaller than either of the two wartime schemes, yet the way modernist and nationalist themes were combined had been subtle indeed. It would be difficult to claim a lineage other than the International Style for the architectural language developed by Tange at Hiroshima. Pilotis, a flat roof, flowing space, exposed structure, and transparency are fully deployed. At the same time, points of reference to traditional Japanese architecture—the plan of Byōdō-in's Hō-ō-dō (fig. 1.7), and column ratios based on Katsura—were unmistakable and clearly expressed. The Memorial Peace Center is both a modernist and a Japanese work. It even embodies the Shintōist space of transparency that is often said to epitomize the *tennō* aesthetic. The problematic of reordering the imported modern style in a context of Japan-ness was finally grasped and given an

1.6 Hiroshima Peace Memorial Museum, Hiroshima, by Kenzō Tange (1949–1955):
northern view of West Building main façade, with cenotaph.

encompassing image by the young Kenzō Tange, ten years after
the inception of the debate in the early 1930s, and a nationalist
image was somehow deftly conjured out of the ruins of nuclear
holocaust.

From Kishida's *Kako no Kōsei* to the dichotomy of Taut's *honmono* versus *ikamono* and the final realization of Tange's Memorial
Peace Center, the problematic of Japan-ness in architecture persisted. In perilous political circumstances, it was sustained, almost
miraculously, through subtle twists and paradoxical reversions. We
have to ask how these discourses on Japan-ness were provoked and
sustained, and why they continued to interest these architects.
Were they really aware of the problematic and its formation? If

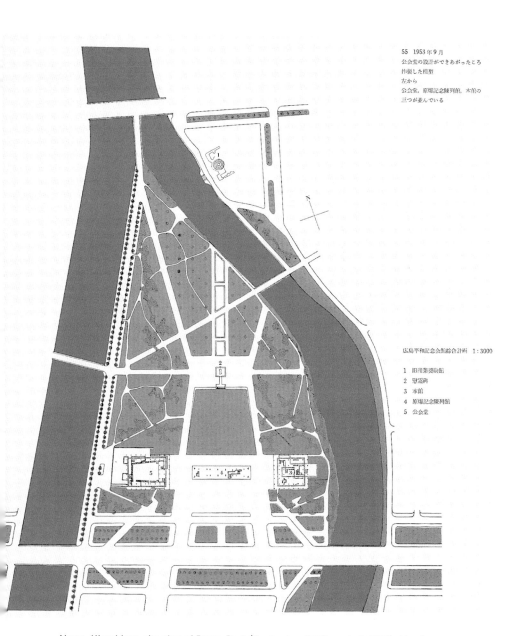

55 1953年9月
公会堂の設計ができあがったころ
作製した模型
左から
公会堂，原爆記念陳列館，本館の
三つが並んでいる

広島平和記念会館綜合計画　1 : 3000

1　旧産業奨励館
2　慰霊碑
3　本館
4　原爆記念陳列館
5　公会堂

Above, Hiroshima, site plan of Peace Park (September 1953; scale 1:3000). Atomic Dome (1), Cenotaph (2), and Peace Memorial Museum (West Building) (4) at center. Flanking pavilion (5) was not realized to Tange's design.

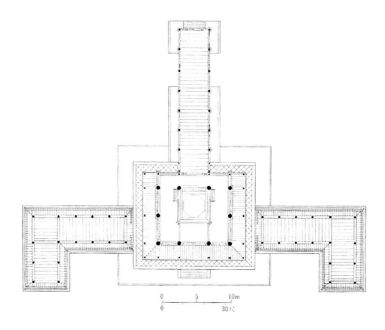

1.7 Byōdō-in, Hō-ō-dō (Amida Hall, so-called Phoenix Hall, consecrated 1053), Uji (near Kyoto), floor plan.

so, it would have been crucial to discover a stance from which to criticize both the modernism that came from without and that Japan-ness being sought within.

In 1942, in the midst of World War II, the conflict being in the Japanese mind near its peak, a broad range of prominent intellectuals—philosophers, writers, critics, historians, aestheticians, and scientists —gathered at a symposium whose theme was "Overcoming Modernity."[13] Significantly, perhaps, there were no architects in attendance, and no discussions on architecture were held. In consideration of the broad range of issues covered, the discussion has been repeatedly referred to at all sorts of critical junctures ever since, now more than half a century afterward. But it seems to me that no critical cutting edge ever evolved, at least not one equivalent to that which appeared in architecture. (The only other productive example is the critical discourse surrounding Japanese film, a field nurtured during twenty years of war and which attained its productive peak in the 1950s.) The "Overcoming Modernity" debate remained essentially sterile because participants simply either praised or rejected the modern vis-à-vis a Japanese aesthetic or ethos. In contrast, architects at least came to see modernity and tradition as two sides of a single issue, articulating a stance by means of which to critique both at the same time. Such was the architectural discourse in Japan produced in the early 1940s, in wartime.

As the war worsened, the government found itself forced to draft those men previously exempted from military service—namely, scholars and technocrats. They, too, were now taught to die for *tennō* and sent into battle, with only the slightest chance of returning alive. Just before this journey of no return, two books were written: Masao Maruyama's *Studies in the Intellectual History of Tokugawa Japan* (publication in 1952)[1] and Ryūichi Hamaguchi's *Nihon Kokumin Kenchiku Yōshiki-no-Kenkyū* (The Problem of Style in Japan's National Architecture) (1944).[2] As it turned out, Maruyama did return to become Japan's representative postwar intellectual historian, and Hamaguchi also became active as an architectural critic after the peace.

In their authors' minds, both books had been written as posthumous works: both were first books, yet neither author had believed that he would write another. Furthermore, the two works shared a similar perspective: first, despite having been produced in a closed and information-deprived country, both authors fully incorporated Western vanguard studies into their own methodologies, and approached their own Japan-based historical topics via such methods; secondly, each succeeded in constructing a unique point of view.

Maruyama extracted two opposed concepts, *sakui* (artifice) and *jinen*, from the political thought of the Edo period (1604–1868). *Sakui* implies a will to construction, while *jinen* is a notion of self-becoming. One might translate the pair of terms simply as construction and becoming, although the equivalence is not exact. Furthermore, *sakui* might also be interpreted as architecture-as-Western-mode-of-thought, which entered Japan as the modern. By contrast *jinen* could be thought of as the Japanese life view: an attitude of letting the natural process of becoming decide its own course, that is, intuiting the course of nature and following it. We may also wish to call this Japan-ness. Not only did Maruyama point out the fact that both these ways of thought were present in the political thinking of the Edo period, but later he theorized that their interaction had formed a determinant scheme throughout the history of Japanese cultural production.

Hamaguchi's book was a critical scrutiny of the results of the competition for the Japan Cultural Center in Bangkok. In recognition of the characteristics of Tange's first-prize-winning and of Maekawa's second-prize-winning submissions, Hamaguchi proposed that this constellation be called Japan's "national architectural style." As its basis, he distinguished the architectonic will of the West—"constructive and objective"—from that of Japan—"spatial and performative [kōi-teki]." He detected Japanese characteristics in both Tange's and Maekawa's designs, but especially in the latter. Hamaguchi's thesis was ignored for a long time after the war because, for one thing, the competition itself was a dead letter, based as it had been upon the ideology that underlay Japan's invasion of other Asian nations and brief cultural domination of its "colonies." More simply put, the concept of a Japanese national architectural style itself became problematic after the war. Hamaguchi, as well as the participating architects, attempted to erase the memory of the competition from their careers, ashamed as they all were of having danced with late-war fanaticism. They wanted above everything to escape the charge of having collaborated with the fascist government that drove the war of attrition and aggression that ended in 1945. However, if and only if we bracket for a moment the historical details of this political situation can Hamaguchi's position be expressed. His argument represents the peak and synthesis of the whole problematic of Japan-ness. Meanwhile, Tange's Memorial Peace Center, completed ten years after Hamaguchi's book, was the very embodiment of his theory in a way only made possible by the collaboration of these two former classmates, critic and architect. These two had together looked for a stance beyond the opposing principles of the modern and the Japanese: those of construction and becoming—objective and "spatial."

This time, no foreign protagonist appeared. Bruno Taut and Frank Lloyd Wright had long since left. Antonin Raymond (1888–1976)—who had followed Wright to Japan and contributed much to the development of modernism—returned after the war but remained aloof from such debates. Maekawa had first worked in Le Corbusier's studio and then with Raymond, but the next generation—Tange, Hamaguchi, and Maruyama—missed the opportunity to study abroad because of Japan's prewar footing and belligerent status. Nonetheless, the methods they found for themselves were by now more Western than those of the previous generation that had experienced the West directly, in the sense that this new generation had at last managed to internalize modernist ideas. Thus armed, they made *Japan* the object of their research and design. In other words, they mined their own interiority, having detoured via an external gaze. In this way, they escaped the vicious circle of self-reference, as the creative vector first achieved an alterity by means of which it could then travel inward. It would be tautological to attempt to elucidate any interior mechanism by way of an internal logic—which would engender romantic aspirations, at best. Until Japan's surrender, intellectual efforts could focus only on honing themselves within the self-enclosed national discourse, a vicious cycle that was only broken by shifting one's stance to the exterior. The problematic of Japan-ness in architecture had in the preceding twenty years matured to such a degree that it could at last construct an external stance within. Hamaguchi's "Problem of Style" first elaborates on the notion of architecture in the West and then analyzes those architectural data which, such as they existed in Japan, seemed almost unarchitectural, if compared to the Western concept. Such logic was not uncommon in the attitude of many Japanese architects during modernization; Hamaguchi's uniqueness lay in a radicalism that finally demolished the boundary between inside and outside.

Hamaguchi begins by criticizing the general method of categorizing styles on which historians as diverse as Heinrich Wölfflin (1864–1945) and Banister Fletcher had relied. In Wölfflin's understanding of changes in style—itself tacitly based upon the Hegelian *Zeitgeist*—a formal apparatus (*der Formenapparat*) is posited behind a creator that determines his production from the depth of his unconscious. If one looks at Japanese artistic production from this point of view, then, indeed, unique Japanese propensities may be singled out; but Hamaguchi asks what use this discovery might conceivably be to the creator. It is plain that behind Hamaguchi's rhetorical doubt was his key awareness of the state's passionate desire for a representation of a Japanese or Eastern "taste" in the formation of the Japan-ness problematic. For until that time, Japan-ness had been commonly understood merely as a kind of "taste." This was not only maintained by the theorist Chūta Itō, the moving force behind this trend (who had dismissed the architectural potential of Ise Jingū); it was also the opinion of almost every member of the Architectural Association. They considered the measure of design to be taste, and taste alone, an echo of the *japonaiserie* affecting other domains. Dealing with the notion of "style" takes time and effort, because one has first to identify the *Zeitgeist* and other references, while the concept of taste is easily managed and convenient enough to account for even the most superficial fashion.

Thus in the wake of the introduction of modernist architecture, Japanese taste represented by the curious eclecticism of the *teikan* style came to be criticized, and the counterthesis of "composition" reinvigorated by rationalism and functionalism gained in favor. The late nineteenth-century West had itself reverted to the concept of composition, likewise as a weapon against eclecticism. In Japan, the same concept now aimed at an elimination of taste in favor of universal principles. When Taut posited Katsura as authentic, the motivation was quasi-political. But in order to interpret the imperial villa as architecturally gratifying, he had to rely upon the expression "visual pleasure."[3] That is, he had to say that Katsura's architectural essence lay in the visual pleasure it confers; and such a stance flows from classicist notions of proportion and harmony—namely, the beauty of composition. This inherited aesthetic criterion still underlay modern Western architecture in the works of the International Style. The understanding of Japanese beauty retained today as stereotype rarely goes beyond the notion of compositional beauty—the same understanding of architectural style rehabilitated to serve its own purposes by the nineteenth-century West.

Ryūichi Hamaguchi was quite alone in Japan in recognizing that the art historians Alois Riegl's and Wilhelm Worringer's concept of *Kunstwollen* (urge to form)[4] might go beyond an understanding of architectural style based upon taste, to further enrich the tradition of architectural theory developed for and by architects which such reformers as Alberti and Palladio had promulgated in the Renaissance and after. By lending attention to this will (*Wollen*) of the creator, it was possible to explain how differences in age, culture, and national politics produce heterogeneity. For instance, in Banister Fletcher's *A History of Architecture on the Comparative Method*,[5] Japan was posited as just an exotic peripheral, in company with India or China—a land where no proper concept of architecture existed. It is true that, in Japan, there was no word "architecture," nor were there architects as we recognize them today. Nonetheless, buildings *were* undeniably made, in which unique characteristics might be discovered. Hamaguchi looked for a basic trend congruent with the whole picture of building history in Japan, rather than for this or that feature in itself.[6] As a clue to furthering the understanding of the collective *Kunstwollen*, he looked especially to differences in the basic methods of composition in the West and Japan.

Western texts on architecture, historically intended as a kind of design manual, have naturally been formulated upon the notion of an architectonic will. But more to the point, the placement of columns was invariably determinant, and it is this characteristic that persists as a principle of composition today, delineated as a matrix of planes and lines. This tendency may be categorized as both *objective* and *constructive*. On the other hand, Japanese architectural texts were based on *kenmen-hō*, the interstitial method developed from the eighth to the fourteenth centuries that counts the number of interstices (*ma*)—a term indicating both the spans in between frontal columns of a main building (or navelike hall), and the number of eaves that extend from the main building itself to its four sides (reminiscent of aisles). By identifying just these few numerical indicators, the whole plan, use, and scale of a building became intuitive, and the elaboration of details was entrusted to the judgment of a master carpenter. Therefore, it might be said, the *kenmen-hō* comprehended architecture both *spatially* and *performatively*. This method had been in general use since sometime around the tenth century, and there was no other. The Japanese architectonic will, the *Kunstwollen*, was thus focused on performative-spatial aspects of construction and building.

A similar inward critical engagement by way of an external gaze also became evident in the later work of Sutemi Horiguchi, who, throughout the 1930s, continued to refine his critique of

Japanese taste. One of his designs was the Okada Residence (1933) in Tokyo, which joins the modern Western house and the Japanese traditional living space—with its *sukiya* origins—in a straight line drawn across the site. This reflected the psyche of the client and the schizophrenic mode of the new Japanese urban bourgeois who might keep as mistress and companion, for instance, a *geisha* who had mastered all the traditional mannerisms and performing arts, such as playing the *koto* and practicing *ikebana* (flower arrangement)—all within the context of a thoroughly contemporary and up-to-date modern lifestyle. Horiguchi's solution was itself schizophrenic: abandoning any attempt at a synthesis of contradictory elements, he juxtaposed these façades by an emblematic gesture—that of drawing a line. He explained this, with irony, as "style without style." There can be no such thing as a style that represents an entire age. Instead, he believed, if we simply follow the materials, techniques, and general lifestyle of the age, we will attain a style. But the fact was that in 1930s Japan, modernity and tradition were split down the middle, therefore there was no other way but for Japanese themselves to be so, too. Horiguchi pursued this idea in many of the residences he designed, while for public institutions he sought a purely modernist architecture.[7]

Meanwhile and at length, Horiguchi researched the historical *sukiya* style, especially its original form in the late sixteenth-century teahouse—as a rural, anti-urban, and even anti-authoritarian architectural type—such being the tendencies he had emphasized in the context of his critique of Japanese taste. He concentrated on reconstructing—performatively and spatially, by way of his analytical writings—a historical architecture, the matrix of which had long been virtually lost other than in records surrounding the tea ceremony. This research constitutes a unique and pathbreaking contribution to modern Japanese architectural scholarship. His work totally omits concerns of architectural style. Rather it imaginatively reconstructs the locus of the tea ceremony qua event. It successfully extracts the essence of teahouse space—which even Okakura's *Book of Tea* did not grasp owing to its author's enlightened, latter-day stance. Horiguchi's success was facilitated by the very setbacks he experienced in trying to transplant modern design in Japan; and by virtue of this struggle, he managed to frame and contextualize Japan in a new way—through a battle-scarred modernist stance, as it were.

As modern design evolved, the concept of "art as composition" was invoked to criticize and moderate stylistic eclecticism. And, of course, during the 1920s, there had to be mounted yet another criticism of the overstylish tendency to treat this same "art as composition" itself as décor. In the later years of the Bauhaus, the Swiss Hannes Meyer (1889–1954), a socialist designer who became its second director, framed a manifesto extolling "construction as life function" in the place of the "art as composition" theme. But the dissemination of his ideas was thwarted by the international fascist movement. We can no longer determine to what extent the echoes of this manifesto ever reached Japan, where internationalism was likewise oppressed. I suppose that the only discourses on Western ideas retained were certain Japanese interpretations of the work of the Vienna School aestheticians, such as Riegl and Worringer.

At this point, I wish to call attention to the similarity between Riegl's concept of *Kunstwollen*—whose interpretation might be stretched to include an architectonic, constructive will—and the concept of artifice (*sakui*) that Masao Maruyama extracted from the political thought of the Edo period. The *saku* of *sakui* signifies construction, while *-i* indicates deliberate making; together they came to signify something like the Greek concept of *poiesis*. It was only after the war that the binary opposition—artifice versus nature (*sakui/jinen*), or construction and becoming—was set at the core of the Japan-ness problematic. (This opposition will be explored in the next chapter.) In any event, we shall construe *sakui*—representing the *constructive* and *objective* architectonic will— as classically Western in nature, and *jinen*—representing a *spatial* and *performative* architectonic will—as belonging to Japan. It will thus be possible to track the crucial formation and development of Japan-ness further, backed by this distinction.

In the project descriptions of Tange's and Maekawa's competition submissions for the Japan Cultural Center in Bangkok, the expressions "environmental order" and "environmental space" are both used in Japanese. Maekawa's particular goal was "spatial composition." With most competitors as well as jurors still concerned with Japanese taste or Japanese spirit, Maekawa's work stood out. Hamaguchi must have been inspired by the notions of "environment" and "space" to write his epoch-making criticism, which he indeed believed would appear only after his own death. And the attractiveness of the terms was also buttressed by the new social situation in Japan colored by the rapid military and political expansion into Asia.

Concerning the two submissions, Kishida, the juror, who had himself once already sought to promote modernism by stressing "composition," was known to be perplexed by their use of a roof with its silhouette derived from *shinden-zukuri*, the Japanese court style of the Heian period (roughly the ninth to twelfth centuries)—by their abandonment, so to say, of the flat roof then deemed imperative to modern design. Yet he merely remarks that taking the model from Japanese court architecture was the right attitude.[8] By contrast, Chūta Itō, who for some time had been insisting upon an eclectic representation of Japanese taste, argues, after viewing these two examples of modern architecture with a traditional Japanese roof, that "the empty words and confused ideas of the modernist style have been wiped clear.... From the start, nothing called international can be worthwhile."[9] (Ever afterward, his claim has been revisited time and again as a notoriously confused pronouncement.) Clearly the theme of this competition was closely linked to Japan's expansion into Asia. The characteristics of Japanese architecture had till then all been explained as *forms produced naturally by Nature* (*jinen*); under the new drive toward imperial expansion, a fresh approach was required. Imperial architecture had to consider new climes, ranging from the cold wastes of Manchuria to hot and humid southeast Asia, as included in the various competition specifications. Beforehand, Tange had stated that "concerning the architecture [of the Greater East Asia Co-prosperity Sphere], a new Japanese architectural style must be created sublime and powerful like God, brave and solemn like a giant. It is best to ignore not only Anglo-American culture, but also the culture of the southern [European] nations."[10] This stance was adopted as a general policy by the Architectural Association. As such the statement has been taken as evidence that Tange was a war collaborator—a blot on his career. This might, indeed, be the case. But the significance of the name "Greater East Asia Co-prosperity Sphere" for Japanese at that time was not dissimilar to what the word "international" signified to Westerners: in other words, it seemed the most inclusive of potential categories. For instance, Walter Gropius had more than once employed the term "international" as inclusive of all nations and states. This is to say that in both Japan and the West an expansive logic of globalization was almost unwittingly formulated to mask an imperialist vocation.

It is indicative that by the 1950s, when a new Japanese style of design, sometimes referred to as "Japonica," was being produced under the influence of American taste, Tange and Gropius were able to shake hands. Then in 1960, the two architects collaborated on a book entitled *Katsura*.[11] This was possible in part on account of a shared logic of global scale. Around that time, a further problematic (one that still persists) was already coming into focus involving new binary oppositions: modernism versus colonialism, a universal modernist style versus particular indigenous styles, international architecture versus national architecture, or globalism versus nationalism. As a matter of course, the problematic of Japan-ness entered into this new framework. But it is important to remember that in the last phase of the war, namely, at the ultimate moment of Japanese spiritual closure, this selfsame notion had been inaugurated by Ryūichi Hamaguchi. He had claimed: "Accordingly, the natures of the two [Bangkok] projects are oppositional. In professional design terms, Maekawa's scheme is functional, while Tange's is monumental. Or in other words, Tange's is reactionary, while Maekawa's is progressive. While both are based upon the Japanese architectural tradition in which a tendency toward the performative and the spatial lingers, the means toward realization veer in opposite directions."[12]

Hamaguchi sees *performative* and *spatial* aspects in Ise Jingū, that archetype of a transparently Shintō space, and in *shinden-zukuri*, the architecture of the court of *tennō*, the descendant of Ise's god. In such a conceptualization, there is a vague, if uncanny, justification of a style capable of taking environmental or climatic differences into account. As noted above, Itō dismissed Ise Jingū as having originated in the architecture of "southern aboriginals." In other words, he professed to believe that the style came from hot and humid South Asia. Thousands of years after its arrival in Japan, the style became first a ceremonial space, and in a final apparition, the residence of *tennō*. The genealogy was inverted by Hamaguchi, and the style made to revert to its origin. Here was a strange knot of *tennō* worship with environmental consideration as its justification. Ironically, this discourse later helped assure the colonization of Japan-ness by modernism.

Yayoi and Jōmon

Throughout history, the invasion of foreign lands and collection of cultural fragments as souvenirs has from time to time stimulated a colonialist fashion for exotic imperial taste. One example, a consequence of Napoleon's invasion of Egypt, was the great archaeological expedition that inspired the Egyptian revival in Europe. An encounter with Islamic culture in Morocco and Algiers subsequently diffused the harem motif throughout nineteenth-century Europe. Via artifacts from *ukiyo-e* to African sculpture, Western capitalist expansion has invariably been eager to look beyond itself to discover the fountainhead of a new taste.

Japan, occupied by the Allied Forces after World War II, was not exempted. For the rank and file of the occupation army, Japan was a place of new cultural encounters. Indeed, some of my contemporaries—Jasper Johns and Peter Eisenman, for example—have told me their interest in Japan was motivated by memories of having been stationed there as military personnel. *Chō-chin* (paper lanterns), *sensu* (fans), *geta* (wooden clogs), and *yukata* (cotton kimonos), among other items, were all brought back as souvenirs in lieu of trophies of war. Such artifacts as had been exported earlier during the Meiji craze for *japonaiserie* were now being handled strictly by art dealers, so more accessible everyday contemporary items became the new craze. In the 1950s these were lumped together as "Japonica."

Meanwhile, as early as its succinctly entitled exhibition "Modern Architecture—International Exhibition" in 1932, the Museum of Modern Art in New York had been the master promoter of modernism in the United States. Two decades after that now famous show, the museum produced its "House in the Museum Garden"—full-scale prototypes of three residences for enlightened clients—and exhibited them serially in the museum's courtyard. The first was a house by Marcel Breuer, erstwhile youngest staff member of the Bauhaus. His project not only celebrated the coming of the Bauhaus to America, but also showcased a certain success in the postwar production of new middle-class housing types, as did the second by Gregory Ain. Third and last, the director of the architecture department, Arthur Drexler, commissioned the Japanese architect Junzō Yoshimura (1908–1997) to prepare a full-scale reproduction of the Kōjō-in's Kyaku-den guest house (fig. 3.1).[1]

3.1 Kōjō-in, Kyaku-den (Guest House of Kōjō-in) as replicated at the Museum of Modern Art, New York, and published in *Kenchiku Zasshi* (Architecture Journal), January 1954. ("General View of Japanese Exhibition House"—photograph by IMB-Thinil.) It was given the name Shōfū-sō, the House of Pine Breezes.

By this time, European modernism had moved to America and through the influence of the 1932 exhibition had come to be known as the "International Style." However, any unified tendency was absent apart from the signatures of a few recognized masters: in other words, although modernism could be understood as a method, it had not yet become a guiding stylistic principle. In such a context, Japonica might be ennobled to provide an ideal theme to fill the absence of any dominant model of style. What is more, the replica of the temple guest house reminded some visitors of the Japanese Pavilion at the World's Columbian Exposition in Chicago in 1893. Yet MoMA's intention was this time to present a masterpiece of formal, elegant *shoin-zukuri* architecture, chosen with more sophisticated taste than that exercised by the Meiji government in 1893, when its didactic copy of the Hō-ō-dō at Byōdō-in is said nevertheless to have inspired Wright. Drexler's undertaking also prompted viewers to look anew at American tradition. Looking back half a century or so and noting how Wright had employed a Japanese model to create his prairie house was a near military coup for Japanese taste. At the same time, Drexler's initiative could now with a single stroke complement the lack of a full-blown modernism.

I would thus like to examine the role of Japanese taste in the context of both American and Japanese postwar modernism, and also attempt to clarify the way Japanese taste was influenced by the cross-contextual exchanges that resulted. Two Japanese-American artists, Isamu Noguchi and Yasuhiro Ishimoto, confined in American camps during the war, visited occupied Japan after the surrender. Both had experienced European modernism at first hand: Noguchi studied sculpture with Brancusi in Paris, and Ishimoto learned photography at the new Bauhaus in Chicago, organized by survivors of the original school discredited by the Nazis. Both began to work with a fresh inclination toward Japan-ness. Noguchi's works of this period—his stage designs for Martha Graham, the well-known table for Herman Miller, and the "*Akari* [light]" produced using the technique of Gifu lanterns— are amongst the best examples of modern design. At the same time, Noguchi would not have found inspiration for these works but for his encounter with Japan-ness. He had been designing gardens since before going to Japan, but after he saw the celebrated examples in Kyoto, his designs became transformed into similar stone-embodied landscapes; his sculptures began to look like ancient clay *haniwa* symbols; and the light coming through the translucent Japanese paper in *Akari* now epitomized Japonica.

These works no longer depended on a crude simile, as had the emblazonment of the *teikan* style of the 1930s. Out of the experience of modernism inflected by Japan-ness came a form of sophisticated and abstract composition. Here again we must note that an external gaze played the determining role. After the war, Noguchi came to Japan as the embodiment of American modernism, having abstracted Japanese beauty from the vantage point of modernism. Only a few years after Itō had charged that "from the start, nothing called international can be worthwhile," the situation was turned upside down. Now *only* what was called international was deemed to be worthwhile—but again the mechanism of assessment turned on Japan-ness.

Twenty years passed after the Japonica boom, and Isamu Noguchi returned to Japan. This time, he went there to live and work. He built a studio in Muré on Shikoku Island, and made stone sculptures. In his new work he deliberately restricted the amount of carving; he sought, instead, to *let the stone speak*. In later life, he told me, "Facing a natural stone in silence, I begin to hear its voice. My work is just to follow the voice; my role is just to help it a little bit." This attitude is the same as the spirit found in *Sakuteiki* (The Record of Garden Making), an early technical manual of garden design, written in twelfth-century Japan: "The placement of the stone must follow the stone's request."[2] The point is that the subject is the stone itself, whose judgment is unquestioned. The intent of the stone must be learned through experience. Design subjectively oriented (and thus often arbitrary) is left behind. The designer must identify himself with nature's objecthood *directly*, without mediation. This norm of erasing the distance that separates subject and object—of becoming one with nature—is common to various Japanese arts: the techniques of several of the performing arts, the secret teaching of *budō* (swordsmanship), garden design, and many other practices. That Noguchi reached the ideation of traditional art by way of a long detour was to the artist himself the final mark of maturity. Noguchi represented yet another external gaze toward Japan-ness, the gaze of a Japanese-American. Meanwhile, for other Americans, he stood at the apex of the new Japonica aesthetic. He had been compelled to return to his (half-shared) origin in Japan, where he sought the voice of nature, since for Noguchi the problematic of Japan-ness had never ceased to exercise its spell-like destiny.

But in America, the Japonica boom constructed as a function of the occupation of Japan did not last very long. In fact it was abandoned by American modernists, and Noguchi's personal return to Japan may have been a sign of disappointment. It was after his failed attempt to collaborate with certain other pioneers of American modernism, such as Louis Kahn and Buckminster Fuller, that Noguchi turned back to Japan. And only then did he manage to discover a unique stance in sculpture. I believe that his achievement could only have been possible in this insular nation, and especially in a remote place like Muré. In the late 1980s, in his last years, Noguchi was chosen to represent the United States at the Venice Biennale as creator of the American pavilion. But he was passed over for the Grand Prix that I believe he ought to have won. His loss, I think (and I observed the whole event from my position as his assistant installer), was due to his strategy of pushing the traditional Japanese aspect of utilitarianism too far. Furthermore, the very expression of Japan-ness had by this time become unpopular on the contemporary international art scene.

The work of the second Japanese-American, the photographer Ishimoto, was unrelated to the Japonica taste focused by the gaze of the former U.S. occupiers. Ishimoto's photo-images of the Katsura Imperial Villa appeared in the 1960 book *Katsura* by Kenzō Tange, to which Gropius had provided a foreword (see figs. 25.3, 25.4, 25.5). They were based upon authentic modernist-oriented camera work that violently decomposed and recomposed objects in accordance with its own logic (oddly, along the lines of Kishida, in a certain sense). Inheriting the method of the new Bauhaus, Ishimoto's work expressed the materiality of Neue Sachlichkeit, by which only such images of line and plane as emphasized sheer composition were abstracted from the Katsura complex. In actuality, the really determinant elements of Katsura's architectural and aesthetic environment are large curved roof planes, trees trained into picturesque shapes, and detailed, if restrained, Japanese-style decoration. The camera work bravely eliminates all this, focusing on the surfaces that define architectural space. Floor surfaces (*tatami* or wood as well as bamboo), sliding screens (*byōbu* or *shōji* and wood panel), walls (of sand and lime plaster), and ceilings of *kasa-buchi* (long split boards) and *tsunashiro* (braided husk)—all these planar elements are articulated by linear motifs: pillars, studs, crossbeams, *nageshi* (lintel joints),[3] window frames, and handrails. Ishimoto focused on abstract compositions derived from these divisions using only his camera frame, so that his shots came to look much like the planar compositions of De Stijl or early twentieth-century constructivism. Inflection by the new photographic techniques of the Bauhaus persuasively, but misleadingly, presents the Mondrian-like method of planar division as a by-product of the architectural elevations themselves. This modernist stance decomposed and suppressed Japanese compositional aesthetic—at a time when the very colors of Japanese ancient temples were washing away and being reduced literally to white planes traversed by black lines. As epitomized in the exceptional popularity of the book *Koji Junrei* (A Pilgrimage to Ancient Temples)[4] about Nara written by the philosopher Tetsurō Watsuji (1889–1960), Japan in the late 1920s and early 1930s had begun to discover its fading past as a premise of beauty. This tendency had gained further momentum since the construction of Sutemi Horiguchi's half-modern, half-traditional Shien-sō (cf. fig. 1.3) and the publication of Hideto Kishida's compilation of photos, *Kako no Kōsei.*

Just as in 1933 Bruno Taut had been invited to Katsura, during the age of Japonica it became the custom to take visiting foreign architects there, especially those who had almost single-handedly created modern architecture, like Walter Gropius. Inspired by his visit, Gropius wrote a foreword to Tange and Ishimoto's *Katsura*, which, unfortunately, was a disappointment: it was largely a reiteration of Taut. Meanwhile, Kenzō Tange seriously wrestled with the interpretation of Ishimoto's somewhat sensational photographs. His authorial passion was due partly to an evolving local climate of restless antagonism toward Japonica.

The painter Taro Okamoto (1911–1996), who had also been exposed to European modernism, returned to Japan from Paris in 1940. He vowed to express the schism inherent in French modern art—between abstract and concrete, or "oppositionalism" to use his term—taking his cue from the surrealists. Intellectually, he sought to rediscover Japan drawing on his proximity to the members of the so-called College of Sociology, that is, the circle of Emmanuel Levinas, Georges Bataille, and Roger Caillois. By way of this new perspective Okamoto was awakened to the beauty of ancient earthenware of the Jōmon era.[5] A little earlier, in response to the Japonica trend, a reappreciation of ancient Japanese pots and utensils had occurred, above all in the sophisticated sense of beauty of terracotta *haniwa* figures from the ancient Yayoi period. But, in opposition to this tendency, Okamoto's propaganda stressed the dynamic beauty of even older, native Jōmon patterns, which are like roaring flames. And it was the challenge of this aesthetic that gained public attention. In line with Okamoto, Tange shifted his architectural aesthetic away from a serene compositional beauty of transparency (reminiscent of Shintō shrines and Katsura Villa)— Yayoiesque, to him, as exemplified in the main building of his Hiroshima Peace Center (1955). His take on the Jōmonesque may be seen in the assertive design for his Municipal Building of Kurashiki city (1960). Thus synchronized in their beliefs, Tange and Okamoto embarked on a long and lasting collaboration.

This archaeological periodization—Jōmon/Yayoi—first surfaced in the mid-1950s. Unlike today's obsessive search for the roots of Japanese culture, the dichotomy was exploited mainly in quest of a measure of aesthetic judgment and a modality of production on the part of both artist and architect. Okamoto's partisanship of Jōmon-style, as opposed to Yayoi-style, earthenware appears to me a return of sorts to an event in the history of European thought some one hundred years before, which occasioned a shift in both temporal and aesthetic consciousness: namely, Nietzsche's opposition of the Dionysian and the Apollonian modes as recorded in *The Birth of Tragedy*. Both distinctions take the past as a norm, yet neither is much concerned with actual historical order, since both seek instead to construct a strategic stance toward the present. Reading Okamoto's championship of Jōmon in a social context, it might be said that while the beauty of Yayoi was what American modernism brought from Japan to New York as a trophy of the occupation (inspiring the line of architecture that resulted in Junzō Yoshimura's Shōfū-sō [House of Pine Breezes] at MoMA in 1954),[6] the beauty of Jōmon encouraged by Okamoto's European modernist stance secretly nurtured a native dynamism opposing the gaze of the occupier.

In architecture, a corresponding discourse was under construction: Yayoiesque Japonism was deemed *traditional*, or elitist, while Jōmonesque nativism was seen as *populist*. It was believed that

Jōmon somehow expressed the energy of the masses. As a consequence, Japonica—tinged with the colonialist gaze—became a target of criticism. For instance, as we saw, Tange's Memorial Peace Center was the concrete embodiment of Hamaguchi's theory of a Japanese national architectural style. As the first realization of transparent *modernist* space in Japan, it achieved a flowing space by taking Katsura as its model and transposing the traditional compositional proportions—*kiwari*—to its steel and concrete frame. Yet after the positing of the Jōmon-versus-Yayoi duality, Tange's work at Hiroshima came to be seen as an aristocratic, antipopulist Yayoiesque architecture. When the occupation was finally lifted and an anticolonialist movement took wing, the Apollonian/Dionysian dichotomy was immediately caught up in the political context of an American imperialism versus the populist struggle against it.

In his essay in *Katsura* (1960), "Tradition and Creation in Japanese Architecture," Kenzō Tange further elaborated the shift from Yayoiesque to Jōmonesque. In place of Katsura as epitome of a dynastic flavor, he dared to depict the villa as the opposite—as populist. With a logic all too evidently overextended, Tange felt bound to undertake this interpretive shift owing to the immediate political climate. Therefore, his essay barely mentions Katsura's architecture or its garden. Around the same time, the new polar opposition was expanded to embrace a contrast between Jōmonesque/Dionysian/lower-class/pit dwelling (*tateana jūkyo*) and Yayoiesque/Apollonian/aristocratic/platform-type housing (*takayuka-shiki jūkyo*). This extension went beyond the circle of architects and critics, touching even those architectural historians who proceeded from a positivist premise, such as Hirotarō Ōta (1912–). Ōta's *Zusetsu Nihon Jutaku-shi* (Illustrated History of Japanese Housing) (1948), for example, explained the genealogy of dwelling types from pit dwelling to platform house as the product of an overlapping history of class consolidation.[7]

Tange spent most of his 1960 essay elaborating the two opposing cultural lineages, and finally posited Katsura as an example of synthesis based on two contradictory terms by resorting to "dialectics," the trendy rhetorical refuge of the time. Here one must call attention to a singular point about Okamoto: although he ought to have been familiar with Alexandre Kojève's sophisticated contemporary reading of Hegel so influential in France, he extolled only the destructive and irreconcilable. Indeed, in later years, he spoke only of "explosion," with no intimation of a dialectical synthesis. Meanwhile, Tange, who was almost certainly influenced by Okamoto's destructive dynamism, nonetheless lurched toward a synthesis of his own devising even before fully corroborating the notion of "fissure," that is, destruction. His essay on Katsura thus dispensed with the energy of head-on conflict far too quickly, while cleverly encapsulating the discursive Jōmon/Yayoi conflict of the time. In his words:

> The *shoin* of the Katsura Palace belongs fundamentally to the aristocratic Yayoi tradition as it developed from the *shinden-zukuri* to the *shoin-zukuri* style. Accordingly, the building is dominated by the principles of aesthetic balance and continuous sequence of patterns in space. And yet there is something which prevents it from becoming a mere formal exercise and gives its space a lively movement and a free harmony. This something is the naïve vitality and ever-renewed potentiality of the Jōmon tradition of the common people.
>
> The Jōmon element is strong in the rock formations and the teahouses of the garden. There, however, the aesthetic canons of the Yayoi tradition act as a sobering force which prevents the dynamic flow, the not-quite-formed forms, the dissonances, from becoming chaotic.
>
> At Katsura, then, the dialectic of tradition and creation is realized.
>
> It was in the period when the Katsura Palace was built that the two traditions, Jōmon and Yayoi, first actually collided. When they did, the cultural formalism of the upper class and the vital energy of the lower class met. From their dynamic union emerged the creativeness seen in Katsura—a dialectic resolution of tradition and antitradition.[8]

Meanwhile, in his preface, Walter Gropius complained a little about the garden of Katsura, favoring as he did the taste for a more orthodox Japan-ness espoused by Taut:

> If we judge by the highest standards, we may also find some weak points in Katsura garden. Though its intimate spaces, its pavements, and its plantings are of enchanting beauty, the overemphasis on

playful details sometimes impairs the continuity and coherence of the spatial conception as a whole. The importance given to overcrowded rock compositions, mainly around the Shōkintei Teahouse, reminds me of the age-old Japanese leisure game of *bonseki*, consisting of a tray, filled with sand, in which pebbles of different size and color are arranged in artful compositions.[9]

The configuration of stones near the Shōkin-tei Teahouse is admittedly the most vulgar spot in the garden, where the stereotypical landscapes of Japanese tradition are miniaturized and reassembled like the *makura kotoba* (pillow word) technique in ancient poetry. Rhetorical clichés refer to renowned scenic spots throughout Japan such as *Ama-no-hashidate* (Heaven's standing bridge), *Sumiyoshi-no-matsu* (the pine of Sumiyoshi), and *Akashi-no-hama* (the beach of Akashi). This criticism is proof of Gropius's own exquisite taste. He recommended elimination of certain elements including the big *sotetsu* tree in front of the *machiai* (or waiting area of the tea pavilion)—which Taut also disclaimed. These *ishi-gumi* (stone arrangements) are indeed vulgarized examples of a style known today as *Enshū-gonomi*,[10] which reverted to a stereotypical pattern during the later Edo period.

When selecting Ishimoto's photographs of Katsura, Tange had rejected any view that was the least kitschlike, even the curved plane of a roof. In his foreword he clearly states his intention deliberately to select and exclude: "This is a visual record of the living Katsura as it exists in the minds of an architect and a photographer. We who made the record may conceivably be accused of dismembering Katsura, and those who come to know the palace from the pictures given here may well be disappointed to find upon actually visiting it that it is different from what they had expected."[11] It was thus almost inevitable that Gropius should criticize certain aesthetic choices as *bonseki*-like, that is, resembling those miniature landscapes constructed of sand and stones on a tiny tray.

In fact, however, the stepping stones arranged around these clichéd elements exhibit nevertheless an intense dynamism, like the broken poetic meter that goes far beyond mere intended irregularity (*kuzushi*). Ishimoto took many close-up photographs of these stones, and Tange was quick to recognize here the Jōmon element. His appreciation of the *ishi-gumi* in this context was based upon the

new historical assertion that gardeners of the late medieval age—
who designed, for instance, the famous stone garden of Ryōan-
ji—belonged to a group of outcasts, the *kawara-mono* (riverbank
dwellers). Indeed Ryōan-ji itself had been another discovery of
Japonism. Philip Johnson once confided to me that as he looked
at the garden, tears came to his eyes. And even today the pro-
logue most frequently resorted to is a newspaper report describing
Isamu Noguchi's excitement on visiting the temple garden for the
first time. This is to say Tange sought to place himself in a position
contradictory to that of Taut and Gropius—but without going all
the way. His dialectic, or his vocation as a synthesizer, rendered his
discourse ambiguous. Many an intellectual discourse of the time in
Japan followed the schematic three-stage dialectic—a token, after
all, of the Stalinist spell.

While Jōmon dynamism was being thus elevated, there was
yet another modernism operating in the background. Le Corbusier's projects in India (in Chandigarh and later on in Ahmeda-
bad) garnered attention in the mid-1950s almost as soon as they
were made public, characterized as they were by the use of so-
called *béton brut*: rough form-finished concrete, without the normal
coating of cement or masonry. In the 1930s, Le Corbusier had used
a kind of wall where rough stones were often piled up beneath a
white stucco superstructure. In the postwar *béton brut* aesthetic,
structure itself was deliberately left uncovered. One might see all
this as having been necessitated by conditions in India (notably, a
lack of technical proficiency). However, at the same time, a sense
of reminding the beholder of an image of cities left in ruins by
World War II can scarcely be avoided. Lives lived out in bombarded and destroyed cities (as seen in the neorealist films of the
Italian director Roberto Rossellini) and the state of objects dis-
torted almost beyond recognition were implied, I would claim,
in *béton brut*. A similar sensibility could be remarked in London in
the mid-1950s, when the "angry young men" in theater and the
Independent Group (the forerunners of pop art) began to be
active. The corresponding tendency among such English architects
as Alison and Peter Smithson was called new brutalism. They left
underlying elements—not only the structural framing, but also
pipes and sashes—just as they were, without covering. Their
designs permitted any and all objects and elements to exist in a
state of pure immediacy. It was a matter of course that when this

3.2 The National Museum of Western Art by Le Corbusier (1957–1959, since modified), at Ueno, Tokyo.

postwar European modernism arrived in Japan via Le Corbusier's Indian work, it was welcomed as a tactic to confront and counter American Japonism. Brutalism quickly merged into the recent context of Jōmon appreciation. Liveliness, brutality, roughness, and the exposure of inner workings, or guts—such elements easily overlapped and accorded with the aesthetic derived from Jōmon earthenware.

When Le Corbusier visited Japan to oversee the National Museum of Western Art in Tokyo (1957; fig. 3.2), he, too, was invited to Katsura. He is famous for having made detailed drawings and notes, rather than for any verbal pronouncements. According to what remains, it appears he made some sketches of the *azuma-*

ya (a hipped-roof arbor used as a place of repose) called *Manji-tei* (swastika arbor), built on an elevation behind the Shōkin-tei Tea-house—but noted only the fact that the stool-like seats were swastika-shaped. By a strange coincidence, he determined the basic plan of his museum as a swastika, but this was based upon the spiral matrix of a museum type he had evolved three decades earlier. He commented that the interiors of the teahouse and *sukiya* pavilions all had too many lines, making the architecture busy. The Japanese architectural public concluded that Le Corbusier was therefore uninterested in Japan-ness. Some even said that he did not have the sensibility to comprehend it. The fact was that by the 1930s Le Corbusier had already begun to depart from the sophisticated, minimalist composition of Japan-ness in the direction of a new brute materiality, voluptuous freshness, and free-form composition. Thus his apparent lack of interest in Katsura. In any case, this oppositional stance was seen in Japan as deeply related to the formation of the new Jōmonesque perspective. Behind the then-flourishing and fashionable discourse on culture of the masses, i.e., "mass theory [*minshū-ron*]," was the shadow of new brutalism. The taste of the time favored this heavy architecture with its raw concrete surfaces and implied rhetoric of strength and dynamism. The Japanese architectural designs soon to win international acclaim were created out of the experience of this turn, and yet once again around Japan-ness.

All in all, during the period it is possible to theorize two kinds of Japan-ness. On the one hand, the sophisticated, tranquil transparency of Yayoiesque/Apollonian/aristocratic/platform housing—corresponding to Japanese taste in general, or to Japonica-based American modernism. On the other, the dynamic opacity of the Jōmonesque/Dionysian/populist/pit dwelling, which coincided with the Japanese version of brutalist European modernism. The former ethos was inseparable from the period of occupation by the Allied Forces led by the United States and was a quasi-military achievement. The latter was related to a stance opposing the terms of peace as determined at San Francisco and the new Japan-U.S. Security Treaty, which countenanced a form of indirect American rule. Tange's *Katsura* adroitly kept step with this shifting political ground, notwithstanding the fact that even the architect's hasty dialectical synthesis retained and exposed his natural affinity with the Yayoi trend. Meanwhile, Okamoto persisted in his Jōmonesque dynamism, speaking to a destructive and explosive aesthetic. In collaboration, each played his part: Tange's stable framework, and Okamoto's bombastic energy. These twin discourses of the period reflected the real and conflicting forces within a Japan under foreign pressure: occupied Japan wedged beneath the American defense umbrella in the new world structure of polarized conflict and cold war; and the youthful opposition to it, deployed under the name Zen-gaku-ren (National Federation of Students Self-Government Associations).[12] The Jōmon discourses were not irrelevant to the movement that culminated in the Zen-gaku-ren's anti-Japan-U.S. Security Treaty demonstration at the National Diet Building in 1960, supported as it was by widespread anti-American sentiment across our nation. This act of protest burst like an Okamoto explosion, yet a half-century-long conservative rule has succeeded it. As part of this latter-day context, the focus of the discourse on Japan-ness was again transformed.

We have already seen how in Japan Bruno Taut took up and promoted Katsura and Ise as exemplars of Japan-ness. Both villa and
shrine were, incidentally or otherwise, imperial edifices, that is,
patently *tennō*-esque. As late as the 1950s, while discourses on
Katsura grew along the lines of the Jōmon-Yayoi opposition, Ise
Jingū was still set aside, excluded from architectural debate, and
isolated on a shelf of ethical nonjudgment. Ise was identified
exclusively with the esoteric national rituals of the imperial household. This limited contextualization was maintained in no small
part by the state's suppression of details of what went on there.
All activities, including the precise dismantling and rebuilding
the shrine underwent every twenty years, called *shikinen-zōkan*,[1]
were shrouded in secrecy.

Ise Jingū is rather simple in terms of its architecture. It was
believed, up until the 1950s, that there had been no major changes
or developments since the first ritualized rebuilding of the shrine
late in the seventh century. At that time, the conventions of historical inquiry into architecture were, so to speak, under the influence of Darwinism, and thus an architecture without stylistic
development was deemed worthless, so that Ise as an obscured
site of secret ritual rejected any architectural interpretation or
judgment. Neither was it taken up as part of the Jōmon/Yayoi debate. According to its look—rough and thick—the shrine and its
precinct appeared Jōmonesque/Dionysian, although in formal
terms it belonged to the platform-style housing reserved for aristocrats (i.e., the *shinden-zukuri*) and in actuality it was the property of
the imperial household. Hence, modification of the standards of
judgment was overdue. Returning to Hamaguchi's "Problem of
Style in Japanese National Architecture," Ise would belong to his

category of the *spatial* and *performative*—to the Japanese architectonic will—rather than the *material* and *constructive* characteristics
of the Western architectonic will. As such, any reassessment of
Ise would mandate a shift of attention from the building itself
(its form and structure) to its formation and origins, including the
environment (i.e., climate). All this was foreshadowed by Taut's
appreciation of Ise. He wrote not only how Ise would in future
become a destination of architectural pilgrimage, like the Acropolis, but also that "[the Parthenon] is the greatest and most aesthetically sublime building in stone as the Ise shrine is in wood."[2]

Taut gave attention and authority to the sacred atmosphere of
the Ise shrine, while at the same time referring to its material construction. He was well aware of the environment surrounding the
shrine—a dense forest, where aged and huge Japanese cedars loom
over the diminutive buildings. Taut's motives of appreciation at Ise
went beyond the beauty of composition and the logic of proportion he experienced as a pleasure to the eye at Katsura, and were
linked to his recognition of the Athenian Acropolis as an absolute
standard of cultural value. The Acropolis had long afforded the
very image of architecture itself for Western architects. Without
hesitation, he made the leap from the Acropolis as the building of
all buildings to the imperial shrine at Ise as a genuine or true object
(*honmono*). Concerning its sacredness, Taut seems to have needed
no further explanation and never offered a distinction in kind
between buildings and surroundings. It was Sutemi Horiguchi's
Kenchiku ni okeru Nihontekina-mono (Japan-ness in Architecture)[3]
of 1934 that appears to have shifted the focus of appreciation of
Ise from its architecture to the sacred atmosphere of the precinct.
This is nearly contemporary with Taut's Ise account and seems almost a response:

> The expression as an architectural ensemble, built within a
> thousand-year-old forest and surrounded by a sacred hedge [*mi-
> zugaki*] and imperial fence [*tamagaki*], has long echoed the feeling
> of the twelfth-century monk/poet, Saigyō: "I know not what lies
> within, but I am in tears with gratitude."[4]

In the context of the 1930s, Horiguchi sought to elaborate the
unmediated "gratitude" that had come to form the basis of Ise ap-

preciation. Though he had been a pioneer of modernism in the 1920s, later in life his position gradually shifted. As he later confessed, he had when young visited the Acropolis and seen fragments of the columns of the Parthenon scattered about. He felt that "one who had grown up at the farthest end of the East could in no way compete with [the ancients] brought up in that rich world." Thus, Horiguchi determined to study Japanese medieval residential architecture (*sukiya-zukuri*) as epitomized in the sixteenth-century teahouse, or at Katsura Imperial Villa, and to design accordingly, in order to "follow a path suitable and familiar to [him]."[5] Here one may glimpse an empirical if veiled critique of Taut's shortcut leap from the timber-framed Ise to the marble Acropolis. Horiguchi is no doubt seeking a way to detach Ise from the power of the Parthenon's materiality. He had by this time come to believe that the evocation in Saigyō's *waka* of an intuitive sympathy for the power of nature went beyond the mere constructivism of Western architecture. Such an appreciation entailed a shift of focus from the buildings themselves to the larger environment—namely, *shin-iki* (the sacred atmosphere).

The more "positivist" historian of architecture, Hirotarō Ōta, likewise sought to shift the Tautian assessment of Ise in the direction of a more Saigyōesque appreciation. He undertook to rewrite Japanese architectural history from a modernist perspective and came to be known for his idea that different social classes produce their own housing types: pit dwellings and then the *minka* (farmer's vernacular dwelling) for the general populace as against platform housing and much later *shinden-zukuri* and *shoin-zukuri* for the aristocracy. He remarked in the late 1960s:

> What, of Ise Jingū, so much impressed Saigyō, who sang: "I know not what lies within, but I am in tears with gratitude"? It has long been questioned whether these lines were really Saigyō's or not. Yet they came to be so widely known because they sound a feeling shared by Japanese. Was it the beauty of architecture such as caused Taut to set Ise as an equal to the Parthenon that impressed Saigyō? Perhaps not. It was more likely the deep forest of Japanese cedar and the precinct of raw wood that serenely surrounds the shrine—it was the harmony between the environment and the architecture that impressed him.[6]

During the thirty years bracketing the defeat in 1945, that is, roughly between 1930 to 1960, the appreciation of Ise gradually shifted from Taut's comparison with the Western standard of the Acropolis to a sympathy with the Saigyōesque awe of nature. Here again Hamaguchi's distinction between Western architecture—*material* and *constructive*—and Japanese—*spatial* and *performative*—comes to the fore. Taut's approach was definitely materialist and constructivist, while Saigyō's sensitivity toward nature was the opposite.

In the epoch-making changes of the time—the Greater East Asia Co-prosperity Sphere, the defeat, the occupation, and the anti-U.S.-Japan Security Treaty struggle—the problematic of Japan-ness was continuously at issue, as part of a search for Japan's own uniqueness. I believe that the Japanese reception of modern architecture went hand in hand with, or even paralleled, this process. It was overwhelmingly apparent to the isolated, insular nation that the modern West existed outside, and that in order to survive Japan had ever and again to confront this Western impetus. I repeat—the momentum for the problematic of Japan-ness belonged to the gaze from without, whose object was Japan as Other. As the Japanese processed Western modernity in their own fashion, they somehow also looked for Japan as the Other within themselves. Such was the discourse of Japan-ness and the design approach that resulted. In the postwar era it was Kenzō Tange, as noted by Hamaguchi, who intuitively—if not quite rationally—understood this complex relationship.

At the time of the Jōmon/Yayoi debate, Tange published a long essay, "Gendai Kenchiku no Sozō to Nihon Kenchiku no Dentō [Contemporary Architectural Creation and Japanese Architectural Tradition]" (1956).[7] As his title indicates, Tange felt able dialectically to synthesize the modern (creation of the new) and the national (conservation of tradition) in a way that continued the "Overcoming Modernity" debate of 1942. What was new was the putative consciousness of class conflict: Yayoiesque = Apollonian = aristocrat = platform housing versus Jōmonesque = Dionysian = popular = pit dwelling. True to form, Tange upheld both issues.

> If the space that Gothic architecture achieved, the space that confronted nature with a new technology, is a space that

humans nonetheless wrested from Nature, the space of Japanese architecture is a space that is given by Nature.... [Japanese architecture] is not that which is based upon a human will to three-dimensionality, but a leaning toward or sinking into Nature.... The Nature apparent in the context of Japanese architecture is appreciated in the above manner, and is not Nature grasped by the act of transforming reality.[8]

Here we must recall Masao Maruyama's earlier paradigms: *jinen* (nature) and *sakui* (artifice or invention). Maruyama's "nature" had been filtered through the Chinese rationalist thinking of the Chu Hsi School,[9] as assimilated and recast by Japan in the late Edo period, while Tange's was closer to the sense conveyed by the Western term, as translated into Japanese (Nature = *shizen*) in the Meiji period. The latter interpretation being more substantive, Tange also believed in a contemporary architectural "creation" where human agents, confronting Nature, subjectively create, in accordance with modern Western notions of subjectivity. On such premises he identifies "the space that humans wrested from Nature" with Western architectural space (for some reason, he always used the example of Gothic architecture), and by contrast, "the space that is given by Nature" with Japanese space. His phraseology suggests a view of Japanese architectural space as nonsubjective, passive, and vulnerable, in which context he posits himself, the architect, as a creative subject. Thus, his attack on the Yayoiesque and aristocratic element as conservative also assumes a measure of self-criticism. Up until the mid-1950s, Tange's only realized works had been the Memorial Peace Center at Hiroshima, its main building clearly modeled on Katsura, and his own residence in the Tokyo suburbs (1953), indisputably a present-day version of *shinden-zukuri*. Yet here a back-formation of subjectivity took place, implying self-critique. Within the Jōmon/Yayoi debate, he now had to shift to the side of Dionysian and populist Jōmon by associating himself with modern Western subjectivity and a concept of creation as "artifice." This, first and foremost, expressed a will to abandon Japonica as American-contrived modernism; he was compelled rather suddenly to shift to the new brutalism, as a European alternative. In this process, Tange emphasized the creative subject as a human agent confronting a benign (but no longer all-encompassing) Nature.

It needs to be stressed that the *jinen* and *sakui* Maruyama had salvaged from the Tokugawa era were thoroughly different from "nature" and "design" as these appear in the context of the 1950s, especially with respect to the notion of the subject. One of the significant figures in Maruyama's book was Ogyū Sorai (1666–1728), a neo-Confucianist philosopher of the mid-Edo period, who had attempted to undermine the preeminence of Nature (*jinen*) in the Chu Hsi School by supplying the role of "sage" as a transcendent subject. Yet another well-known figure, Motoori Norinaga (1730–1801), a scholar of *kokugaku* (the study of national classics) and *Kojiki* (the mythical story of the birth of Japan), had proceeded to take a different line of argument against the domination of Nature—that found in *kokugaku*—and so posed another version of the transcendent subject. Maruyama explains:

> Therefore in order to maintain the primacy of innate naturalness over human invention, while avoiding any ideal absolutization of Nature itself, there was no alternative but to posit a superhuman, absolute personality behind innate nature, as its foundation. Thus Norinaga introduced the theory of "*Nature as the invention of the Gods.*"[10]

Both Sorai's sage and Norinaga's gods were, in different terms, transcendent subjects. Such invocations of transcendence were a logical sine qua non: only a superhuman could have constructed the cosmos. Thus the question of the transcendental was not easily overcome. Meanwhile, in the discourse of the 1950s, it was commonplace to short-circuit the whole issue. Subjectivity was blended into Nature, while as a limiting case the human being was nonetheless entitled to act as the agent of creative artifice.

In broad terms, therefore, one might interpret the pursuit of Japan-ness spelled out in the "Overcoming Modernity" debate as Japanese tradition *qua* Nature overcoming Western modernity *qua* artifice. But at this point Tange attempted to sabotage the equivalence. In his creation versus tradition essay quoted above, he was clearly on the side of modernist *sakui* and even declares his intention to destroy Japanese tradition once and for all. On this premise, and by openly espousing the new brutalism, Tange completed his Yoyogi aquatic stadia (1964; fig. 4.1) for the Tokyo Olympics,

4.1 National Olympic Stadium complex, Yoyogi, Tokyo, by Kenzō Tange (1961–1964).

a state undertaking that in every way signals the postwar era in Japan. This work embodies Dionysian dynamism, and furthermore, the gigantic suspended roof structure is so Japanese as to remind us of the great hall of Tōdai-ji in Nara. The National Olympic Stadium complex, then, would seem to prove the paradox that the destruction of tradition, which Okamoto had spoken of in somewhat ironic terms, was the most positive way of rehabilitating the traditional. It was a landmark creation of substantial uniqueness, no longer relying on a subexotic Japonica, nor even upon identifiable brutalist themes borrowed from Le Corbusier at Chandigarh. Tange's iconic work marks the high point in the Japanese reception of modernist practice as regards the problematic of Japan-ness.

The very fact of being a state-sponsored project speaks to the nature of this problematic. All of Tange's major projects and works—the Greater East Asia Memorial Building, the Atomic Bomb Memorial Park, Hiroshima, and now the Yoyogi Olympic complex (1964)—had addressed themes that enabled the nation of Japan to express its will in a sequence of political climates. And the appraisal of Tange as the architect most adept at satisfying and expressing the will of the nation still persists. One should probably also interpret Tange's desire to produce Expo '70 in Osaka as his intention to discharge this perceived responsibility as state architect. But, as it turns out, no trace of the Japan-ness problematic was visible in this exposition. For by this time the state was losing hold of any theme on behalf of which to express itself. The postwar economic recovery had succeeded, and the rehabilitated nation-state could be called a techno-giant. This nation-state brought into being by the Meiji Restoration came at last to be represented in its economy and technology, no longer by its traditions or culture. Expo '70 was the thematic turning point at which the Japan-ness problematic began to metamorphose drastically, or more succinctly, merely to decompose.

Hence, beginning in 1970, Kenzō Tange, after following a straight party line of Japan-ness as subscribed to by the nation, had suddenly to work without a theme. Japan no longer required an architect who represented the state. Therefore, like the popes who dismissed Michelangelo for a period of time, or deserted Francesco Borromini on a whim, the Japanese state abandoned Tange. He went, so to say, into exile, being invited by royalty to work in the newly rich oil-producing countries, like Giovanni Lorenzo Bernini coaxed to France as a guest of the nation to design the Louvre palace in Paris. After completing not a few literal palaces, and the like, in more than twenty countries, Tange returned to Japan, this time to work as a thoroughly commercial architect.

Twenty years before his exile, Tange had chosen to stand on the side of artifice—"the space that humans wrested from Nature"—as opposed to "the space that is given by Nature." He is still remembered for introducing (or reintroducing) the architect as a modern subject in the role of protagonist in a supposedly *jinen*-dominant Japan. That is, the human as universal subject—a mythical yet real protagonist as opposed to Sorai's sage or Norinaga's gods, these having been hitherto the only protomodern transcendent subjects.

I worked in Tange's studio for ten years after the mid-1950s, and was a partner for ten years after that. During that time, I was deeply fascinated to hear his clear advocacy of the modern subject as the originator of imagination. Historically, this subject was a stranger who had come from the West at the onset of our reception of modernity. To become this modern subject in Japan was to view Japan—one's own origin—by taking up the role of a stranger; it was to understand the Japanese self as Other. Even Chūta Itō, who was able to see that the buildings of Ise Jingū must have originated in some more southerly climate, had spoken from the stance of the modern West, despite his later fanatical nationalism. In the case of Tange, the architect besought the locus of artifice (intention), while somewhere in himself he had always been strongly drawn to "nature" in the sense of Saigyō. This was evident in his essay on Ise, written after *Katsura*, in the mid-1960s, for by that time he had begun to shift his point of view from the material/constructivist theory of the architectonic back to the spatial/performative theory of environment.

> The ancient Japanese sought their symbols and divine images in nature—in rocks, trees, and water. This way of looking at nature is still at the very core of the spiritual make-up of Japanese today.
>
> Ise came into being through the sublimation of symbols into a basic form. The final achievement of the quintessential form represented by Ise also meant the completion of the corpus of Japanese religious mythology and approximately coincided with the end of the process of melding the Japanese people into a whole. The vigorous conceptual ability of the ancient Japanese who fashioned the form of Ise was sustained by the energies released during the nation-building process. The form of Ise partakes of the primordial essence of the Japanese people. To probe this form and the way it came into being is to go to the very foundations of Japanese culture.[11]

Buildings themselves were no longer even spoken of. Tange gradually transposes the grounds for appreciating Ise to anthropology, deploying recent achievements in historiography and archaeology. He wrote, "Out of it, out of nature's darkness, the rigorous conceptual ability of the ancient Japanese gradually fashioned various symbols of the spirit culminating in the creation of the form of Ise. Here primeval darkness and eternal light, the vital and the aesthetic, are in balance, and a world of harmony with nature unfolds."[12] Previously, from the point of view of a will to artifice (intention), he had been critical of Japanese architecture as passive before Nature; in this appreciation of Ise, he still followed the modernist ideal, yet now grasped its architecture as a world in harmony with nature, tending toward an appreciation of the Saigyō-esque gratitude and awe. Simply put, his loyalties were split.

In fact the proof of this divide, such as it appeared at the time, was the advent of a *new* Japan-ness at Expo '70. As the producer of the entire event, Tange also had to oversee the design of the central space, Omatsuri Hiroba (Festival Plaza), rather than the less centrally placed Japanese pavilion. Taro Okamoto joined the team as thematic director with the result that Okamoto's giant sculpture, *Taiyō no Tō* (Tower of the Sun), penetrated the big roof of the modernist space frame (fig. 4.2) covering the plaza. This was a clash of differences—modern versus anti-modern. I designed the devices for staging grand events in Festival Plaza, and was one of the supporters of having a huge roof. But alas, when at last I saw Okamoto's tower (looking like a giant phallus) penetrating the soft membrane of the roof, I thought to myself that the battle for modernity had finally been lost. The primordial—which Tange had poetically cast as "primeval darkness and eternal light"—ended up as bombastic kitsch, in all too candid a manner. The smiling mask affixed to the tower felt somewhat eerily like a presiding alien—upsetting enough by itself. But, what was worse, you had to acknowledge the fact that Japan-ness was so omnipresent and in such a sad way. In the thirty years since, the predicament has come clear: the big roof was demolished, and only the vulgar Tower of the Sun remains—in fearful witness to the final celebration of the state, Japan.

Thus far I have attempted to sketch the history of Japan-ness, which the island nation of Japan constructed in the process of assimilating modern architecture in the roughly thirty years from the 1930s to the end of the 1960s. Thereafter, until the late 1980s, the world was polarized beneath a sublime nuclear umbrella. Be-

4.2 Festival Plaza by Kenzō Tange, with *Taiyō no Tō* (Tower of the Sun) by Tarō Okamoto, at Expo '70 in Osaka. Photograph by Shinchōsha Press, Tokyo.

tween the defeat of the worldwide "cultural revolution" (1968) and the destruction of the Berlin Wall (1989), the epoch customarily known as postmodern, demarcation of the traditional line separating interior and exterior in this insular nation has been altogether transformed. Throughout the period, the gaze of Japanness has been redirected from within to without. I also participated in this process of reorientation.

Since the beginning of the 1990s, cultural space around the world has been redesignated as a series of archipelagos, as it were, with multiple centers. Inevitably, the insular Japan has become one of these mutually heterogeneous configurations. That is to say that the very border that once gave substance to Japan-ness has been decomposing. Now it must be observed that the problematic of cultural identity exists in a new form: mutual exchanges across oceans, the *intermundia* (of Epicurus, or of Marx), and the space-in-between communities—all that was previously deemed void. The autonomy of such island groupings is no longer assured by a dialectic of internal and external gaze, let alone any physical boundary. There is no more need to flaunt our cultural identity (whether Japan-ness, or Englishness, or Germanness, or French-ness, or something else). Within the cultural space organized between our newly delineated archipelagos, the problematic of nationhood has at last been rendered obsolete. Now it is events occurring over the sea or in space—no longer merely those happening on land—that are likely to be problematized.

Ka (Hypothesis) and *Hi* (Spirit)

The theme of the eighth of the Congrès Internationaux d'Architecture Moderne (CIAM 8), which took place in 1951, was "Heart of the City: Towards the Humanization of Urban Life." The invitation was a call for strategies enabling modern architects to contribute to reconstruction of cities bombed during the war. From Japan, Kunio Maekawa and Kenzō Tange traveled to Hoddesdon, England, presenting Tange's scheme for the Hiroshima Peace Center. Reflecting and responding to the climate of the time, the project and its theme garnered tremendous support.

In traditional Western cities, the plaza has often provided a core. Notably, in the first half of the twentieth century morphological analysis of the town was conducted by the Austrian Camillo Sitte, among others. Those architects who gathered at CIAM in 1951 were about to undertake a reconstruction of the traditional urban plan. Le Corbusier's proposed radical restructuring of Paris and Hilberseimer's proposal for Berlin, both of the 1920s, prophesied that the concentric structure of the city center familiar since late medieval times was no longer functional. Moreover, during the 1930s and 40s, the significance of the city center had shifted from an intimate space framing and nurturing everyday life, and full of nostalgia, to the focus of political events, such as rallies and demonstrations. Recalling only a few such events, there had been the Nazis' mass rally at Nuremberg, the Rockefeller Center Plaza parade to celebrate the Allied victory in World War II, and the annual May Day celebration in Red Square in Moscow—and, much closer to our time, the Tiananmen Square declaration in Beijing. The masses gathered in plazas and squares were no longer acquaintances meeting in the intimate center of a traditional community but multitudes of David Riesman's "lonely crowd."[1]

Modern architects were charged with exploiting new technologies to reaccommodate the anonymous displaced denizen of the already overcrowded metropolis. The obvious solution was to construct cubicles—high-rise cages detached from the ground. Meanwhile, Martin Heidegger's fervent hope for a return to the land through the exercise of *technē* had resulted in turmoil and disaster. Nightmarish scenes had filled the town squares when ordinary Germans strove to recapture their homeland. It appeared that the only place people could live was in the air or on the water. The architects of the time tried to seduce them by saying: we have built you cages in the sky, and while you may not be able to fly, you will use elevators to reach them.

But then, after the war, modernist architects began seeking once again to *recover* the role of the plaza and its traditional urban function. A compromise, or setback, had occurred, perhaps a humanist revisionism would be the term. The "Heart of the City" conference was the last to include the original generation of CIAM participants. When the organization was at its peak, Le Corbusier had repeatedly stressed the image of his Ville Radieuse, which took the human body as a model—the central nervous system of the brain (political and administrative center), the internal organs (residences), and the circulatory system (traffic). All this was assimilated to the architect's concept of an ideally proportioned *modulor,* an anthropomorphization of the golden section of ancient Greece, modeled after Renaissance humanism. Le Corbusier sought to realize his scheme, above all in the master plan of Chandigarh, the capital of Punjab. The idea of "The Heart of the City" likewise implied a new anthropomorphism. Its premise was the shift of modern society from *Gemeinschaft* to *Gesellschaft*, as articulated in the urbanism of the 1920s. It was an irreversible process through which the organic space of the plaza was to be standardized in the form of a mass-produced dwelling machine for anonymous masses. Likewise, Mies van der Rohe's cubical grid also rising high in the air was imagined as a response to social change.

Le Corbusier and Mies van der Rohe are considered the founders of the modern movement in architecture, even though operating from different continents after Mies's move to Chicago. Le Corbusier, for his part, persisted in remaining in Europe. He was invited once to Soviet Russia, where he was ultimately rejected by Stalin; he also failed in approaching Mussolini; and he was even disliked by the pro-Nazi Vichy regime in France. Meanwhile, while sketching the vivid flesh of Algerian whores, he hit upon the idea of recomposing architecture and the city as the silhouette of the human body. By contrast, Mies van der Rohe in America composed cubic grids to accommodate *das Man,* who had by now lost any personal features. In the space of such a grid, everything would be possible but could be left in a state of incompleteness. The city would proliferate endlessly as a combination of grids, but without an internal principle to relate and connect them. Were our fate simply to accept contemporary society as *Gesellschaft* and the wandering of the displaced, Mies van der Rohe's method—which, incidentally, cast a subtle shadow over the claims of Japonica as modernism, via America—would appear a superior solution. Meanwhile in Europe, Le Corbusier had experienced the horrendous outcome of fascism's impetuous attempt to recover the nation and land for *das Man* in terms of a pervasive ideology. Thus he proposed anew his anthropomorphic system and method.

As we have seen, when this modernism arrived in Japan as brutalism, an antagonistic matrix was born: American modernism as Japonism, in opposition to European modernism (with its subsequent transformation into the Japanese neohistoricist problematic of Yayoi versus Jōmon). We may say, then, that the methodological debate within CIAM clashed in the Far East, after having encircled the earth from opposite directions. The plaza became the crucial subtheme of this collision. Taking into account the differences in the origins of European and American urbanism, we are forced to realize the inevitability of such a clash. European cities had organically embraced plazas as their heart and livelihood, while American cities, from the beginning, were composed on the abstract infrastructure now known as the Jeffersonian grid, where although there may be spots called squares, these are really only voids. CIAM recognized such conflicting interpretations of the plaza, yet it failed to create a compromise. In Japan, consequently, the issue played out as simply a contorted and exotic problematic.

Indeed, were there plazas in Japan? No, not in the European sense. Nor was there any neobaroque city plan or even a Jeffersonian grid. Japanese cities consist, instead, of various layers: first, there may be the labyrinthine structure of an original castle town; on top of it, there is a radiating network of modern streets; often, before that network is even complete, highways, built over the canals of castle towns, will have overlaid the streets. All this is a chaotic mishmash of historical layers and social events. Taking flight with subsidies earned from the Korean War in the early 1950s, Japan's economic growth got under way in earnest; its cities were strained by overpopulation, and subsequent layers have never been more than stopgap; in such a space, there was no margin to devise a plaza from zero.

By the time the 1951 CIAM conference was held, some two decades had passed since construction, by way of the external gaze, of the Japan-ness problematic of the 1930s. During that time a constellation of unbalanced responses was formulated—discourses generated by a process of urban modernization: one solution was a vision of a future city to solve the problem of burgeoning population, while another sought to prove that there might, after all, be an equivalent of the Western-style plaza in Japan. Here the gaze was directed equally toward future and past. The real cities beheld by the Japanese were an incorrigible mess by the 1960s, although it took another thirty years for us to rhetoricize this condition as "chaos." Envisioning a future city, constructing goals, and launching a progressive movement—all this was equal to a belief in the progress of modernity and followed the ideals of the early twentieth-century avant-garde. One response appeared in the guise of a project to extract the uniqueness of historical Japanese urban structure (in contrast to the West or the rest of Asia) by way of a morphological analysis of its development. The results were expressed in the anthology *Urban Space in Japan* (1963).[2]

A different response was contained in a manifesto by the Metabolism group presented at the Tokyo Design Conference in 1960, and it epitomized the Japanese response to Western ideals. The manifesto began as follows:

> Metabolism is the name of a group that seeks to present a concrete vision of the coming society. We posit human society as a process in the cosmic development from atom to nebula. We use the biological term "metabolism," because for us design and technology are nothing short of extensions of vital human power. For this reason, we do not simply accept the metabolism of history as natural, but seek to develop it actively.[3]

Metabolism had matured as a part of mainstream discourse. After the 1951 "Heart of the City" meeting at Hoddesdon, a younger generation had emerged from CIAM—the so-called Team X. They were skeptical of the idea of reconstructing cities with plazas at their core and maintained that the contemporary city and its architecture must be grasped in the rhetoric of "growth and metamorphosis." The main members of Team X—Alison and Peter Smithson, Louis Kahn, and Kenzō Tange—regrouped at the Tokyo Design Conference held in 1960. And Metabolism, an even younger generation of Japanese architects, thus in turn directed their manifesto to Team X. The manifesto was drafted by Noboru Kawazoe (1926–), while the architects Kiyonori Kikutake (1928–), Kishō Kurokawa (1934–), Masato Ōtaka (1923–), and Fumihiko Maki (1928–) further contributed their personal visions of the future city.

The image Metabolism deployed comprised a permanent core supplemented by a shorter-term growth module. The former was a megastructure that may be likened to a tree trunk or spinal cord; the latter resembled the branches of a tree or organs of the body, constantly renewing its cellular metabolism (fig. 5.1). Especially remarkable was a mass-produced, interchangeable capsule unit for living, which Archigram later took over and termed a "plug-in" or "plug-on" system.

The Metabolism group possessed all the characteristics of an avant-garde architectural movement in the quintessential modernist sense, driven by a humanist revisionism that stressed biomorphic metaphor. It incorporated the previous models of the human body—i.e., Le Corbusier's Ville Radieuse, the spine of Tange's Tokyo Plan (1960, but earlier presented at MIT), and CIAM's "Heart of the City." But while the previous generation had based its models on the relatively static structure of bodily organs and systems, the new Japanese group shifted their attention to a dynamic of molecular structure and did not hesitate to link the idea to the mechanics of (re)production, a notion expressed in the manifesto. If nineteenth-century architectural history records mere stylistic changes, that of the twentieth century followed artistic movements whose manifestos challenged all conventions. Metabolism was the last avant-garde to publish a manifesto and later movements, such as Archigram, no longer produced them. Around that time, the idea of drafting a new vision of coming society had

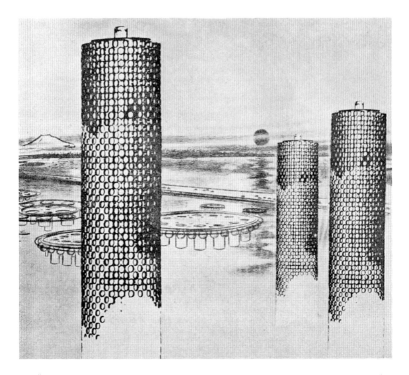

5.1 "Ideas for the Reorganization of Tokyo," visionary scheme drawn by Kiyonori Kikutake presented by Kenzō Tange at CIAM meeting in Otterloo, Holland (1959), and published in *The Manifesto of Metabolism* (Tokyo: Bijutsu Shuppansha, 1960).

come to be discarded, for utopia was already realized, in a sense. And what a shocking scene it presented. Meanwhile, the diastrophic events of 1968, that fatal blow to utopian thinking, were imminent. Furthermore, in his celebrated essay "A City Is Not a Tree," Christopher Alexander set out to prove the fatal paradox inherent in the idea of planning itself: namely, the vision of the city that modern architects embraced would never achieve the semilattice structure natural cities characteristically embody, nor could it ever escape from its own metaphorical tree structure.[4] This was the end of the avant-garde.

For Japanese architects, the Tokyo Design Conference in 1960 signified the completion of the reception process of Western modernism. The works and movements discussed presented a perfect mimicry of Western modernism. It was only this mimicry, however, that allowed the discussion to be shared cross-culturally; and only in the mimetic domain could a counterweight to the lopsided external gaze be construed. Nevertheless, this did not signal the disappearance of the Japan-ness problematic that had always belonged to the external gaze.

The architect Kiyonori Kikutake expounded his participation in the Metabolist manifesto by way of the etymology of an idea: *ka, kata, katachi*[5]—inspired by the epistemology of the physicist Mitsuo Taketani (1911–) and its three categories: the phenomenal, the substantial, and the essential. Analogous to the development of ancient Japanese phonemes into fully fledged nouns, Kikutake sought an aspect of form production in accordance with each category. Here *ka* indicates hypothesis, *kata*, form, and *katachi*, shape: an order corresponding to the order of the design process itself. That is to say, a designer first poses a hypothesis, next looks for a form (or matrix), and at last realizes a concrete shape. This procedure may also have echoed Louis Kahn's assertion in reference to Plato's theory of *poiesis* that in any design process, form must precede shape. Kikutake added the stage of hypothesis, and transposed the whole into *wago*, the ancient Japanese language.[6] This was a new turn away from Western concepts (epistemology and *poiesis*) and a reversion to Japan-ness.

For Japanese modernists—and I include myself—it is impossible not to begin with Western concepts. That is to say, we all begin with a modicum of alienation, but derive a curious satisfaction—as if things were finally set in order—when Western logic is dismantled and returned to ancient Japanese phonemes.[7] After this we stop questioning.[8] The discourse of Japan-ness in architectural design also takes refuge in the uncanny force of gravity possessed by old Japanese phonemes. These simple enunciations are bound by something that appears original and arcane. The moment of problematizing Japan-ness is effected more or less by allowing it (and us Japanese) to be drawn down to the ancient layer of words.

From the beginning, it was quite futile to look for the Western-type plaza in Japanese cities of the past. Nonetheless, there were equivalences and correspondences: *tsuji* (crossroads) used for posting *takafuda* (placards for government notices); and *kawara* (riverbanks) as a place of asylum for various social outcasts. Any such an interpretation had inevitably to follow concepts of Western urbanism, that is, it had to search out something like the

Western plaza. This was the same as attempting logically to interpret Ise and Katsura according to Western architectural logic. The research group Japanese Urban Space,[9] in which I participated, hoped to grasp the particular characteristics of Japanese cities through field research into townscape and typological research into the tradition of fifteenth- and sixteenth-century urban dwellings (*machiya*) built for artisans and the merchant class. Our conclusion was that no Western-style tradition of picturesque urban scenery was to be found in Japan; rather, temporal or virtual enclosures were set up here and there for rituals or festivals. We are reminded again of Hamaguchi's distinction between *material/constructive* Western space-making and *spatial/performative* Japanese space-making, except that one is here speaking of the larger domain of an urban space. In Japanese cities, the territorial extension of communal events at *tsuji*, in street markets, or in festivals and rituals held in temple precincts and shrine approaches is never fixed, but is instead temporary and amorphous, even if there are markers and a shared understanding regarding them. Such ambiguous demarcation is called *kaiwai*. It is impossible to mark the spots clearly on any map; they are just vague areas. That is to say, Japanese cities did not have plazas—but rather *kaiwai*. Our group concluded that it was this difference that required definition.

These virtual and temporal characteristics of Japanese urban events are produced by a particular spatial formation. I would say that this derives from the way the locus for inviting gods (*kami*) is marked. Gods normally exist outside architectural appurtenances. As a ritualistic device to invite them inside, a *himorogi* is temporarily constructed, customarily surrounded by evergreen trees (*tokiwagi*) or an imperial-style fence (*tamagaki*) in courtyards and shrines (fig. 5.2). This space is called *niwa*, today meaning garden, but it was originally an empty space. During this ritual, the sacred *sakaki*—an evergreen tree favored by Shintō—into which the gods are to be invited is set up. But when, after the ritual, the tree or branch is removed, the gods are gone. Their visit is only temporary. This kind of space can be created anywhere in principle, such as at new construction sites, and it is designated *virtually*, so to speak.

The empty area—*niwa*—is initially purified and rendered a potential ceremonial space. Thus it becomes *yuniwa* (a ceremonial garden) where the *himorogi* is installed. The ideogram for *himorogi* means gods' fence—it is a device to enclose or keep guard over

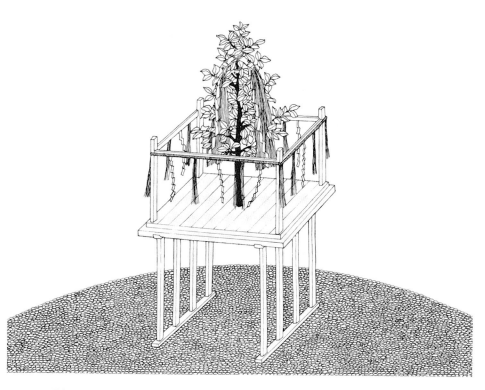

5.2 Illustration of *himorogi*. From *Ma: Space-Time in Japan*, catalogue of the exhibition, Paris (1978) and Cooper-Hewitt Museum, New York City.

gods/spirit (*hi*). On this occasion, what is significant is that *hi* is never visualized or idolized; it is merely considered to lodge in the *sakaki* tree, and, after the ritual is over, it disappears with the removal of the tree. The space, normally a construction site, is nowadays left empty again. Its clearest example is the configuration of Ise Shrine where, since the alternating construction recurs every twenty years, there are two identical sites, one of which is always left empty (*kodenchi*—the old site) with just pebbles and demarcations for primary columns. The transposition of *hi* (spirit) is thus clearly demarcated. The point is that any permanent form of altar is omitted.

As the term *kaiwai* indicates, the demarcation of ritual space (which often does overlap busy areas of cities) is essentially ambiguous, because the many comings and goings of *hi*, as events, have formed a complex of layers. Here, then, exists a correspondence between the presence of *hi* and that of the crowd. When many events have accumulated, the *niwa* becomes soiled and has to be reemptied and purified, but then it is again soiled and again purified. This repetition blurs the contours of the locus. Here *himorogi* is symbolically required, but we should attend carefully to the movement of *hi* as it lodges in *himorogi*. It is clear then that Japanese urban space is filled with invisible *hi*, which is never fixed but is constantly on the move. In Japan, city space has always been like that. In an astoundingly similar way, contemporary urban space, not only in Japan but everywhere, is reaching a state in which it is veiled by a fog of signs, flickering and wavering like the movement of *hi*. Metaphorically, this resembles Japanese cities of old veiled by the flow of *hi*.

While Kikutake was envisioning the future city as a megastructure with metabolic functions following the etymology of *ka*, *kata*, *katachi*, I was beginning to conceptualize a new way of envisioning cities calling up the concept of an "invisible city" that would consist of the flow of signs with different densities, in reference to *hi*. Both methodologies relied on Western logic in their technical details, but also on ancient Japanese phonemes and concepts for their imaginative roots. Neither looked for Japan-ness on purpose, but neither could escape the original seduction and linguistic power of phonemes. In an attempt to summarize twentieth-century urban design methods I wrote:

> The expressions of space inherent in Japanese culture—such as *kaiwai* and *kehai* [sign, or a not-yet-manifest indication of something]—point precisely to the way we sense urban space in a daily life not made up solely of physical attributes. Urban space is the whole of what surrounds us, entailing our five senses, or what our five senses receive. In order to describe and record this content, one has to rely on all sorts of signs. Once we recognize that cities are filled not only with visible but also invisible entities, we may be able to reorganize the city as method, delving deeper into its concrete image. The traditional Japanese way of sensing space teaches us this. The spatiality of *kaiwai* and *kehai*, where demarcation remains vague and in flux—here is the origin of an imagination that countenances an undifferentiated, intuitive space going well beyond any mere mechanistic articulation. This is

reemphasized by the condition of contemporary space filled with continuous and invisible electronic impulses trafficking and communicating with one another.[10]

In the early 1960s I linked the *kehai* of *hi*, or the manifestation of spirit, with the new invisible electronic media. At that time, we were not yet fully in a cyber age (although there was indeed much talk in Japan of cybernetics), while electronics was just at an incipient stage. My aim was to pinpoint a method of describing the city hazily flickering like fog. Also I believed in the not-so-remote possibility that the phantomlike future city—what I then referred to as an "imaginary model"—would appear somehow in the air, underground, on the ocean's surface, that is, not just at the periphery of real cities. At that time, no one could have imagined that the theme park would become such a pervasive twenty-first-century model. I actually envisioned an apparitional *yamagoe-amida* (the advent of Amitabha, rising over a mountaintop to welcome ascetics), and called this vision my "virtual city."

Today's conceptualization of the virtual city is remarkably different from what was called fantasy, or utopia, in the 1920s. It is, in a sense, equally fantastic but has become a methodological necessity—for only by way of such visions can any model be approached. Even if the virtual city is totally different from, or perhaps contradicts, the real city, inasmuch as it can be turned into a model, it may also one day be simulated. All this is connected to the possibility of computer-generated design. Perhaps for our contemporary cities, such notions as formal synthesis and visual order will become old hat. Instead we may develop various other concepts of cities—ocean cities, sky cities, labyrinthine cities, cities of the dead, and so on—constructing models of these and superimposing them on real cities. Urban designers can no longer rely on preexisting concepts because present-day cities are such that they are generated by interminable dialogue. Thus, a decision can be reached only if conditions are frozen at a certain moment in time. The procedure of urban design is, therefore, becoming like a war of pushing buttons.[11]

Until recently, urban projects used to extend existing cities along a temporal axis toward some point in an imagined future.

Such exercises assumed a certain progress toward utopia. Be it the picturesque European version or the American city laid out on a grid, the scheme was always similar in that it was made to conform in time progressively and sequentially. Not least of all, these were the only procedures that bureaucrats could grasp and control. In all such schemes, among the myriad tasks to be accomplished for a total realization, all that could be realistically hoped for was what was possible at any given moment. Yet, after a certain time had elapsed, the image of the goal had faded amongst the innumerable revisions. Long before the inevitable setback of the socialist project in the late 1980s, and already as early as the 1960s, any notion of urban design had reached gridlock regardless of politics or national tradition.

The death of utopia thus pronounced, who, then, could have imagined the spectacle of the theme park conceived by commercial entrepreneurs and about to proceed beyond the limits of states and bureaucrats? Walt Disney began the EPCOT Center in Orlando with intent to construct a prototype of the experimental community of tomorrow. From the beginning, Disney envisioned this construction of a future community where visitors might observe the real lives of residents. After his death, his notion was retooled and became what today we know as the theme park, modeled to some extent on world's fairs. What struck home was that a nonlinear time frame—the realization of a city, or community, at a single stroke—had now become thinkable, surpassing all former piecemeal bureaucratic projects. Outside any lived-in city appears an urban unity totally unrelated and alien, like a mirage. In that it has no past, it is a city of absence; in that it is detached from existing social institutions and might appear at any time and in any place, it must be called an atopic city.

Utopia exists in no known place (u-topia, or no-where). If it existed, the fact would be contradictory. So it was that a theme park cannot be a utopia but is at long last an experimental community. The death of utopia in 1968 coincided with the self-destruction of the historical avant-garde. Yet in the background of these events we can scarcely afford to ignore the rise of the theme park. If so, it could even be said that utopia did not self-destruct, but was merely killed off by the advent of the theme park.

I have already touched upon Expo '70 with reference to Tange, but that event had other ramifications. Creating a model for the future city was the theme common to all the pavilions and other facilities at Expo '70. The official slogan was "progress and harmony," reflecting the notion that Japan, in the throes of new economic growth, was pursuing the very ideal of modernism, as if anticipating in a certain measure EPCOT Center. Like EPCOT Center, Expo '70 appeared to sustain a faith in modernity as progress. A strain of utopianism, however much exposed to the critique of currents siding with 1968, survived in it. But Expo '70 was no longer an avant-garde, artistic/political movement. It was rather a commercial project in the manner of EPCOT Center, except that it enjoyed state sponsorship.

Expo '70's idea of the future city was inflected by a curious bias. Even a future city, inasmuch as it is a city at all, was understood to require a core (as, for example, in CIAM's "Heart of the City"). Such a core had most commonly been a plaza. But this world's fair was a temporary event, lasting only for six months. In the cultural context of a traditional Japan, the festival was itself and alone the most elaborate and conscious generator of urban events. Thus these two urban elements from different sources— "festival" and "plaza"—collided, and delineated the core of Expo '70 as a model for the future city. This naming was proposed by a Kyoto team led by Uzō Nishiyama (1911–1994)—one of two teams, along with the Tokyo group led by Tange, that conceived the facilities. From the first, the name "festival plaza" (*Omatsuri hiroba*) impressed me as totally uncool, the kind of cheesy term one would even hesitate to pronounce. But surprisingly, it was a hit. Since then, in fact, many expositions all over Japan have adopted the *Omatsuri hiroba* as their core element. Whenever such an event is being planned, this facility with the strange, vulgar-sounding name—festival plaza—an entity that has never existed either in Japan or in the West—furnishes the core attraction.

Again, according to Japanese etymology, the word for festival —*matsurigoto*—originally means politics. This same equation makes sense in other places, too. Public arenas in Nuremberg as well as Tiananmen Square were all places for the declaration and exhibition of a new state apparatus, whereby politics and festival were conterminous. In the Western tradition, the plaza where daily markets and religious rituals took place in alternation was deemed the city core. In ancient Japan, the *yuniwa* in front of Shi-Shinden (the purple main pavilion) of Kyoto Palace was the place where gods were invited, and at the same time policy was made and declared; this venerable politico-religious event is the archetype of the festival. That is to say that the vulgar, made-up term "festival plaza" manages to subsume the whole range of Japan's historical and geographical heterogeneity. And the strange ambivalence of the term—the *temporary* festival and the *enduring* plaza—retains the contingency of the festival, its ephemerality.

Such a scheme was uncharacteristic of Uzō Nishiyama. After investigating the urban slums of Osaka during World War II, he had come to advocate the separation of spaces for sleeping and eating,[12] a rebuttal of the Japanese traditional lifestyle, which foreigners had admired (e.g., in Ozu's films). In the traditional living space, everything can be spread on *tatami* flooring; every element of life, including *chabu-dai* (dining table) and *futon* (sleeping mattress), is movable and may be exchanged or replaced. Nishiyama concluded that such a lifestyle was an index of feudal premodernity. Nishiyama proposed that sleeping and dining areas at least be separated. His idea was intended to disqualify the ambiguity of the Japanese traditional living space as well as the familial model of patriarchy. This new notion influenced the postwar standardization of urban lifestyle, especially designs for public housing. According to Nishiyama, as a correlate to the modernization process the Japanese living space must be split up, articulated, and functionally reorganized in a manner consistent with Western rationalism. In his festival plaza proposal, however, this Japanese neorationalist sought to merge two quite separate cultural orientations, if necessary by force.

What we learn from the way previously avant-garde architects, artists, and theorists intervened in Expo '70 is that in the final analysis the gaze searching for Japan-ness discovers itself most dramatically in the realm of bad taste. In Okamoto's *Tower of the Sun,* a black mask faced the Festival Plaza with a rough and eerie grin. We must heed the bitterness projected by that mask, for Japanness readily descends into sheer vulgarity, to the extent of the horrifying.

After World War II the issue of the automobile versus the city center came to the fore everywhere. The Team X initiative for "growth/metamorphosis" undertook to discover an improved circulation for pedestrians and cars. The Smithsons proposed a network of pedestrian decks in the center of Berlin in 1957; Louis

Kahn's project for Center City in Philadelphia of the same year would have constructed garage towers throughout the downtown area. Neither scheme was realized. Soon after these projects were published, Japan began its first and only nationally sponsored promotion of urban planning in the postwar era: Tsukuba Academic New Town. There appeared many other so-called new towns, which, however, were just bedroom communities on the edges of existing cities. Tsukuba was the sole project prepared to construct all the independent functions of a city from scratch. In its central area a network of pedestrian decks was installed and a large plaza was planned. In major Japanese cities, there had been numerous empty sites called plazas, most of which were mere traffic roundabouts or parking spaces, having never been designed for pedestrians (let alone public gatherings). In the late 1960s, when protest demonstrations accompanying folk concerts occurred spontaneously in the famous sunken West Plaza of Shinjuku Station, the legal pretext resorted to by police to remove participants from these sit-ins was a stipulation that in Japan there were no plaza spaces where pedestrians could legally foregather. In other words, any such public space existed only for pedestrian circulation.

When, much later on, in 1983, I designed the Tsukuba Center Building and its plaza as the hub of Tsukuba Academic New Town (fig. 5.3), I discovered that all the by-laws governing the facility were legal fictions. The site of the new town had never corresponded to any town or village. The place had no history, no memory. There was no compelling reason why the institutions of the university and its research center should move there. The choice was almost arbitrary. If there were a purpose, it must have been to eliminate the population pressure on Tokyo by creating an overflow zone in this vicinity. The planning methods adopted at Tsukuba consisted of little more than zoning and reapportionment: versions of the most characteristic and commonplace zoning regulations in use in the West for urban and suburban redevelopment. Nevertheless, our bureaucrats had also introduced certain of the ideas developed by leading modern architects from CIAM to Team X, including the aforementioned center with its diminutive plaza and network of pedestrian decks. This project not only served to divide pedestrians from traffic, but also designated an urban space solely for pedestrian use. The Western notion of the plaza, transformed by a certain neohumanism, reappeared here as

5.3 Large-scale watercolor rendering of "Tsukuba Center Building in Ruins,"
1983, by Arata Isozaki.

model for a "future city." This idea was Western in origin through
and through, and quite fictional in the immediate cultural context
at Tsukuba.

But at the end of the day, Japan-ness was inscribed and
embedded, without anyone's having noticed it. The Japanese new
town was a state project realized by mobilizing an entire nexus of
researchers, academics, politicians, bureaucrats, and artists; the government of Japan officially drew up the plan and executed it in its
totality. But as the first (residential) phase of the Tsukuba Academic New Town neared completion, its population attained just
one fifth of the estimate projected. The enterprise turned out to be
unpopular and was spoken of as a serious failure. It was said that
the government's prestige was at stake, and countermeasures were
widely discussed. To redress the problem, it was decided that cultural facilities would have to be constructed sooner than had been
planned. As mentioned, the center of these facilities was to contain
a plaza. Although it was never stated in so many words, the buildings around this plaza were, I felt, expected neatly to embody

"Japan-ness" as an aspect of national policy. Was it possible to represent the Japanese state in terms of architecture? I asked myself. Since the very beginnings of an imported modern architecture, Japan-ness had recurred at each political juncture, and behind it always had been the State. On every occasion was the recurring question of how to render its features: the *teikan* style, the ideology of *hakkō ichi-u* (the whole world under one roof),[13] Hiroshima Peace Park, and the Tokyo Olympics—all were envisioned as official manifestations or events, as expressions directed toward the outside. Tsukuba Academic New Town was thus also intended as an urbanistic expression of the postwar Japanese state.

To build an illusive city around a plaza in Japan, a land where there had never been a plaza in the Western sense, was to engender a double fiction. Acting out the fictitiousness of the construct, I conscientiously eschewed any element that appeared to be of Japanese origin. Then I elaborated the Western model—but as an inversion. I inverted, or reversed, the plaza Michelangelo designed for the Campidoglio by constructing surroundings that appeared to collapse like Giulio Romano's work at Palazzo del Te at Mantua. I further quoted Borromini as well as Ledoux, architects who had both transposed Western classicism in an idiosyncratic manner, and arranged my two sources so as to index and offset each other. Michelangelo, Giulio, Borromini, and Ledoux each devised unique and distinctive urban contexts, yet without indulging in any private fantasies. When quoted at Tsukuba, however, these schemes were transferred from an authentic Western context to the *un*authentic context "Japan," that is, beyond their own time and space, and thus became fictions, in such a way that context and meaning were totally displaced. Nevertheless, their four diverse architectural signatures persist, refusing any metamorphosis and marking a stark contrast with the International Style modernism that permeates the whole scheme as an abstract model, all being selectively transformed by the new context at Tsukuba.

In this kind of transplanted urbanism, when foreign urban concepts are quoted, only the contour of such notions are transcribed as signs. This is quite different from the displacement, say, of excavated artifacts with a professed physical substance. At Tsukuba signs were materialized anew in their new location. Images without gravity came floating to the surface so to speak, precisely as if assimilating the traditional character of Japanese urban space, replete with the *kehai* of *hi*. Transcription, transposition, metamorphosis, and an arbitrary subjective reformation—such operations yielding floating signs were all the more effective in an originally fictive place like Japanese urban space. In this fictional arena, the flow and compositions of *hi* merged as an identity. In this way, the plaza comprising the Tsukuba Center Building and its surroundings morphed into a topos of accumulated signs all in the process of being materialized and reconstituted. The project brief read as follows:

> When you visit the building, you notice a sunken oval plaza in the courtyard, part of which is collapsed, as if ruined. Your gaze nevertheless does not descend immediately into the plaza, but instead moves along the surrounding surfaces of the hotel on the east and the concert hall on the south. You may at this moment wander into the buildings, but do not go down to the oval plaza. Walk along the rim of the upper level, all the while looking down at the sunken center. The center point is at the bottom, absorbing the two sources of water—one from a waterfall and the other from the base of a bronze laurel tree portraying Daphne's metamorphosis at the edge of a stream. In the pavement's original context—the Campidoglio in Rome—this center is the very spot where a statue of Marcus Aurelius was set, but here all relationships are inverted and the center becomes an aperture, in which both rainwater and your gaze are absorbed.[14]

Inversion in the midst of the transposition of signs—here was the crux of my plaza scheme. Michelangelo first conceived this plaza in front of the Roman Senate—whose image was later to govern the prototype of the plaza as a symbol of power in many other Western cities. At Rome, placed in the center and at the apex was the statue of an emperor astride his horse. Transcribing and inverting this center point, I transformed it into the lowest point of all, that into which water streams. This operation was a measure taken to forestall the apparition of Japan-ness within the plaza at Tsukuba, which is a mere metaphor, that is to say a rife fiction.

> I understood the architect (read *myself*) to have been commissioned by the state (read *Japan*) in place of a king, requested in other words to make a portrait of the State. Nonetheless, the fea-

tures of that state did not appear so clearly as those of an actual king would have; and even had they done so, I would not have wanted it. I was entrapped in my own dilemma. The only solution was to supply a central void. In producing such an inverted space, I needed to create a metaphor of disappearance, namely, descent into the void.[15]

In *The Empire of Signs*, Roland Barthes's book on Japan and Japan(ese)ness,[16] a central void is said to indicate the presence of the Japanese emperor and imperial court as zero cipher as implicit in the conceit of darkness at the heart of the forest. Akira Asada commented on the realization of my Tsukuba project that the inversion of the Campidoglio as a measure to prevent the advent of Japan-ness paradoxically triggered a Japanese cultural matrix: the void as center.[17] This was correct. The erasure of the equestrian figure of Marcus Aurelius produced a void that may be akin to the old vacated site—*kodenchi*—of Ise Jingū, the actual prototype of *yuniwa*, as I now see, writing this at a distance of twenty years. I intended, at the time, not only to eliminate Japanese historical motifs but also judiciously to include four signatures originating in Western art. Nonetheless, the void-as-center was capriciously generated in consequence of the inversion I effected—an unexpected turn of events. My inversion of the iconic Western matrix unwittingly overlapped the ancient ritualistic practice of inviting—then sending off—gods in the *yuniwa*. Japan-ness, even eliminated, reappeared in an unexpected manner. But the reason is clear: namely, the crux of Japan-ness is not this or that particular image, symbol, or sign, but rather the very mechanism of constructing a fiction around the zero sign, thus producing an ahistorical nonplace. The *tennō* system is forever reductive to the zero sign, and thus omnipresent. Like the *hi* or animistic gods, it can appear anywhere—in every detail, even within a blade of grass. Once the visualized center of its being is removed or discarded, it nevertheless remains like an elusive fog gathering at the site of every event. My attempt at inversion accidentally invited this structure of the emperor system, the epitome of Japan-ness, as I now see. Yet this issue won't go away easily. Because, from the very beginning, the nation somehow concurred that matters pertaining to the emperor belonged to an invisible, or forbidden, domain.

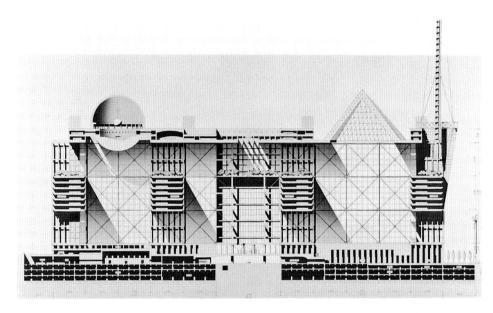

5.4 Silkscreen section rendering with cast shadows of unbuilt competition project for Tokyo Metropolitan Government Building, 1986, by Arata Isozaki.

In principle, postwar democracy in Japan drew a picture that excluded the emperor from the domain of *hi* (gods). This is more or less evident in the shifting succession of projects by Kenzō Tange. The shrinelike space of the Greater East Asia Memorial Building and the plaza at the Atomic Bomb Memorial Park in Hiroshima were both designed in formal terms as *empty* spaces. These two works by the same architect, which stand no more than several years apart, although on either side of a major war, thus have an undeniable formal affinity. But significantly, in Hiroshima, the abstract figure of the emperor was erased, and a new *hi*, called the populace, filled the space, as befitted the postwar democracy. Then, about forty years after this revision of *hi* (signifying the end of the *tennō*-ist state), the same architect designed a vast plaza in Tokyo, in front of the seat of the Tokyo Metropolitan Government (1991). It was still an empty space. But by this time the protesting mass (*hi*), which had filled the West Plaza of Shinjuku Station twenty years earlier, was absent. Today neither *tennō* nor the masses are present, so what is going on in this plaza? In Tange's design the ideal plaza argued for in the "Heart of the

5.5 Perspective rendering of unbuilt competition project for Tokyo Metropolitan Government Building (interior), 1986, by Arata Isozaki.

City" conference at Hoddesdon forty years before still persisted; like my project realized at Tsukuba, this was a transplant of the Western notion of such a place. Notwithstanding the fact that Tokyo Metropolitan Government Plaza is the supposed embodiment of postwar institutionalized democracy, however, even the *kehai* of *hi* (or, indeed, any sign of *anima*) is absent. It is, therefore, sheer void. The architect did not sense the fact that postwar democracy had weathered somewhat, and he still followed the model of the Western plaza as simile. Anachronistic and sclerotic, without the operation of any inversion or concept of transposition, what it has come to embody is the disastrous bubble economy of the 1990s in Japan—naturally enough, empty of all cultural content.

Meanwhile, the *hi* that used to fill Japanese urban space had scarcely vanished, it is just that it had moved. One should never have assumed that in Tokyo, say, the *hi* would simply appear in any Western-style plaza designed as an adjunct to a building. In Tokyo, the *hi* has now moved to inhabit interior space. To the extent that workable public space could no longer be attained in an outside space, sheltered indoor spaces such as underground malls, atria, and interior circulation spaces have been created throughout the city. *Hi* fills up these interiors as an alternative to the plaza. My own proposal for the Tokyo Metropolitan Government Building (1986) focused squarely on this issue of the new internalization of the plaza (figs. 5.4, 5.5). I reasoned that the way to design a plaza, after the symbol of the emperor had been eliminated and postwar democracy had matured, was to surround and cover—no longer just enclose—the noise of chaotic signs filling a given urban space. Thus a gigantic receptacle would be needed, and my solution for the Tokyo Metropolitan Government competition was to create a public space doubling the interior volume of the basilica of Saint Peter's in the Vatican. Only to such a vast space would *hi* nowadays return. The idea of creating this simple yet vast internal space was rejected as quite unrealizable. Instead, the Tokyo Municipal Government premiated a pastiche solution based on a defunct Western cliché, setting it down in the midst of a prolific forest of "Towers of Bubble."

Around 1975 I began to reflect on the experiences of 1968 that had marked my European debut on the stage of the international architectural scene.

> I was in Milan for most of the month of May 1968 preparing my exhibit for the 14th Milan Triennale, which was to begin near the end of that month. The organizers invited relatively young designers and architects from all over the world, gave each of us a room, and let us do whatever we wanted. With the help of the photographer Shōmei Tōmatsu, the graphic designer Kōhei Sugiura, and the composer Toshi Ichiyanagi, I created an installation called "Electric Labyrinth [fig. 6.1]."

> We installed Hokusai's ghostly *ukiyo-e*, "The nine stages of the process through which a beautiful woman decays after death [*Ono no komachi no Kusō-zu*]," and photographs of the burned and ineradicable [lithoid] shadows of Hiroshima victims—images [on buildings and pavements] that variously implied the death and rebirth of the city. These were keyed to rotate at a certain signal and thoroughly perplexed [visitors to the Triennale]. On an adjacent large wall space we spread an image of a hypothetical atomic destruction of a future megastructure (in other words, the future city) collaged over scenes of Hiroshima immediately after the A-bomb blast; on top of this we projected plans of a great metropolis undergoing the throes of death and rebirth.[1]

In architecture a number of international associations were born during the twentieth century. CIAM, already mentioned, effectively competed with the UIA/IUA (International Union of

6.1 *Electric Labyrinth* (view of revolving panels), 1968 installation at fourteenth Milan Triennale, by Arata Isozaki.

Architects), made up of representatives from each nation's own local association of architects. CIAM was an avant-garde movement that had set a goal in the utopian future, which it approached piecemeal; in retrospect, its relationship with the UIA was like that of the Comintern to the UN. After the war, CIAM was driven to abject collapse by members of the succeeding generation, Team X. Milan's Triennale had presented international design exhibitions at regular three-year intervals since 1923. The fourteenth, held in 1968, was frozen by a lockout immediately after it opened, influenced by the May events in France believed to foretell "the death of utopia." That year the organizers had invited members of Team X, as well as a group of even younger architects. These would later be called the RATS (a name coined by the Dutchman Aldo van Eyck to signify radical neorationalist architects).

The list of featured participants that year prefigured a future network of very young architects: the so-called Tokyo-London-

6.2 *Hiroshima Ruined Again in the Future*, photomontage wall mural made for *Electric Labyrinth* in 1968, by Arata Isozaki.

Vienna-Florence axis. The roster included Hans Hollein (Vienna), Peter Cook of Archigram (London), myself (Tokyo), and on the side of the lockout, those students who eventually founded Superstudio and Archizoom (both in Florence). Since the situation was in flux, it was unclear who was locking out whom. It was rather the venue that counted, and everyone shared alike in the sense of utopia's death. Within ten years, architecture had begin to march to the tune of postmodernism; the onset, I believe, was the Milan Triennale in 1968.

The eventual axis members were Metabolism (Tokyo), Archigram (London), BAU (Vienna), and the aforementioned Superstudio and Archizoom—a network that functioned as an exchange of information via universities, conferences, exhibitions, and periodicals. In the beginning, it was all rather informal and consisted of the groups as units, but eventually, the individuals became the links. This was because the fate of the revolution of May 1968 had rendered any notion of organizing a group around a manifesto obsolete. Thus, members were now listed as individuals. In addition to those already mentioned, there was also Cedric Price in Britain, who had designed the Fun Palace (1960) that suggests itself as a prototype for Tange's Festival Plaza at Expo '70 in Osaka.

What now remains from the installation *Electric Labyrinth* is a large collage entitled *Hiroshima Ruined Again in the Future* (fig. 6.2).[2] As described, the whole work was a multimedia installation, acclaimed, later, as a pioneering work in the genre. For myself, it represented a significant debut on the international stage. I had been invited to the international division and had no special duty to represent Japan. Yet the images I brought together were all related to Japan. My guiding intention was to represent Japan's newly regenerated urban space as a process akin to the human life cycle—birth to death. By this time, our nation had had a 100-year history of exporting, as its face to others, all the hit commodities of exotic Japan, prestigious Japan, colonial Japan, and so forth. The infrastructure of its postwar reconstruction was now complete, and the country had shifted into high gear in terms of economic growth, while reviewing and casting off a number of utopian plans for the future city. To me, however—and especially as a native of western Japan—the experience of Hiroshima had to be accepted as the indelible origin of the reconstruction process. I belong to the generation that had experienced once and for all the bankruptcy of Japan as an export commodity, the destruction of its cities, the transformation of the social structure, and above all, the end of history at Hiroshima. Stained upon my eyes was the scene of destruction and extinction that came *first*, before the beginning of everything else. Yet the reality of construction and growth proceeded apace. Though the architect and urbanist are dedicated to progress, it is nonetheless impossible to escape altogether a recurring premonition of total collapse. The basis of architecture is construction, and urban space is understood as its extension. But over against such ideas as had long persisted in Western thought, I intended to pose the example of Japan's passage through collapse and extinction. So it was that I naturally began by choosing these apocalyptic Japanese images.

In order to posit Japan as Outsider in contrast to the West *qua* center, my *Electric Labyrinth* tried to show collapse-as-difference versus construction. This had been an intuitive response to my first invitation outside Japan, namely the Triennale. Amidst all the other protests that sought to challenge and overturn preconceived ideas, my project was hardly out of place. There remained however, in my own mind, an aporia related to the thematic of "Hiroshima." Had the murderous holocaust and destruction been caused by a human impulse? Or might this extinction of an urban space and its humanity have occurred as inevitable destiny? Even Hiroshima's stupefying disappearance may be reduced to the binary of human construct, on the one hand, or act of nature, on the other. According to the hermeneutics of Japan-ness, even instantaneous annihilation could be broadly regarded as an act of nature.

The inscription "we will not repeat this mistake" on the Hiroshima peace monument merely expresses a general antagonism toward constructive logic, provoked as it was by the event's awful nature. By superimposing the eerie imagery of bodily deterioration, monsters, and genocide over the human shadows etched that day onto the marble steps, I hoped to reverse the internalization of Japanness, which had developed mainly in response to the provocation of the external gaze. My point in the Milan exhibit was that even *nature* might and, indeed, must be considered *construction*. To discover any tacit constructive sense in my *Electric Labyrinth* would entail such a reversal.

The death of utopia owes less to the dissolution of any image of a future society delineated by the historical avant-garde than to the nullification of the overall notion of *project* that proceeds with more or less regularity toward a predetermined goal. During the twenty-odd years between 1968 and the collapse of the Berlin Wall, the world was suspended between two ideological poles, so that the very fact of the death of utopia (or of the term "project") was obscured. It was still being claimed that everything could be planned and, indeed, a number of projects were already planned a century ahead. Then, the Soviet Union—the ultimate planned state—disintegrated. The whole teleological ideal died, and with it much goal-oriented planning ground to a halt. Instead, a network of singularities—that is, of individuals in cities throughout the developed world—was generated. We had to wait until the end of the century for the World Wide Web to supplant these individuals by more impersonal terminals; however, in the late 1960s we had a premonition that this was going to occur. In between was the twenty-year detour of postmodernism.

In contrast with the *écriture* of other artists, the architect's métier is tremendously conditioned by the epoch, to the extent that a work of architecture is often permeated by the gamey scent of its time. An architect must always assume the existence of the Other, namely the client. The technologies on which we depend are always socially and industrially conditioned, likewise constructed by an Other. These various frames define a paradigm governing the formation of each new generation in architecture. The historical avant-garde was formed in roughly fifteen-year waves: CIAM, Team X, and the RATS. The average age cohort represented some twenty-five years. Most of these individuals are also writers and this domain of their activity is also ruled by, and at the same time reinforces, the paradigmatic scheme. Paradoxically, if an architect refuses intervention by the Other, an *écriture* flows freely, but in that case the architectural design will never be realized.

Over time it became the custom for hopeful Japanese avant-garde architects to debut with an unbuilt project. There was no question that having a project actually constructed was the fundamental condition for achieving credibility, but presenting a project set clearly beyond the frame of realizability afforded a different kind of fame. This unbuiltness prolonged the utopian impetus and provided the new and unwritten manifesto of being avant-garde. In Japan, from the 1930s to the 1960s—in parallel with the international avant-garde movement—the strategy solidified. In fact, all the architects of CIAM, Team X, and the RATS debuted with celebrated yet unbuilt proposals.

The rejected plans for the Tokyo Imperial Museum competition (1936) by Kunio Maekawa (who belonged to CIAM), the Greater East Asia Co-prosperity Sphere Memorial (1942) by Kenzō Tange (Team X), and the *Incubation Process* (1962) that initiated my own participation in the RATS were all debuts with the nature of manifestos. Thinking about it now, one is surprised to note how each of these unbuilt projects figures deeply in the problematic of Japan-ness. Maekawa's Imperial Museum was a modernist counterproposal to the *teikan* style of the winning submission for Tokyo National Museum by Jun Watanabe. Maekawa's design embodied the pure forms of quintessential modernism, but at the same time contained the seeds of many of those later compositions that were to be formalized as Japan-ness in the postwar epoch. Tange's Greater East Asia Co-prosperity Sphere Memorial contained specific elements still regarded, at that time in Japan, as denoting ancient magnanimity. Tange went on to combine modernist elements with the Shintōesque *yuniwa* structure, and this combination of modern and traditional developed as the hallmark of Tange's early career. Unlike Maekawa, who had openly criticized the mishmash of traditional and modern in the *teikan* style and fought consistently to transplant a purist modernism, Tange subtly wove together conflicting modern and traditional elements. Precisely because such debut works were unbuilt, one could read their *écriture* head-on. Over multiple decades as a skilled entrepreneur/architect,

6.3 *Future City* (*The Incubation Process*), 1962, photomontage by Arata Isozaki.

Tange renegotiated the problematic encountered at his debut at key critical junctures of his career, while struggling with ever-intensifying bouts of Otherness (in the person of his clients). In similar fashion, my *Incubation Process* (fig. 6.3) has continued to hold me captive, and the *Electric Labyrinth* produced for the Milan Triennale had been a version of this scheme as it related to urban problems and cities in Japan.

Incubated cities are destined to self-destruct
Ruins are the style of our future cities
Future cities are themselves ruins
Our contemporary cities, for this reason, are destined to live only
    a fleeting moment,

Give up their energy and return to inert material
All of our proposals and efforts will be buried,
And once again the incubation mechanism is reconstituted
That will be the future[3]

In the *Electric Labyrinth*, the image of *Hiroshima Ruined Again in the Future* was juxtaposed over a vast enlargement of Hiroshima photographed as soon as the A-bomb had been dropped. This image is imagined as a *future* scene of urban megastructures in collapse. This notion in turn revisits the, for me, iconic drawing entitled *Incubation Process*, where the "joint-core system" I imagined in 1960 as a trabeated unit of the future city is supported by the columns of a ruined Doric temple. Both photomontages aim to portray cities in the recurring cycle of growth and death and both sought to represent the way cities self-destruct. As mentioned, the idea derived from our own generation's experience: we who had seen the death of cities and took this as our point of departure. To us, such cities as were supposed now to be built had already decayed. The trauma of urban collapse had been so severe for us in Japan that we were uneasy in accepting urban reconstructions put forward in place of the bombastic and pseudo-humanist Greater East Asia Co-prosperity Sphere-type proposals of our recent wartime past. I could only hope to depict the trauma itself. Bringing the city to be constructed back to the city that had been destroyed emphasized the cycle of becoming and extinction. I had written: "The city is a process, and there is no concept more certain than this."[4] But upon reflection wasn't the worldview centered on flux already part and parcel of those ages of social dissolution in Japan's ancient past? Leitmotifs that flash in the opening passages of two great classics—"those who prosper will inevitably fall," in the *Heike Saga*, and a reference to "the flow of the passing river," in *The Record of a Small Hut* (*Hōjō-ki*)[5]—both address the inevitability of destruction and rebirth. Even the great haiku poet Bashō's *Narrow Path to the Deep North* (*Okuno Hosomichi*)[6] pursues this topos of impermanence through the author's desire to wander. Finally, the aesthetic embodied in the phrase "dried and emaciated" (*kare kajikeru*) of the poet Munetada (1421–1502),[7] or the medieval concept of *sabi*, both represent the frozen landscape of death.

Observing the process of decay closely and then deliberately pulling the end nearer instead of patiently awaiting it—my post-war trauma unwittingly made me take up a motif our culture had repeatedly reexamined at least since medieval times. "Dried and emaciated" landscapes appeared again and again in the ruins of the fires of World War II, the barricades of locked-out universities in the late sixties, and more recently, rubble-strewn landscapes in the wake of the 1995 Great Hanshin-Awaji Earthquake centered at Kobe. All such landscapes are of destruction and dissolution. From my earliest projects, a gaze that entailed anti-construction as pure process was elected and inscribed, so that the mark of trauma itself came to be my signature. After all, this is the core of what Japan-ness is to me. That said, I did not intend merely to represent Japan, and I pursued my universal theme of becoming and extinction.

Time encroaches on all materials, and being decomposes and begins to flow away. This suggests an ontology of architectural time par excellence as found in the chapter "Being Time" in *Shōbō Genzō*, the teaching of the celebrated Zen priest Dōgen (1200–1253). His proposition claiming, "time comes flying," indicates that there are multifarious times. Even ruins are one of these. Only by means of such a view can one grasp the very instant of transition.[8] Therefore, I struck out to define the phenomenological moment by overturning the ordinary view that space is exactly localizable while time is mere occasion. In contradistinction, I believe that "space appears only in the *time* that humans perceive, therefore it is always specific, concrete, flickering, and never fixed."[9] At this juncture, my conception of time had begun to deviate wildly from the convention of space/time based upon modern science, as portrayed by the modernist architectural historian Sigfried Giedion and other midcentury critics. Architectural space can only be experienced through corporeal sentience. What we call space is that flickering *imago* appearing after the five senses have performed their diverse operations. I characterize it as follows:

If we posit the substantial three-dimensional space that in daily life is the object of human perception as a pair of axes, one represents a series of magical and symbolic spaces (deep psychological space) associated with the image of darkness; the other is a series of abstract, multidimensional spaces (semiotic space) affiliated to an image of emptiness.

The space of darkness probes an individual's consciousness to its very depths, while the space of emptiness logically analyzes an individual's personality in a diversifying, complicating sweep.

In hindsight I wonder whether these two expansive conceptual movements actually connect or cross. At present I cannot say for sure.[10]

Thus I declared my deviation from the neo-Cartesian point of view considered as the universal basis for modern architecture, in favor of a position that leans more in the direction of phenomenological epistemology. My main point of reference was the celebrated essay by the fiction writer and essayist Junichirō Tanizaki, *In Praise of Shadows* of 1933/34 (in fact, I prefer to say *In Praise of Darkness*), in which he persuasively analyzed various characteristics of Japanese architectural space. Tanizaki stresses that "darkness" comprises not only space but also time. That is to say, both are returned for the purposes of argument to a state of undifferentiated being. Though forty years ago I suspected the view could somehow be linked with the new invisible network that an incipient information technology had began to construct, I was unsure and rather hesitant to say so. I had, in any case, already embarked on my own detour. Analogously to the way in which the Japanese myth of origins *Kojiki*[11] begins with an undifferentiated state of heaven (*ame*) and earth (*tsuchi*), I believed it necessary to return to an undifferentiated state of time and space. In Japanese, when the concepts of time (*jikan*—時間) and space (*kūkan*—空間) were first written down, the Chinese ideogram *ma* (間)—an interstice—was used as the second character for both.[12] I determined to search for clues in this space in between.

Ten years after the May events—in 1978—the Festival d'Automne in Paris mounted a show on Japan. Michel Guy, its director, asked four artists for proposals: the painter Shūsaku Arakawa (1936–), the film director Nagisa Ōshima (1932–), the composer Tōru Takemitsu (1930–1996), and me. He had hoped to ask Arakawa to present his series "The Mechanism of Meaning," and Ōshima for a short film about Japanese lives in reference to Roland Barthes's views about Japan,[13] but the budget was too meager. It was possible to realize and present only Takemitsu's work on voice, reflecting both traditional and contemporary Japan, and my own contribution, an exhibition entitled "Ma."

To explain how I came to my interpretation of *ma* requires yet another detour. The basis of all modern scientific operations is the measure of absolute time from a singular point of beginning toward a singular point of completion—in linear fashion and accompanied by a continuous ticking. The other assumption is the homogeneous and infinite space that expands around the Cartesian axes *x*, *y*, and *z*. As we have already noted, modern architectural discourse was similarly formulated on these regularized articulations of time and space. The avant-garde pursued a straight line toward its utopic telos. For instance, Le Corbusier's manifesto proclaiming the Cartesian city portrayed an image of the future city anchored within an abstract, homogeneous space. Sigfried Giedion's *Space, Time and Architecture*—the erstwhile bible of modernist architectural historiography—was an attempt to synthesize time and space via a shift of viewpoint, taking a clue from Minkowski's *four*-dimensional space. Even the medium Marcel Duchamp navigated so ironically consisted of regularly articulated time and space.

It was only after I tried to ground architectural time and space logically and came up against confusion, a real cul-de-sac, so to speak, that I started to think about returning to a mutually undifferentiated condition of time/space with reference to process and to darkness. Then, several years after the Milan Triennale, I came face to face with an even more serious aporia, the actual impossibility of differentiating the two elements. I was to take part in a meeting to help prepare an inaugural exhibition for the Cooper-Hewitt Museum, entitled "ManTRANSforms" (1976/77) and curated by Hans Hollein. I was irritated by my inability to express myself in English, but then I eventually realized my own idea was of an order that could be adequately constructed only in Japanese—no translation was possible. My contribution was an installation I called *Angel Cage* (fig. 6.4), about the membrane that separates and connects the interior of and exterior of an architectural, space or, indeed, any receptacle. I decided to install various birdcages from the museum's collection and also hung photographic images of the views outside the cages—as seen by the birds trapped inside. The bird's-eye view is usually understood as an overhead perspective, but in this case it was just the opposite. The

6.4 View from within the *Angel Cage*, 1976 installation at "ManTRANSforms,"
Cooper-Hewitt Museum, New York City, by Arata Isozaki.

various designs of the exterior framework in no way affect the
view from within, so that I attempted to present the indeterminate
quality of the architectural design process as irony. To enable the
spectator to experience this more dramatically, I installed a life-
size model of one of Fra Angelico's angels inside a cage shaped
according to the vital measurements of Marilyn Monroe. At last,
the spectator was drawn into the cage. In order to bring home the

ambiguity of this "membrane" or interface that divides interior and exterior, I discussed in the exhibition catalogue various meanings of the Japanese homophone *hashi*.

> Under *hashi* in any Japanese/English dictionary will be meanings that seem totally different or even at odds: bridge, chopsticks, veranda, edge, and so forth. They refer to quite different species and forms of object. But if we pay attention to the way they function, all can be seen to share a similar feature. Everything is related to "edge," that is, the end of one thing (or one world)—and at the same time the beginning of a world beyond. In Japanese, everything that connects this side and that side may be called *hashi*.
>
> So it is possible to understand *hashi* as a concept that relates couples of contradictory terms; the term disjoins and also connects two worlds.[14]

My theme was above all concerned with issues of translation, in part to exhibit its difficulty, or the ambiguity inherent in communication itself. Whereas my primary intention had been to show the undecidability that clings to designing planes and surfaces, the second was to reveal the imperfectability of translation and at last the virtual impossibility of any real cross-cultural communication. Man Ray, an American who worked in France, constructed any number of visual diagrams that play on the space between French and English, visual wordplay games decomposing French words by an external gaze. Even between sister languages sharing many of the same roots, as English and French do, there are gulfs and crossings. But who could take pleasure in such phenomena as occur between Japanese and any major Western language? I felt strongly nonetheless that there was no choice for me but to set myself on the *hashi* and dance upon its edge, however shaky the borderline or tricky the tightrope.

When for Paris a year later I proposed curating a show about the concept *ma* (figs. 6.5, 6.6), my concerns were various. Instead of illustrating the way Japanese speakers customarily use the concept, I wanted to look into the deeper linguistic origins and later ramifications of *ma*—how the notion had been grafted onto both time and space when these elemental Western concepts arrived in Japan in the mid-nineteenth century. But the original nature of *ma* was little modified even when appropriated for the translation of

6.5 View of installation of "Ma: Space-Time in Japan" (1978), Paris, Festival d'Automne, by Arata Isozaki, 1978.

new concepts. Moreover, it lurked behind a wide range of activities in Japan from everyday life to artistic production. Was it really possible to translate this dualistic concept of *ma* to the language of speakers whose culture had two quite separate and unmediated concepts of "time" and "space"? Was it possible to formulate such questions in a public exhibition? I strove to devise a form by way of which the conceptual maneuver might be effected.

With the necessary translations:

(時間 = 時 + 間)　time (i.e., duration) = (Greek) *chronos* + *ma*

and

(空間 = 空 + 間)　space = void + *ma*,

the term *ma* itself came to be glossed as follows: "originally means the space in between things that exist next to each other; then comes to mean an interstice between things—chasm; later, a room

6.6 Tendai Sect chanting ritual at "Ma" exhibition, 1978, detail of dummy figure installation by Arata Isozaki.

as a space physically defined by columns and/or *byōbu* screens; in a temporal context, the time of rest or pause in phenomena occurring one after another."[15] Such definitions tend to confuse original uses with present-day meanings—those that came into being after the introduction and translation of Western concepts of time and space. Extensions of meaning such as "in-between space" and "pause" must have attained common usage only after the importation of Western ideas. It seems to me that *ma* ought best be thought of as "gap," or (as with the original Sanskrit meaning) an original "difference" immanent in things. Only much later did the term come to signify "marginal void," a latter-day usage of *ma* that is scarcely explicable.

I wanted, at all events, to grasp *ma* at the moment at which time-and-space had not yet been disentangled and rendered as distinct notions. I hoped to present the ways in which *ma* shows up in different modalities of thought and speech: logical, visual, and performative. Such was the basic form of the exhibition I was then working to realize in Paris. I sorted *ma*-like phenomena into nine frames of reference, and to each I applied a concept, a historical example, and the work of a contemporary artist.[16] At that time nearly thirty years ago, presentation of analytic conceptual art (e.g., the work of Joseph Kosuth)—featuring the juxtaposition of a word, dictionary definitions, and an object—was already popular. But I wanted to present *ma* in all its linguistic and nonlinguistic, i.e., performative, aspects by invoking bodily experience through installations the onlooker might participate in, rather than to set forth a mere static concept.

In architecture, the genealogy of the Japan-ness problematic, which had long been associated with the external gaze, reflected at each stage such issues as were then current in the West. The enthusiasm for Beaux-Arts and modernist composition (implying Art) as well as for function and technology from the Wiener Werkbund to the Bauhaus (enjoining Life) were invariably applied in the search for Japanese beauty. And, of course, the Jōmon/Yayoi debate relied on a revival of the timeless Dionysian/Apollonian dichotomy, enlisting a native logic in its attempt to compel a selection between populist and aristocratic taste. Such exchanges were present in the exhibition of Japanese avant-garde art at the Pompidou Center in Paris in 1986, entitled "Japon des Avant-Gardes," since it is an incontestable fact that twentieth-century avant-garde art movements first evolved in Europe and were then disseminated throughout the world. However, the curators of the Pompidou show grasped this dissemination as a simple one-way process and selected works produced in Japan but made in the image of Europe, so it was perhaps natural that a harsh critique characterized the undertaking as yet another example of Eurocentrism and/or colonialism. The show failed miserably and scandalously to the extent that the organizers in both France and Japan approached these issues only in terms of their respective national cultures. They somehow failed to notice or record the gradual climatic change that had already set in—effecting a mutual inversion, and even collapse, of the external gaze.

It was a historical peculiarity of the Japanese situation that the avant-garde movement there was confused with an enlightenment movement whose aim was to accelerate modernization, and it has generally been believed in Japan that the avant-garde was just a part of this process. A hundred years later the world's avant-garde began to veer out of control at the beginning of the 1960s—and finally self-destructed in 1968. The motivation of Japanese artists in this phase no longer directly relied on the external gaze, but was driven by the chaotic realities facing them. The co-participants in "Ma" were precisely these artists, and the sense they shared was that Japan and the West, whether avant-garde or post-avant-garde, were equally alienated. When Bruno Taut compared Ise Jingū with the Acropolis, we infer that he was motivated by the net political implication of the *tennō* system as true value (*honmono*). In contrast, to the minds of the artistic vanguard of my own time, both Ise and the Parthenon represented equally remote, even irrelevant sites. It had become clear that for Japan the borderline that had once divided interior and exterior was already disappearing. The anachronism of the Pompidou's show lay in ignorance of the fact that the external gaze that had long provoked Japan-ness was at last irrelevant; yet even if the organizers had recognized the significance of this, the framework of a formal culturo-diplomatic agreement between sovereign states might not have permitted any shift in agenda.

By way of contrast, "Ma" ten years earlier was an event that undermined the image of an exotic Japan. Nevertheless, I determined not to bring it to Japan, and not only because it would have been meaningless to exhibit "Japan" in Japan. Worse, the show would likely have been appropriated by the media always eager to sell Japan-ness to an international market, where *japonaiserie* or Japonica were somehow still believed to be in demand. Any such *japonaiserie* or Japonica would have blurred my interpretation of *ma*, constituted as it was by an unequivocal awareness that the borderline had been disappearing. After twenty-five years I recently brought the Paris "Ma" show to Japan, because at last the time had come when we were able to view Japanese Japan-ness from a meaningful distance.

Once more (and at long last) calling scenes of ruins to mind has itself faded, the very act becoming a sort of ruin in itself. After about half a century, all scenery wears out. Yet, again, an actual heap of rubble has appeared—the Great Hanshin Awaji Earthquake (1995), precisely a half century after the initial reconstruction of Japan began following World War II. The exhibit I curated at the Japanese Pavilion of the 1996 Venice Biennale was,

6.7 Photographs by Ryūji Miyamoto of Kobe earthquake of 1995 and floor installation by Yoshiaki Miyamoto, Japanese Pavilion at Venice Biennale, 1996, commissioned by Arata Isozaki.

therefore, entitled "Architects as Seismographers," directly provoked by this disastrous earthquake in the region of Kobe (figs. 6.7, 6.8). The director Hans Hollein chose architects who were mostly former members of the RATS. Hence, for the international section, I reexhibited my *Hiroshima Ruined Again in the Future* that had been made for the *Electric Labyrinth* in 1968. I was named commissioner for the Japanese Pavilion, where we exhibited basically rubble itself: the wall space was covered with photographs by Ryūji Miyamoto, which attempted to grasp the scene after the earthquake from the viewpoint of people standing on the ground; on the floor, the architect Yoshiaki Miyamoto installed actual debris collected from Kobe; and the architect Osamu Ishiyama demonstrated the breakdown of communication networks and the

6.8 Installation by Osamu Ishiyama outside the Japanese Pavilion at Venice Biennale, 1996, commissioned by Arata Isozaki.

security systems of the city by showing robots wearing the uniforms of the rescue teams amid broken computers. The exhibit won the Golden Lion award; but strikingly it had nothing to do with Japan-ness in terms of cultural representation; it simply expressed the frailty and vulnerability of contemporary cities confronted by disaster. Since then, as, of course, before, similar scenes have appeared the world over.

Since the 1960s, when I first began my cogitations as an architect, I have frequently called to mind the scenery of ruins. By ruminating on the images of Japanese cities bombarded in 1945, I believed I might be able to construct a point of view with which to confront world history. It was only from the springboard stance of a return to that point where all human constructs were nullified that future construction would again be possible, I thought. Ruins to me were a source of imagination, and in the 1960s it turned out that the image of the future city was itself ruins. Professing faith in ruins was equal to planning the future, so much were the times deranged and out of sync.

After the May revolution of 1968, the world seemed to be suspended. Clues as to how to plan for the future had vanished, so that other times in history when the image of ruins were cherished had to be recalled. At that point, time began to be inverted, and in the 1970s ruins reappeared as nostalgia. What then of the 1980s? The new face of technology enabled us to perceive the existence of another space at the heart of electronic media, and, strangely, many of the images of the future city that appeared in cyberspace were equally of ruins. The future city now reappeared as a virtual image from within the ruins. Throughout all this the imaginable scenarios, whether visiting history or imagining the future, were of ruins. This taught us indeed how tightly 1945 bound our imagination, true archi-experience.

In the 1990s, the real and the virtual flip-flopped within the world experienced in real time. The Gulf War was interpreted by some as if localized in the media. Certainly, it was hard to tell if the images of targets destroyed by missiles were real or fake. Heavy concrete bunkers must have been devastated and human blood spilled; however, the images on everyone's TV screens were like those in dreams. Judgments of right or wrong, of winning or losing, were never made.[17] Then, only rubble was left. Virtual images are concocted of rhetoric. By contrast, rubble is the bare materiality of things. It is the bankruptcy of that mode of being signified as architecture, or urban design, or even mere décor. What is dramatically revealed here is the materiality, the thingness, that had been hidden all along. This is the last stage before disappearance. Such scenery is an extreme and precise form of the Japanese expression *kare kajikeru* (dried and emaciated). Rubble is thus scattered to the space of the interstice *ma*. I had introduced *sabi*—the sense of extinction—as a section in "Ma," because undoubtedly it is in *ma* (in its relation to the primordial Greek *chora*) that such disappearance occurs; and I believe that the ultimate state of *ma* must be continuous with a *productive* emptiness like the place prepared and purified to receive the gods, *yuniwa*.[18]

Fall and Mimicry: A Case Study of the Year 1942 in Japan

For roughly a century, modern Japanese architects were obsessed with Japan-ness as the primary means of locating their own identity. This search shaped the ways by which we in Japan responded to the external gaze, transmitted as architectural form. This enduring problematic unconsciously relied upon the immobility of the physical border of our insular nation: the ocean. There had never been a need to construct actual fences or walls on the ground, as in lands that were part of the great continents. The ocean, to this nation, was an unquestionable given. The shape established for the nation is a datum of the ocean, not the land. The geographical boundary that divides inside and outside ebbs and flows, merging with the tides our cultural border and that of Nature.

This fosters the illusion that territory, language, and race are identical and homologous, all owing to Nature. And far worse, the illusion has been accelerated and intensified by the modern world's glorification of the nation-state. Today there are scientific arguments that undermine the myth of homogeneous Japan-ness thanks to research into the cultures of the Pacific islands and the origin of the Japanese language, as well as new information about ancient seafaring peoples, like the Wako. However, things have not changed all that much owing to one geographical fact: enclosure by a border that is itself the ocean.

Japonaiserie, japonisme, and Japonica all came and went in the course of a century. And beginning with the postmodern scene at the end of the 1970s, what I call the japonesque came to embrace Japanese techno/comic goods and images. But these are all names given to the quest for "curiosities" within our insular nation, to which in response corresponding bouts of cultural production have arisen automatically. The problematic of Japan-ness was built up of transferals between external and internal gazes, with the resulting self-consciousness acting as a virtual border, having served to reinforce insularity.

At the end of the twentieth century, however—as we have seen—the borderline began to blur, accelerated notably this time by the cyber revolution. The global information network enables any event to be communicated instantaneously around the world. This simultaneity may at last weaken the impetus to sustain nation-states that has been so much a function of borderlines. Already, it is easy to imagine the resultant densification and intensification producing a new globalization. We have had to ask if the problematic of Japan-ness would be sustained. I think the answer is a resounding no. Indeed, it is already disappearing.

In the face of a disappearing borderline, it becomes difficult for an insular nation to sustain the production of cultural value by sheer differentiation. Our borderline has long been a locus for the exchange of commodities as "curiosities" that began in the Meiji era. Or, to take a slightly different view, the criteria of selection are changing. Now almost anything that produces a value difference can be called a curiosity. What the external gaze appraised in the nineteenth century as curiosities used to be, more or less, rarified high art. But now, as e-commerce has accelerated and any commodity, high or low, can be exchanged instantaneously and en masse, what is reckoned low kitsch in one place can be valued as a curiosity in another, by a simple criterion of externality. Or it may be that what has hitherto been ignored by the external gaze as frivolous will now be commodified as "sign" within the cyber network. Therefore, anything can present itself as an equally curious (or *non*-curious) commodity to any gaze, be it external or internal.

I take for granted that the globalization precipitated by the cyber revolution will in the not too distant future put paid to the map of modern society divided by nation-states, rendering the whole globe smooth and flat. Still, it should be noted that in an information-based society where anything may be a commodity, there are nonetheless remnants that can never be turned into signs. When a major earthquake hits, precisely as happened in Kobe, say, the signs that until then populated the urban field disappear. What remains is rubble or sheer materiality without meaning. In like manner, human bodies remain as a form of excess baggage to our world of signs. In truth, in our ever-evolving techno-age, the human body is bound to present a major obstacle and source of resistance.

In any event, once globalization is pushed to its limit, the discourse of cultural particularity—i.e., Japan-ness—will no longer be able to dominate the formation of cultural identity. Here another possibility hoves into view. There may yet be an alternative way of tracing an outline of Japan—would it not then be possible to grasp a notion of Japan by focusing fetishistically on material remnants dropped from the new superflat information surface? This time the dynamic is no longer situated at the interface between external and internal gaze, but rather in the relation between the upper surface and the sediment below. Criteria would no longer be furnished by the gaze, but by more subtle modalities like selection, determination, and attitude. This, too, was once a way of pursuing Japan-ness. I want to look at a few such examples, but first let me describe the historical matrix.

What is known to political economists as the Kondratieff wave (or K-wave) denotes a production cycle occurring about every sixty years. There are also a few smaller waves that last only from twenty-five to thirty years, or even fifty years. Wavelengths vary in accordance with which events are sampled, but the hypothesis of the wave cycle itself is consistent and could also be applied to the shifts in discourse about nationalism. According to my analysis, Japan-ness moves roughly in 25–30-year cycles. In the context of Japan's ongoing discussion of modern architecture, in the first decade of the twentieth century, there was the "what the future architectural style of our nation should be" debate;[1] in the 1930s, there was the *teikan* style debate; in the 1960s, there was the debate on tradition versus the masses. If we project the thirty-year wave cycle forward along this line, the next cycle should have been produced in the 1990s. At that time, there was no notable debate, because the basis for discussion itself had crumbled, affected by the turmoil of the times: collapse of the cold war apparatus, burst economic bubbles, and a rising tide of globalization. What began to occur in architecture, however, was a broad-based renewal of pseudo-japonesque design, given that the self-imposed taboo against returning to a nationalist aesthetic had by then disappeared. Debate was silenced, meaning that any serious analysis of Japan-ness as ideology was considered out of the question. Instead,

"Japan," like so many other signs, became an object of almost random sampling.

Globalization—if irreversible and unequivocal—must eventually lead to a stateless and borderless condition. Paradoxically, the number of centers turning out illusory images of national identity must multiply exponentially, since everywhere would be superflat and anyplace might become a "center." The discourse seeking to explain and confirm such a scenario has been organized hastily. Returning to the notion of quarter-century K-wave cycles, a similar matrix applies to the globalizing trend and recurs roughly every half century. That is to say, well before the 1990s Japan could already have experienced its own mini-wave of globalization, say in the 1940s under a different name, accounting, I believe, for the age of the Greater East Asia Co-prosperity Sphere. That former globalizing upsurge was clearly motivated by imperialistic expansion, while the origins of the current blip are less clear-cut. But there is an isomorphism favoring the general search for identity beyond the nation-state, provoked one could say by politico-economic factors.

Architecturally speaking, whenever a cyclical curve peaks in consistent fashion, one can assume that the underlying ground is in crisis. The 1990s crisis expressed itself symptomatically as an impetus to bury architecture and/or erase its proportions and contours by dissolving its visible surface. Moreover, architects tended to suppress architecture by shifting attention to the surrounding environment. The worldwide trend in architecture of the 1990s was an extreme effort to liberate building from modernist ideals of order and proportion. The goal was to dissolve architecture in external elements—the city, the environment, and nature itself—in a kind of architectural osmosis. The process was similar to the scheme by which the insular nation of Japan was dissolving its contours into the ocean—or into an electronic sea of liquid crystal.

It was apparent that the capacity of architecture—since classicism and the end of modernism—to express and maintain its own internal equilibrium had collapsed. Even the semblance of a façade disappeared. Interiors, as they approach a fluctuating virtual space, now dissolve toward the external environment. I categorize this dissolution into two types: one inclines toward the cyber city (*sub-culturalism*) and one toward Nature (*environmentalism*). The former may be considered an antidote to "formalism" by positing the forms of architecture as semi-autonomous, while the latter counters "contextualism" in prioritizing architectural continuity with the historically generated city as new Nature. Such were the two main tendencies in the age of postmodernism, that is, between 1968 and the collapse of the Berlin Wall. In any event, this was a drastic shift. Both trends marked an abandonment of any claim to discover the basis of architecture as spatial content. However, this opening out of architectural principles will be stranded sooner or later, as we come to see that what spreads outside is little more than a vast superflat horizon.

In 1940s Japan—well over fifty years ago—the issue of the Greater East Asia Co-prosperity Sphere was the crux, as that of globalization is today. Naturally the problematic of Japan-ness faced the daunting task of justifying the outward expansion of an insular nation. As I mentioned above, Japanese architects were accordingly required to familiarize themselves and their practices with the climates of different colonies, such as Manchuria and those of Southeast Asia. The resultant forms of the Japan-ness debate were hardly suited to the freezing temperatures of Manchuria or the heat and humidity of subtropical regions. To this end the problematic of Japan-ness had to be undone and reformulated. Like the Japanese invasion of Asia with national dignity on parade in the 1940s, seizing the initiative in global exchanges in the 1990s entailed the necessity of reinventing autonomy. As today's debates stress, a nation is a communal embodiment of a certain collective imagination.[2] The retooling of such constructs demands tremendous national effort. Curiously enough, in both the 1940s and the 1990s, the clue to reconstruction was the notion of "environment," namely, an external concept from which a new paradigm could be mined.

Describing their respective projects for the competition for a "Japan Cultural Center in Bangkok" (*Nittai Bunka Kaikan*, 1943), Tange used the expression "environmental order," and Maekawa, "environmental space." As I mentioned above, Ryūichi Hamaguchi remarked of these expressions: "Maekawa's work is functional, while Tange's is monumental. Or, in other words, Tange's is reactionary while Maekawa's is progressive."[3]

In order to stress the difference, Hamaguchi paid attention to the nouns "order" and "space." Nevertheless, both architects employed the modifier "environmental," and this points to a different aspect of both proposals. The proposed location was Bangkok,

Thailand, and the project was supposed to be a Japanese cultural center. In the preparatory discussions, it was asked whether a Japanese-style building would be appropriate for this hotter, more humid climate. In other words, and this was the very question: could Japan-ness, physically and in formal terms, be exported beyond the border? The term "environment" thus arose as a response and was used as an excuse for both architects, whose proposals were among the top selections, to force an opening of the formulaic system toward its surroundings. It seems that the term "environmental" may even have been chosen by tacit mutual agreement.

Up until then, for Tange, the external raison d'être for buildings had been the city—the kind of city it was possible to plan (in the sense that persuaded CIAM architects to adopt the Athens Charter in 1933). When the Japan Architectural Society requested architectural guidelines for use within the Greater East Asia Co-prosperity Sphere, Tange proposed the following:

> Concerning architectural guidelines, if the building is set in a proper location in Greater East Asia and exerts a clear nexus of signification, it will function properly and its beauty will be apparent. The architectural development of Greater East Asia must begin with an allotment of space. It is urban planning that affords a context. In this way individual architectural creations will achieve a self-evident meaning endowed with maximal freedom, without which such works would be unprincipled. Thus a vigorous form of southern urban planning and construction, motivated by a new Japanese spirit, will emerge.[4]

"It is urban planning that affords a context," Tange had stressed. Throughout his career of more than half a century, urbanism consistently grounded Tange's architecture, the selfsame principle he expresses here. In the same year, he took first place in the competition for the Greater East Asia Memorial Building—which was to have been his debut. The overall scheme is well known from the submission drawing of a building modeled in perspective after the utmost orthodox Japanese shrine architecture *tenchi-shinmei-zukuri* (divine-light-shed-upon-heaven-and-earth style). It was to be built at the foot of Mount Fuji (fig. 1.4), and the official name was a long one: "Plan for a Memorial Building Connecting the Greater East Asia Highway—Chief Motif: Plan for a War Memorial to the Construction of a Greater East Asia." That is to say, the stimulus for the memorial was a highway. Its starting point was to be the Imperial Palace (Kyū-jō) in Tokyo; the road would run southward and continue all the way to the east side of Mount Fuji, where it would veer to the right and go straight to the top of the mountain. The "sacred precinct" was set perpendicularly to the highway, whose axis was to bisect the domain framed by the war memorial facilities and an adjacent plaza for commemorative events. To situate the building, modeled after Ise Jingū, the highway linking the Imperial Palace with Mount Fuji was employed as a *tracé régulateur*. To Tange, urban planning "grounding" a building meant this kind of solution. The memorial highway—metaphorically, a foretaste perhaps of today's network of fiber optics—was the infrastructure grounding his entire project.

In the case of the competition for a Japan Cultural Center in Bangkok, siting was predetermined, and no urban scheme could be introduced to provide a context. The transferal of one culture to another climate was the ostensible task, so "environment" was invoked as a mediating concept. Any attempt to link principles of "order" or "space" to the vague concept of "environment" was quite irrational, yet such thinking had been mandated. This mindset might be compared with today's tendency to dissolve all borders and internal points of reference in favor of an external datum that is superflat, and hence without qualities.

Just when Japan-ness in architecture was compelled to reinvent itself and open up toward new horizons of geography and climate, Japanese intellectuals were confronting a complementary issue that I have termed the "Overcoming Modernity" debate. Participants belonged to various fields: philosophy, literary criticism, religion, and science, as well as the arts. The arguments revolved around Japan's position vis-à-vis recent Western modernism, and Japan's new presence throughout Asia was thoroughly implicated in the conclusion that her ancient traditions were greatly superior to any Western-style revisionism, whether in thought or deed. The debate was aired in 1942 in two consecutive issues of the new and influential literary journal *Bungakukai* (Literary World). Opposed premises such as tradition/modernity and Japan/the West were argued, and superiority of the former over the latter was conclusively pursued. Among Japanese architects such contradictions had never seriously plagued the reception of modernity (as

I have argued in chapter 1). For this reason, their more elusive design problematic easily survived the turmoil of war and defeat.

In 1942, the year after Japan had provoked war with the U.S., the impending reality of the Greater East Asia doctrine must have been keenly felt—much more so than the advent of today's homogeneously superflat world in recent times. Shōichi Inoue, in his book *Japanese Architects during the War,* saw fit to publish the following comment by Kunio Maekawa:

> During wartime, I was attacked by Ryūichi Hamaguchi and Kenzō Tange (whom I believe to a certain extent to be responsible for this). They asked me outright: "Why indeed hasn't a Japanese architectural style been created? What would you say?" I replied, "Only in the sense that the brand-new Japanese warships *Aoba* [Blue Leaf] and *Furutaka* [Venerable Falcon], known to be strong, light, and swift amidst the raging waves, are deemed Japanese, can a Japanese architecture be said to exist nowadays." Their reaction was pretty bad. They treated me almost as a traitor [laugh].[5]

The episode has been widely interpreted as referring to the time when Kunio Maekawa, who persisted in the rationalist formulas of early modernism, was indicted by his students Ryūichi Hamaguchi and Kenzō Tange (somewhat like Red Guards during the Chinese Cultural Revolution). The latter not only themselves accepted but also actively promoted the militant slogan of the time *hakkō-ichi-u* (the whole world under one roof) that advocated actively mixing Japanese tradition and the new expansionism into Asia. I myself later heard Maekawa recount this episode, so the younger men's reaction must have been correctly reported. Moreover, Kunio Maekawa also told me the sequel. When the signs of defeat were at last indisputable, Hamaguchi advised people to leave Tokyo for the countryside or the provinces. (He in fact went to Hokkaido, as far as one could get.) Tange, instead, extolled the state slogan *ichioku gyokusai* meaning the "whole million" (*read* the whole populace) must die rather than surrender. Luckily, all three men survived the defeat; inevitably, they were to become the postwar bearers of the discourses concerning Japan-ness. Hamaguchi became overinvolved in Japonica and suffered a setback. Tange reinvented himself in grand urban schemes such as his Tokyo Plan of 1960 (which was, not to mince words, a resurrection of the Greater East Asia highway scheme already referred to). Meanwhile, Maekawa's rationalism was never tailored to suit the matrix of Japan-ness. These were three individual responses to the overpowering obligation of opening up the system to the outside.

Maekawa's reference to battle cruisers as the *real* Japanese architecture was not at all uncommon for the time. In the context of constructing Japan-ness whilst importing modern rationalist design in the 1930s, it had often been argued that Japan's battleships embodied the very ideal of both beauty and function. In the instance cited, Maekawa resorted to this explanation simply as pretext. In the same year as the "Overcoming Modernity" controversy in 1942, the unique novelist and essayist Ango Sakaguchi (1906–1955) wrote something similar but more explicit.

> Why are these three things [Kosuga Prison (in Tokyo), a dry ice factory, and battleships] so beautiful? No artificial aesthetic makes them so. No column, no steel structure has been added for the sake of beauty. No column, no steel structure has been removed for the sake of non-beauty. Whatever is necessary was simply placed wherever required; all unnecessary things have been removed. Under such conditions, unique forms underwritten by need, and need alone, gradually come into existence. They look like nothing but themselves. Following the dictates of necessity, columns are unequivocally twisted, steel plates are stretched irregularly, or rails all of a sudden protrude. The whole conforms to necessity. No idea from the past could compete with this inheritable necessity. In such fashion these three artifacts looking like nothing other than themselves have come into existence.[6]

Here Sakaguchi articulates the essence of the Neue Sachlichkeit (new objectivity) that modern German design attained around 1930. Even when, after the war, we restudied the principles of modern architecture such as function, rationality, the external expression of plan, and so forth, no other explanation was as clear and lucid as Sakaguchi's. His acute appraisal was based upon the strategy he had thought through in the climate of 1942. He was already suspicious of the dualism in the "Overcoming Modernity" debate— modern/traditional and West/Japan—from which Japanese were apparently able to extract only two options: good or bad, and win or lose. Brilliantly Sakaguchi conjectured that one of the predisposing causes of such dichotomizing was Bruno Taut's discourse on the rediscovery of Japan. Furthermore, he saw right through the construction of Japan-ness precipitated by the external gaze:

> Nevertheless, in between the fact that Taut rediscovered Japan and its traditional beauty and the fact that we ourselves are Japanese whilst losing the Japanese tradition, there was a distance that Taut could scarcely have imagined. That is to say, Taut had first to discover Japan, while we are already Japanese, prior to having to discover Japan. Although we may have lost our ancient culture, we can hardly lose sight of Japan. What is Japanese spirit?—we need not pose the question. It is unthinkable that Japan could be born from such a rationale, or that the Japanese spirit as such can ever be explained.[7]

Written in the same year that the "Overcoming Modernity" debate and the plan for the Greater East Asia Memorial Building were receiving publicity, Sakaguchi's essay nevertheless ignored the kind of discourses formed in an effort to respond to this ideology. However near to being a Japanese version of Neue Sachlichkeit, Sakaguchi's writing boasts an incomparable radicalism: it attempted a vertical leap into materiality, or the ineluctable weight of existence, with a forceful enunciation that at times sounds almost decadent. Even when the situation had drastically mutated after the war, Sakaguchi persisted. His famous "Daraku Ron" (Essay on the Fall) (1946) radicalized his message, and "Kokuhō Shobō Kekkō Ron" (Never Mind if National Treasures Are Burned Down) (1951) represents the high point of this argument.[8]

Among actual architects, it was only Sutemi Horiguchi whose pose was comparable to Sakaguchi's. His essay "Yoshiki naki Yoshiki" (A Style without Style)[9] was an ironical interpretation of Japan also from a *sachlich* position. He studied the Japanese teahouse from the standpoint of the compositional notions of modern design, and first published *The Teahouse of Rikyū* in the middle of the ongoing war in China, in 1940.[10] It is even possible to interpret his aim to have been a reconstruction of the teahouse from the "performative/spatial" perspective advocated by Ryūichi Hamaguchi. In the prewar period, Horiguchi had confined himself to Jikō-in, near Hōryū-ji, in Nara. There he was immersed in scrutiny of teahouses of the Sekishū school, so influential during the Edo period, all the while disregarding the expanding problematic of Japan-ness. This after all was grounded in the modernist compositional approach whose construction he had participated in during the early 1930s. Perhaps increasingly his degree of self-involvement was almost that of a modern-day dropout. If I may say so, Horiguchi's works of this period have survived longer than any of the rest because he focused on facts and facts alone. For that matter, Sakaguchi was also loyal to the *sachlich* point of view and to facts alone. This argument far surpassed in subtlety the contemporary zeitgeist that applauded ancient Japanese religious architecture in line with the discoveries of Taut.

Sakaguchi did not in the least share the scruples that the modernist Maekawa had expressed. Sakaguchi, again:

> Being slim and sharp in appearance is not enough to achieve true beauty. All is a matter of substance. Beauty for the sake of beauty is not honest nor can it be genuine—it is empty. I argue that such emptiness will never move people and must finally become obsolete. It would not trouble us in the least if both Hōryū-ji and Byōdō-in were to be burned down. If necessary, let us demolish Hōryū-ji and construct a parking lot.[11]

All assessments of Japanese beauty, including any architectural aesthetic, are flatly refused by Sakaguchi as a fiction. He insists that beauty should be assessed in any number of possible ways according to circumstance, while the zeitgeist that seeks an absolute principle of judgment must be resisted. His bravura assertion that it wouldn't matter if Hōryū-ji burned down, or were demolished, is an ironical expression of this unique rationalism. When Kinkaku-ji (the Golden Pavilion) was destroyed by fire after the war, he claimed: "Neither Kinkaku-ji nor Ginkaku-ji [the Silver Pavilion] nor Hōryū-ji is anything that one can call beautiful in itself. The nature of their beauty is merely canonical, colluding with historiography to fabricate a plausible art historical narrative."[12] Finally, he adds that it is quite enough to keep to the given architectural model and its data.

As I have said, Sakaguchi's position remained perfectly consistent both before and after the war. And especially in the prewar years, when Japanese beauty was being aggressively exported beyond its own borders under the slogan of *hakkō-ichi-u*, it must have required significant courage to assert that both Japanese aesthetics and its history were arbitrary fictions. Even Maekawa's reticence was subjected to a kangaroo court; it was an age when one could only let time pass, obsessed with some innocent object like Horiguchi's teahouses.

In the same year came another pronouncement from a position parallel to Sakaguchi's, yet originating from a broader perspective. Its source was the literary critic Hideo Kobayashi (1902–1983), who wrote:

> Previously we felt it difficult to escape from the doctrine that a new way of seeing and interpreting history was needed. Such a thesis affected me with its apparent wiles. Meanwhile, as I read history more closely, it appeared less and less a discipline alterable by any means. History refuses to give up an inch to any new interpretation as such, for it is not so weak as to be defeated in that way. As I realized this, I felt history to be increasingly beautiful. There is a morsel of accepted wisdom that the great novelist Ōgai [Mori] late in his life "degenerated" into a mere researcher after facts—this is frivolous. At the very point when he began his intensive scrutiny, he was at last able to intervene in a spirit of history. When reading *On the Ancient Records* [a celebrated commentary on the *Kojiki*] by Motoori Norinaga, the originator of Edo nationalist scholarship, I had again this sensation. Only that which rejects all interpretation and is not moved an inch has beauty—this was the most forceful opinion Norinaga held. Yet today, in a time filled with interpretations, it appears a most esoteric notion.[13]

"Only that which rejects all interpretation has beauty" became Kobayashi's most renowned dictum. One extreme position within the complex discourse woven around Japan-ness is thus encapsulated. The fact that Kobayashi took into account the book on *Kojiki* by Motoori Norinaga is suggestive of a variety of issues surrounding Japan-ness. Motoori categorically refused any interpretation of the mythology of Japan's nationhood, instead simply pursuing its philology. His attitude was a direct consequence of the linguistic power and authority confronting the discourse on Japan-ness from the very beginning.

Though my goal is to pursue the way Japan-ness is prob-lematized in architecture, I have nevertheless introduced non-architectural writers such as Sakaguchi and Kobayashi because I hope to understand why their essays on Japan cast such a long shadow. Sakaguchi's "A Personal View of Japanese Culture" and Kobayashi's *A Thing Called Transience*—both published in the same year (1942), at the height of the war effort—had a long and lasting influence upon the postwar climate, if compared with more ephemeral architectural writing of the same generation. And, as I stated, my hypothesis is that the prewar transition compelled by the state ideology of *hakkō-ichi-u* and the official policy of the Greater East Asia Co-prosperity Sphere exercised a similar function within the Japan-ness problematic as the superflattening of all dif-ferences by the IT-driven globalization of the 1990s. On these quite different occasions, the common denominator was that sud-den erasure of the border which had previously guaranteed a more rigid internal order. After a new 50-year cycle (ending in the 1990s), Japanese history is beginning to be reinterpreted in diverse ways. And the new overall tendency stresses the unique superiority, and thus the universality, of Japan-ness in a way similar to the pre-defeat epoch of *hakkō-ichi-u*. In both cases, the undoing of the older framework has coincided with an expansionist process, owing to a perceived reinforcement of Japan as center. Along with an expansion of the topos of the insular nation welcoming a new architecture, both phases have repeatedly called upon the environ-ment as the main thematic. In the earlier phase, the impetus per-ished after breaching the border, resisted elsewhere in Asia. By contrast, the latter-day scenario of globalization is ongoing and boasts an overwhelming certainty and power. The assumption shared by both eras was and continues to be that of global percep-tion and its inevitability.

Sakaguchi, by deliberately regressing to a realist, or *sachlich*, proposal, suggests that the falsified Japanese beauty that had become a cliché could now be relinquished and abandoned. Kobayashi, rejecting all manipulation of history as fiction, advo-cates a more risky stance—a mimicry of the foundation myth or story of origin, in other words a reenactment of origin. We should pay heed to the fall (into materiality) and mimicry (of origin)—agendas that are veritably Japanese, and which prewar intellectuals adopted in order to combat an overpowering official ideology. In today's superflat context, any such claims would call attention to a residue—one that could provoke an alternative problematic. Whatever terminology we decide to employ—"Japanese" or some new name—Sakaguchi and Kobayashi (and to a certain extent Horiguchi)—exemplars from the 1940s—may afford a model that helps us to reconsider globalization, offering an approach to what is excluded from the forever-circulating signs of national culture.

Japan-nesses—all those terms with the prefix *Jap*—have always had an external origin. Whether a one-way or mutual gaze, their locus is always the border. These case studies from 1942, that desperate moment of uncertainty for the future of the insular nation-state, should help us learn what could be done now when the border is once again disappearing. Indeed by fall and mimicry our two writers sought fresh ways to combat the secular annihilation of the border. Yet, after the surrender, the old frame was quickly reinstated. Meanwhile, the architects of the wartime period tried to effect a dissolution toward the environment, but, even before the results could be judged, they had to submit to the Japonica boom that came with the occupation.

Today a new destruction of architecture is afoot, stimulated by the World Wide Web. It is in this context that the agendas of fall and mimicry might be revisited. They were both ways by which to tackle what is actually this fact of Japan, even when the broader fictitious Japan-ness was dissolving. Sakaguchi's intention of dismantling Japanese "beauty" as a dominant fiction by descent into sheer materiality corresponds, I believe, to the late twelfth-century "architect" Chōgen's agenda that is the subject of part III. His was a *sachlich* revelation of the bare structure of Tōdai-ji's Nandai-mon (Southern Gatehouse) by way of a persistent attack upon the disintegrating Japanese-style beauty created by the Kyoto establishment of the time. Likewise, Kobayashi's mimicry in his *Motoori Norinaga*,[14] in which he retells Norinaga's own retelling of the origin myth, *Kojiki*, replicates Ise Jingū's tradition of periodic rebuilding—a creation of the eternity of form by a repetition, or the mimicry of its own origin. (This side of Ise is discussed in my part II.) Both, I would like to insist, in no way rely on the border that supported the masquerade of *Japan*-nesses. Both "drop" straightforwardly and vertically, and that is all. What arises in turn will resurrect an island with *specificity*. In contradistinction to the nation-state etched upon the broader atlas of world power, this is just an island habitually called Japan, one of innumerable such islands throughout the world. In our contemporary state of affairs—superflatness—any precipitation would form an island; more islands would form an archipelago. But, of course, it is more than ever imperative to encourage ways of perceiving islands/archipelago other than, and beyond, a mere archetypal descent to materiality or reenactment of origins.

A Mimicry of Origin: Emperor Tenmu's Ise Jingū

By the 1930s the buildings and setting of Ise Jingū (fig. 8.1) had at last begun to capture the imagination of contemporary Japanese architects. Until then, Japanese building history had simply contextualized these enigmatic edifices as a single example of one among many different types of shrine architecture. *Nihon Kenchikushi-yō* (Summary of Japanese Architectural History) (1927) by Shunichi Amanuma,[1] a comprehensive and fully illustrated compendium of Japanese buildings, included a brief description of Ise—in contrast to its detailed accounts of other shrines—noting summarily, but significantly, that shrine carpenters (*miya-daiku*) called this type the "original style of shrine architecture in heaven and on earth"— *tenchi-kongen miyazukuri*. That was the extent of it. A generation earlier, Chūta Itō had surveyed Japanese shrine architecture in "Nihon Jinja Kenchiku no Hattatsu" (The Development of Japanese Shrine Architecture) (1901).[2] His first inclination was to categorize Ise's buildings—the *nai-gai kū* (its central, as well as outer satellite, buildings)—as *shinmei-zukuri* (radiant style of the deity), but he avoided any further mention except to avow that "one is too much in awe to describe the Great Shrine in detail." The upshot is that both scholars seem to have believed the style of Izumo Taisha[3] in Shimane prefecture—*taisha-zukuri* (cf. *Sumiyoshi-zukuri*)—to be the more original of the two in terms of Japanese Shintō typologies. Izumo Taisha exhibits the *tsuma-iri* structure (fig. 8.2), where the entry is below one of the gable ends, while Ise has the *hira-iri*, where the entrance is beneath one ledge of the sloping roof (fig. 8.3). Both authorities maintained at the time that the latter style had appeared only with the introduction of religious architecture from the continent, and thus could not be purely Japanese.

8.1 Ise Shrine: inner precinct, Shōden (main sanctuary), and the two Hōden (Western and Eastern treasure houses). Photograph by Yasuhiro Ishimoto.

In his essay on Hōryū-ji (1893), Itō famously speculated that the entasis of the columns of Hōryū-ji, one of the oldest buildings in Japan, had originated in Greece.[4] At any rate, he was the first architectural historian in Japan who attempted to grasp Japanese building history in its global context. As early as 1930, in his essay "On Ancient Architecture,"[5] Itō pinpointed the origins of two major modes of ancient Japanese building: *taka-yuka* (elevated-floor) style, derived from the south, and the *azekura* (log-cabin-style storehouse) from the north. But Itō dealt mainly with temples and very little with shrines. Moreover, it seems that he hesitated to classify the Ise archetype as a truly ancient form, considering its strange periodic rebuilding and dismantling procedure that may have incorporated various transformations or even new elements.

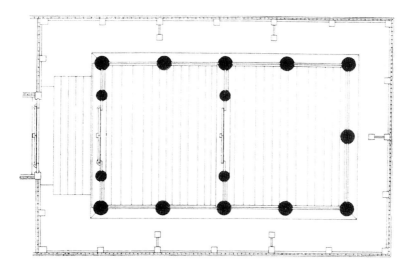

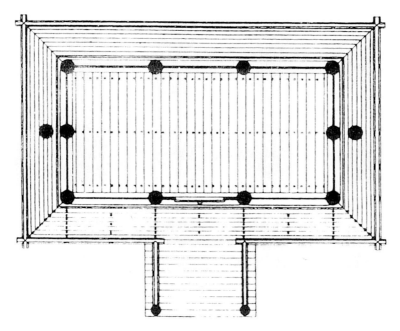

8.2 Typical plan illustrating *tsuma-iri* entrance style of ancient Japanese shrine architecture.

8.3 Typical plan illustrating *hira-iri* entrance style of ancient Japanese shrine architecture.

As we have already seen, it was Bruno Taut who made Ise a focus of attention in the 1930s, employing the existing aesthetic distinction between *honmono* (high art) and *ikamono* (low art) and linking that with the dichotomy of *tennō* versus the shōgunate. Taut's agenda was evident in his two books published at this time, which tossed the issue of Japanese architecture directly into the political arena even before submitting it to existing aesthetic standards.[6] The new direction became evident at once. For instance, Itō announced:

> I believe that Japanese architectural history is a very special sort that does not exist anywhere else. Much of the ancient Japanese architecture we see is that of shrines, whose features are said to have originated in the South Seas: the materials are organic, the structures are simple, the appearance is rough and humble. The shrine seems to be an infantile architectural type, but one with a deep and pure beauty. Concerning all this, the famous German architect Bruno Taut, who has recently come to reside in Japan, has a good deal to say. He marvels at the architecture of the great Ise Jingū. He has praised it as the ideal architecture, the true Architecture of architectures. When I met him, I requested that he explain which aspect of Ise he admired so much. He answered that it was difficult to list actual points, but the main criterion was its purity. Although it has neither ornament nor complexity, the purity of form and structure attests to a certain spirituality. It is an architecture before which one naturally bows down. It is not merely the acme of Japanese architecture but also of world architecture. Though I felt more than a little flustered and was even made uncomfortable by Taut's overpraise of the shrine, I realized that this was not mere flattery. What Taut says contains a great deal of truth. The purity of this architecture is like that of an infant; its innocence has a divine character. The survival of ancient South Seas architecture is a unique phenomenon—seen only in Japan.[7]

It is worthy of note that Itō never claims Ise is original to Japan. Furthermore, this passage appears without warning, after he has described how Japanese architecture developed under the certain influence of Korean, Chinese, and Western styles of building.

Such was Itō's way of expressing his disconcertion at Taut's forthright appreciation of Ise and the growing attention given to it. The fact was that Itō had never much appreciated Ise before. "At the time we adopted standards of Western architectural scholarship in the first year of Meiji (1868), Ise was regarded as a primitive work of the southern aboriginals and ignored as insignificant."[8] This much he admitted.

The exchange between Itō and Taut occurred as part and parcel of the Japan-ness problematic, and as such it even aroused excitement. On the heels of Itō, it was Sutemi Horiguchi, among Japanese modernists, who first and most consciously engaged the issue of what is Japanese in architecture. For him, the essence of Japan-ness had to be "an original product of the Japanese people."[9] Accordingly, he pointed to certain types of shrines, residences, and teahouses. In contradistinction to Itō, Horiguchi claimed Ise as the foremost example of Japanese architecture. How does one account for this difference in their positions? When Itō consigns Ise to the South Seas, he is speaking of *origin*. But when Horiguchi enlists Ise as the epitome of Japan-ness, he refers to a *beginning*—*wayō-ka*, the Japanization of foreign imports. Therefore, it is necessary for us, too, to distinguish between *origin* and *beginning*. Yet, notwithstanding their differences, both men are meeting (or had forcibly been thrown into) the same problematic head on. Thus, Horiguchi, like Itō, responded passionately to Taut.

> The expression that comprises the whole of Ise, built amid its one-thousand-year-old forest and surrounded by a sacred hedge [*mizugaki*] and imperial fence [*tamagaki*], has long evoked the feeling recorded in the twelfth century by the monk and poet Saigyō: "I know not what lies within, but I am in tears with gratitude." Recently the German architect Bruno Taut saw it and in his awe rose to the heights of rhetoric: "There is no architecture superior to Ise in terms of the purity that one observes in its harmony between material and structure. Just as Japanese people revere Ise Jingū as a state sanctuary, Japanese architects ought to revere it as an exemplar of design. Its beauty defies mere description. Architects throughout the world must revere it as a holy site of architectural pilgrimage. This unique Japanese creation is also one of the world's most important masterpieces."[10]

In the same way that Itō mentions Ise as if he had just remembered something out of context, Horiguchi quotes Taut almost incidentally. What Horiguchi evokes by means of the idea of Japan-ness are the native qualities of *wayō-ka* vis-à-vis Chinese forms and influence: asymmetry, columns without stone bases (*hottate-bashira*), periodic rebuilding, and lightweight construction, among other things. Quoting Taut does not seem to be essential, but Horiguchi does so anyway. Why? Was it because Horiguchi, as a modern architect and architectural historian, had simply to take into account this new and important judgment delivered by a foreigner that dramatically rent the eerily blurred Japanese cultural veil of the time? Not exactly. It was far more likely because Horiguchi found Taut's appraisal so simple and strong. Taut did not enunciate great complexities, but merely pointed out that Ise might will be compared with the Parthenon:

> The shrines of Ise are Japan's greatest and most completely original creation in terms of world architecture. They afford an encounter differing entirely from the most beautiful cathedrals or mosques, the Indian and Siamese temples or pagodas, and even from those of [nearby] China. The Parthenon on the Acropolis is to the present day a visible sign of the beautiful gifts that men of Athens bestowed on their collective symbol of wisdom and intelligence, Athena. It is aesthetically the greatest and most sublime building in stone, as are the Ise shrines in wood. But still there is a great difference. Even if the Parthenon had not been blown to ruins it would today still be only a monument of ancient times, as life is missing from it. How very different are the shrines of Ise! Not only are the religious rites and the everlasting stream of worshippers a living presence, the shrines have yet another vital quality, which is entirely original in its effect, intention, and perception. This is the fact that the shrines are always new.[11]

In his 1937 book, whenever Taut praises the features of Ise, he contrasts every detail with the Parthenon, painting Ise in glowing words. In any event, it is evident that the Parthenon offers Taut an absolute measure of value. In Japan the translation of the term "architecture"—*kenchiku*—was first proposed by Itō in his essay "Discussing the Essence of ARCHITECTURE, in Hopes of Avoiding the Conventional Term *Zōka-gakkai* [Building-House

Society] in Its Translation."[12] It seems clear that Itō had come to understand what the concept of architecture signified in the West. On the other hand, Horiguchi was a founder of the earliest Japanese avant-garde architectural group, the *Bunri-ha*; he had grasped the concept of architecture with a capital A in the very effort of its organization. But, for both these Japanese, it may still have been difficult to appreciate Ise as architecture, even in pointing to this or that unique feature. Thus Taut's assessment—especially his sweeping comparison with the Parthenon—intervened as an unexpectedly opportune reference. At the time, there was a common notion that, in evaluating modernity, the Parthenon was crucial to appreciating architecture as high art. Taut's paradigm inscribed Ise's position on a Western scale of value.

In fact there was a subtext to Horiguchi's assessment of Taut's sanction of Ise. He seems to imply that Taut's impression was a modern version of Saigyō's poetic homage. Saigyō's *waka*, "I know not what lies within, but I am in tears with gratitude," expresses an awe inspired by the sacredness of Ise. The *waka* formula requires no logical explanation; the simple statement enters the hearer's heart and reverberates there—it is sheer power of language. In Japan, poetry is believed to convey the power of the primordial word, or *kotodama* (word-spirit). The Japanese *parole* was felt to transmit the anima of the speaker to that of the listener in an unmediated fashion. There is a kind of phonocentrism here that beggars logical explanation as unsophisticated. In the event, the awe and power of Ise are fully accounted for in Saigyō's lines, and that suffices. Horiguchi himself was a serious amateur of *waka*: later in life he was appointed a juror for the annual New Year's poetry reading (*uta-kai hajime*) at the imperial court. He must, therefore, have had faith in *waka*'s power. Nonetheless, quoting Saigyō, well known as was this poet, is not deemed enough in his attempt to reevaluate Ise, thus he reinforces his own words by paraphrasing Taut. Eventually, however, Saigyō's poetry did become the cornerstone for the reevaluation of the topos of Ise. Much later Hirotarō Ōta, who pursued Japanese architectural history with a slightly different agenda, after Itō and Horiguchi, also mentions Saigyō, touching upon Taut, by then deceased.

What about Ise Jingū so much impressed Saigyō, who sang: "I know not what lies within, but I am in tears with gratitude"? It was long questioned whether this line was really Saigyō's. Yet it has become so widely known because it portrays a feeling shared among Japanese. Was it the beauty of architecture—which made Taut value Ise on a par with the Parthenon—that impressed Saigyō? Perhaps not quite. The deep forest of Japanese cedar and the sanctuary of raw wood that it surrounds in such serenity—this harmony between the architecture and its environment inspired him.

What about *Hōryū-ji*, also a religious structure dating to around the same time as Ise? Today there are a few pines around the middle gate, but the whole, including its innermost precincts, must simply have been spread with white sand. At Ise, the central area enclosed by the sacred hedge—*mizugaki*—is covered in pebbles, while the surrounding cedar forest possesses a scale and volume that envelops the whole complex. The sanctuaries stand quiet and in secret within.[13]

Ōta set great store by the Saigyōesque appreciation. Touching upon Taut's position only briefly, he seems less preoccupied with the Parthenon analogy. His chief point is the effect of the harmony between the dense cedar forest and these buildings made of the same trees. That is to say he tacitly shifts the standard of architectural appreciation to the building's surrounding, the natural environment. Reconfirming the poetic topos persisting in Japan since ancient times, Ōta pays homage to the continuity of architecture and nature. Implied is the Japanese idea of gods—*kami*—as closely linked to the vital power lurking within nature: the Shintō shrine was conceived as a device, or machine, to worship the gods in nature. Ōta's stance has today become commonplace. In one of his several books on Ise, the Metabolist architectural critic Noboru Kawazoe comments as follows:

It is unthinkable for the great poet Saigyō not to have known that Ise's deity is the Sun Goddess—Amaterasu Ōmikami—or to have been unfamiliar with the mythology surrounding her. But these facts do not directly affect visitors. For neither does the deity admonish: love thy neighbor, nor does it call: I am with thee, nor does it extend a helping hand. Instead, simply pray and.... Furthermore, in Saigyō's time, there was no *tennō*-ist ideology;

that appeared with the Meiji Restoration. Since ancient times, Japanese people have believed in mysterious forces of nature operating behind human society. But this has never been the kind of thing grasped by logical reflection. It is very well expressed by, "I know not what lies within, but ...".[14]

For Kawazoe, the Saigyōesque approach by itself is a sufficient appreciation of Ise. Later he quotes Bruno Taut, but merely to remind us that Ise must be experienced with awe: "[Taut] wrote how one could not understand Ise's beauty until visiting it and that architects from all over the world should make a pilgrimage to Ise."[15]

Thirty years passed (from the 1930s to the sixties) during the shift in Ise's appraisal—from Taut's transposition of Ise to a Western value system to the return to a Saigyōesque appreciation proper to Japan. World War II had intervened. These years afforded, among other things, a process through which Japan sought to recapture confidence in its cultural integrity by "overcoming" the modern West. In the 1930s, the Japanese modernist architects who had invited Taut were hoping to combat, or at least modify, the nationalism of the teikan style, but by the 1960s the tendency to stress national values—albeit in a very different way—had once again taken precedence. In the background was the rise of a new postwar nationalism of sorts. This no longer supported political identification of Taut's Ise with the tennō system but nevertheless preserved the cultural agenda of discovering Ise's uniqueness. It is now widely understood that under the new postwar constitution, tennō was redefined as a symbol of the state rather than as a sovereign. The new nationalist tendency left tennō in the background, and shed fresh light on Ise as a cultural product. But why, then, did Ise absorb so much attention? How could it become a problematic in itself? Though all knew that the myth-engendered power of the tennō system lurked behind the siren call of Ise, no one tackled this rapport, owing in large part to the fact that by the 1960s tennō was no longer considered a powerful—or dangerous—entity. Nonetheless, highlighting Ise as an object of cultural analysis unwittingly rendered the tennō system—if not this or that individual emperor—liable to resurface as an object of cultural worship. Even more, the shift toward a Saigyōesque awe of nature was part of the whole tendency. It was Kenzō Tange, the new spokesman for modernism in Japan, who was prepared to elaborate the discourse.

> The creation of the quintessential form of Ise was also a process of discovering symbols. A world of religious mythology is shaped according to the fantasy of a people through discovery of reflections of the myths in tangible symbols, which make the system visible and apprehensible. The ancient Japanese sought their symbols and divine image in nature—in rocks, trees, and water. This way of looking at nature is still at the very core of the spiritual make-up of the Japanese today.
>
> Ise came into being through the sublimation of symbols into a basic form. The final achievement of the quintessential form represented by Ise also meant the completion of the corpus of Japanese religious mythology and approximately coincided with the end of the process of welding the Japanese people into a whole. The vigorous conceptual ability of the ancient Japanese who fashioned the form of Ise was sustained by the energies released during the nation-building process. The form of Ise partakes of the primordial essence of the Japanese people. To probe this form and the way it came into being is to go to the very foundations of Japanese culture.[16]

What Tange refers to here as "form" is reminiscent of Louis Kahn's influential methodology publicized around this same time. Kahn argued that architectural design must be differentiated from manipulation of mere surface shapes; on the contrary, it should be a discovery of form that energizes existing potencies into a system.[17] Tange attempted to draw an equivalence between the "becoming" of form, a favored phrase of Kahn's, and the formation of a whole Japanese culture. In his thoughts that continue the above excerpt, rather than analyze Ise's architecture Tange examines above all the gods (kami) and nature at Ise with reference to archaeological materials; what he perceives is animism. Ise as a total culture involves a number of ritualistic utensils—natural objects as well as fetishistic devices—used in summoning kami. Citing the example of Japan's oldest Shintō shrine—Miwa Jinja in Sakurai, Nara prefecture—he finds it likely that shrines originally had no buildings at all. A temporary altar complex—himorogi—was built for each ritual. Thus it is only natural that the performative aspect be taken into consideration in analyzing Ise's architecture. What was crucial to understand is that in the 1960s, the modern archaeological attitude that lends serious attention to animism was also employed in a new appreciation of Ise. The transposition of an underlying appreciation to the concept of *kami* comes close to Ōta's equivalence of architecture with the natural environment. In Saigyō's celebrated introit nature appears full of awe. Ritual was the means to draw on that power. Tange once again:

> Tradition by itself cannot function as the driving force for creativeness, but it always bears within itself the chance to stimulate creativeness. To find this chance I have roamed through tradition until, at its furthest limits, I was confronted by Ise, by the fountainhead of Japanese tradition.
>
> I found the form of Ise; behind it lies primeval nature.
>
> Out of it, out of nature's darkness, the vigorous conceptual ability of the ancient Japanese gradually fashioned various symbols of the spirit culminating in the creation of the form of Ise. Here primeval darkness and eternal light, the vital and the aesthetic, are in balance, and a world of harmony with nature unfolds.[18]

Once again, the ultimate standard is the awe-inspiring power of nature, with little difference from Saigyō's *waka*. Harmony is achieved by simply bowing to *kami*—a natural force. As Taut had said: "One involuntarily bows in front of it." In other words, Japanese people were themselves to be seen bowing in front of it, and Taut's metaphor of pilgrimage derives from his observations of a devout Japanese populace. The Parthenon, on the other hand, was useful in constructing a metaphor of appreciation: a place of pilgrimage but also the quintessential and perfect Western building. For Taut, "obeisance" and "pilgrimage" were perhaps rhetorical, even though based upon actual observation. For Japanese, however, bowing was no mere figure of speech; in the most literal sense they are filled with awe.

Comparison with the Parthenon, for Taut, is the Western architectural reference par excellence, while the transmutation of architectural value to an awesome natural force restates the Saigyō-esque topos. Both topoi seek an origin in a spatially and temporally distant point, even at the risk of focusing beyond the forms of Ise itself. Here is a hint of the mindset haunting modernity and its conflation with genealogy: discovery of origin is all that is needed to perform an evaluation. Every account of Ise—architectural, but also anthropological, historiographical, or mythological, and so forth—has been penetrated by genealogical inquiry. It became an obsession. And as we shall soon see, the question of origin is precisely what haunts us about Ise.

In ancient times, Ise was the locus of early imperial ritual. In the middle ages, Ise perpetrated a grandiose doctrine in syncretistic fusion with Buddhism. In the Edo period, there occurred a nation-wide mass frenzy of pilgrimage to the Great Ise (*O-Ise-mairi*). In the Meiji period, Ise was the center for diffusion of state Shintōism (*kokka shindō*). And half a century later, in the mid-twentieth century, the ancient state-centered system disintegrated in defeat; but even afterward, the form of its rituals was kept intact, even purified. This amounts to an unheard-of duration of thirteen centuries, whose mystery could be dangerously tempting even to modernist thinkers. And almost all research substitutes an investigation of *origin* in place of any inquiry into the cause of its endurance. Such logic as may be found here dictates that should an origin come to light, the cause of the mysterious, seductive power of duration would thereby be explained. Hence, the trick that is configured by Ise and the mechanism of its renewal.

At Ise, the very veiling of the origin—*absent* in any strict sense—engenders seduction. The veiling of its architecture, rituals, historical foundation, and so forth is the very fountainhead of the problematic called "Ise." Ise is a mechanism whose origin itself must be somehow fabricated, for there is no *origin* as such. Insinuation that an origin exists has sustained the seduction. What is seen deep in the cedar forest is a swindle—or veiling—of sorts. The sanctuary is surrounded by its four layers of sacred hedges; the ritual of renewing the shrine takes place in secrecy—we sense its occurrence from without but cannot verify it. Moreover, even in *Nihongi*—one of the two catalogues of national mythology—its inception is blurred. The ambiguity of mythological narrative also obscures the fact of its own fabrication. The investigation into origin thus causes us to lose the point, abandoning the real object. Thus are we drawn into the swindle. I believe what we have to do is to pay attention to the rhetoric of veiling employed in this fabrication of origin—the only real "truth" at Ise.

The crux of the "Ise" problematic is the institution of *shikinen-zōkan*: dismantling the old shrine on one site and rebuilding the new one on an adjacent site at a predetermined interval. Then there is also the ritual of transposing the *shintai* (god's body). The last of these transpositions took place in 1993, the sixty-first on record. The rebuilding is said to occur each twenty years, but reality is neither so simple nor regular. In earlier times, it was nineteen years; and due to turmoil in the middle ages, there occurred a complete interruption of more than one hundred years. Records say that the first *shikinen-zōkan* took place in the fourth year of Empress Jitō (r. 686–697) as prescribed in the fourteenth year of Emperor Tenmu (r. 673–686). But these dates are not quite precise because the records were recast by the shrine scribes at a much later date.[19] But that Empress Jitō solidified the institution in the late seventh century seems certain, at a time when the social system was undergoing a major reformation. Since ancient times, whenever a new emperor ascended the throne, the capital had been moved. But when Emperor Tenmu willed the creation of a permanent capital, Fujiwara-kyō was laid out in present-day Nara prefecture. After this, the capital moved again several times: to Heijō (710), Nagaoka (784), and Heian (794), but these reinstallments no longer coincided with the enthronement of a new emperor.[20] Moreover, the seventh century was also a time when new statutes were enacted, marking the beginning of the ancient legislative state (*ritsuryō sei*). This defined the shift from a theocratic system to a constitutional system and required tremendous institutional restructuring. If we regard the rebuilding of Ise as part of this whole process of reformation, it is reasonable to consider the great shrine's inception as belonging to the late seventh century.

Such was Ise's *beginning*. Afterward, a series of narratives unfolded confirming the political intention behind Ise's foundation. But to return to the architecture of the late seventh century, it was a time when simple imitation of all that had been brought from the Korean peninsula was starting to be surpassed in terms of both technology and style. After all, a century and a half had passed since Buddhism's arrival, and a large number of temples had now been constructed in Japan. But at Ise, the design fixed upon for the great shrine was rather primitive. The very motivation for such a choice is veiled by Ise's *beginning*. A more detailed functional and tectonic elucidation of the Ise archetype, rather than any hypothesis of foreign origin rooted in archaeological research, could help to clarify this. For ultimately, what must be explained is the continuation for thirteen centuries of the regular rebuilding tradition. There must have existed some deep-seated aspect of the social system that made the repetition desirable, and that was directed, one assumes, to ensure the preservation of the *tennō* system. Each emperor is enthroned according to the ritual of *Ō-name-sai*,[21] in which the physical body of the new *tennō* is designated as host to the spirit of the *tennō* lineage. It is even said that there is a sexual implication—since the goddess is said to visit *tennō* to sleep with him. This treatment of the physical body of the emperor is analogous to the treatment of the buildings at Ise—after rebuilding/ relocation, the new shrine is host to the *hi* (spirit). Ise Jingū was always restricted to worship of the ancestral god of the *tennō* family, so that this analogy has solid grounds. And Taut's aesthetic judgment—Ise = *tennō*-esque = authentic—appears in retrospect as a reconfirmative speculation.

In the several chapters that follow, I wish to discuss the overall problematic of archetype and duration produced by the event of *beginning*, with regard to Ise's architecture.

Sutemi Horiguchi wrote an essay for a photographic monograph on Ise intended to describe the transformations that had been incorporated into the reproduction mechanism of the great shrine over time.

The major objects of Ise's periodic rebuilding are the Shōden [main sanctuary] and the two Hōden [treasure houses]. Looking at photographs taken in the Meiji period, we might well be surprised by changes in terms of their respective locations. In the photographs taken by the Ministry of Education in 1872 (Meiji 5), for instance, the arrangement of the inner shrine, Ise Naikū, after the rebuilding of 1869 (Meiji 2) was different from the arrangement we have today. In this version, the inner precinct comprised the main sanctuary and the paired (eastern and western) treasure houses set on either side of the main building. This inner precinct was surrounded by double fences: the outside wooden fence [*itagaki*] and the sacred hedge [*mizugaki*]. Such differs from today's version of four layers of fence protecting the inner precinct, where both treasure houses now stand behind the main building.

Beginning with the rebuilding of 1889 (Meiji 22), the arrangement became what it is today. Furthermore, according to another old picture, said to have been taken by a foreign visitor to Ise around 1873 (Meiji 6)—that is to say, it must depict the 1869 (Meiji 2) rebuilding—there was an eave over the front steps to the main sanctuary. Today's version does not have this, but instead features an *akunoya*—a cypress structure (originally temporary) with roof and columns for ceremonies—detached from the main building. There have been many changes for such a brief period of time.[1]

It is not permitted for us commoners to step inside the sacred fences—at either the inner or outer shrine (Ise Gekū). Today's version, as noted by Horiguchi, has four layers of fence. The outermost is of thick wooden board (*itagaki*), totally sealed without any crevices, so that the inner precinct is completely invisible.[2] The pictures of the 1869 version that Horiguchi refers to were taken over the fences, and captured the scene as far as the front steps (*kizahashi*) of the main sanctuary. This indicates that there must once have been a higher position from which to peep inside. Furthermore, the arrangement of the main building vis-à-vis the eastern and western treasury buildings as pictured was of a sort first established at the forty-first rebuilding in 1462, after the 123-year interruption due to wars. The famous pictorial representation of the Edo period, *Ise Sanpai Ezu* (Pilgrimage to Ise Jingū), shows this exact arrangement.

With regard to the disposition of buildings in the Ise Naikū referred to by Horiguchi above, and supposing one could somehow approach and view the whole, the buildings as set frontally must have afforded a more powerful volumetric arrangement than today's, where the treasure houses are recessed behind the main sanctuary. Nevertheless, it is said, the 1889 rebuilding revived an older arrangement. The architectural historian Toshio Fukuyama has pointed out that, along with rearrangement of both inner and outer shrines, the plots of the two sites were drastically modified in size.[3] We know, in any case, that by the time of the Edo depiction, the outer shrine is the same as today's in terms of configuration of both buildings and site.

On the other hand, in the post-Edo version constructed between 1869 and 1889 (the one in which the buildings in the inner shrine are aligned) the site of the inner precinct was wider and not as deep as either the current or the Edo versions. Notably, the outline inside the sacred fences was almost square, and this, too, must have influenced the arrangement of buildings. The frontal configuration is evidently a product of the Japanese manner of spatial composition formulated during the medieval period—based upon a simple layering of planes parallel to the gaze of the spectator. By

9.1 Aerial view of part of Ise Jingū (Ise Grand Shrine) and its precinct (originally fourth/fifth centuries C.E.), Mie prefecture.

contrast, the ancient arrangement was more idealized and schematic, architecture being grasped as a dense mass rather than layers of superimposed planes. In any case, no design permits us to conceive of the space at Ise in anything like a picturesque, or remotely perspectival, manner.

Fukuyama reconstructed the arrangements of the inner and outer shrines of early medieval times by way of conjecture from the first known Meiji version. Accordingly, the sites of both shrines in the middle ages would seem to have been much narrower: about half of today's width. This forces us to accept that the fence immediately surrounding the main sanctuary and treasure houses must once have been very close to the buildings. That is to say, the function of the fence must have been less to prohibit entry or observation than symbolically to delimit the sacred domain by way of simple enclosure. One imagines there to have been practically no margin between buildings and fence (just as Sumiyoshi Jinja in Osaka appears today). Furthermore, the treasure houses in the outer shrine, until the early medieval period, seem to have faced each other, instead of both facing in the same plane as the main sanctuary.

At Ise the periodic alternation of sites takes place between identical and adjacent plots, despite minor variations in slope or topography. Transposition involves the complete construction of new buildings accompanied by various rituals on the alternate site. The main object is conservation and transmission of data preserved in each previous twenty-year period. Not only the forms and procedures of ritual, but detailed information on all 65 buildings (including related minor shrines) to be rebuilt, as well as the 1,567 ritual utensils to be refabricated, must be acknowledged and handed down. A vast network of carpenters, craftsmen, construction workers, and precinct caretakers (*ujiko*), who perpetuate the daily routine of worship at the shrine, has always to be maintained and sustained.

The 123-year interruption in late medieval times occasioned a moment of severe crisis during which the organization failed. Among the shōguns of the Ashikaga reign (1392–1573), there were even a few who declared themselves emperor (*tennō*). Oda Nobunaga, in the late sixteenth century, was actually masterminding his own establishment toward a position even higher than that of the emperor. Notwithstanding such challenges, however, the *tennō* system finally achieved lasting durability by renouncing all secular power. By strategically undercutting imperial authority, Nobunaga thus sought to unify Japan. Nobunaga's plot paradoxically reinforced the *tennō* system and allowed it to revive the hallowed rebuilding pattern at Ise. The information underlying the entire Ise system (having almost become extinct) was revived and reanimated. Fukuyama writes of the situation at that time:

During the 85 years that followed 1500 (Meiō 9), the year in which the main precinct of the rebuilding of 1462 (Kansei 3) collapsed, no authentic embodiment of the main precinct existed. *The Record of Rebuilding in Tenshō 13* (1586) describes the joint effort: shrine officials collected information concerning detailed measurements of each structure and gave it to the carpenters; when this data contradicted the master carpenter's records, officials and master carpenters settled on a compromise. They were forced to determine scale, structure, and form of the new main sanctuary by combining bits and pieces from old records and plans.[4]

We may be sure that these architectural plans were not drawn up using today's methods. It was only after the seventeenth century that any systematic effort to produce measured drawings is recorded. And this was far simpler and more primitive than the system we know at present. By the time of the Tenshō era (1573–1592) rebuilding, the previous structures had all been dismantled or destroyed; without a physical example of the architecture to be replicated, the master carpenters and shrine officials gathered and sought to recover the old prototype by combining what information they did have, as recorded in the *Record of Rebuilding* and recounted by Fukuyama. What I find fascinating is that they sometimes chose to split the difference and compromise on a middle way, meaning they had almost to resort to guesswork in reaching their decisions. In this system of shrine construction executed in wood, written data were confined to the simplest instructions and the rest transmitted by word of mouth. In this tradition, there were certain margins of free judgment, as opposed to rigid rules. This meant that techniques of individual carpenters, as well as the taste of the time, were bound to intervene.

As an example, Fukuyama mentions the *tsumakazari*—decorative structural elements of gables—in the main precinct of the inner shrine. He says that detailing before the long interruption— as inferred from documents of the Muromachi period—would have been of a totally different *kiwari*—proportional measurement system—from today's.[5] The beam on top of a *tsuma kabe*—the transverse wall—and the girder that overlaps it were inverted. Furthermore, the proportions of this older version were much more subtle than today's *tsumakazari*. It may be that the change was effected when rebuilding was revived in the Tenshō era. Fukuyama explains: "In olden times, the girders used to be laid on top of the beams, but in modern times, they were placed below; meanwhile both elements became stockier; in consequence, all timber pieces for *tsumakazari* became shorter and thicker. The ancient lightness and élan were lost and the dull form favored today was conventionalized."[6]

In today's version, as Fukuyama tells us, everything is uniformly large-boned (even merely symbolic or decorative items, such as *gogyō*—the wooden seal celebrating completion of the building). In conformity with other elements of the main precinct, the *tsumakazari* shed their ancient lightness. And it is believed that the more ancient forms were similar to the *tsumakazari* of Hōryū-ji's Kondō (Golden Pavilion, or image hall). If that is so, then similarity to the detail of Buddhist temples was deliberately erased at this juncture (some 400 years ago); it would also seem that the intention to maintain a purely formal architectural conventionalism—not merely revival of an older style—at Ise was reinstated at this point.

There is no doubt that the overall site configuration remained after the buildings had been demolished. But, instead of reusing the existing scheme, spatial arrangement and scale were now intentionally formalized to accord with the new medieval trend toward frontality. In that case, it would be inaccurate to claim that the twenty-year rebuilding interval maintained a strict identity of form. Instead we must admit that in the gesture of replication, a certain will to readjust the design toward a perceived authentic form by eliminating indeterminate elements must constantly have been at work. So it is that this "pure" form is not necessarily an original form. Rather, all in claiming to rehabilitate older forms, Ise has been significantly *re*designed at crucial junctures.

What mechanism is at work? More than anything else, Ise may recall the mechanism by which life forms sustain their identities: selection from a pool of genes in response to certain external conditions. In life forms there is a written code—the genome, in which, however, only certain elements function in response to a particular context, thus sustaining a pattern of formal identity. In the same way at Ise, can we assume there is a code that in its unconscious drive authorizes convergence toward a pure form? I believe that Japan-ness is precisely such a code, namely that cultural apparatus prescribed by the *tennō* system, which enforces a convergence at the Ise shrine.

The alteration at the Ise site in 1889—after the shrine had been defined as the center of state Shintōism—undid the frontal configuration documented in the Edo period and restored the older formal precedent. But this time, the site was also greatly enlarged well beyond its size in the pre-Muromachi era, while the main precinct was rendered more luxurious with metal fittings added as a new element of décor. The site itself was blocked off by new fences built much closer to the buildings, and veiling these from view. All this was not irrelevant to excessive mid-Meiji design trends. Suddenly, it was felt that bare simple wood was insufficient to express the requisite nobility of the undertaking. In the 1954 rebuilding—after World War II—most of these decorative metal fittings were removed. This was Ise reinterpreted under the aesthetic of modernist architecture. Though continuously transformed throughout the ages, Ise perpetuated an identity via feedback in favor of a return to pure authentic form. (As we shall later see, this bears a relation to changes in the Japanese language as reflected in the text of the national myth, *Kojiki*, imposed by Motoori Norinaga.)

How far back in time are we justified in going in order to posit the beginnings of the architectural form of Ise? According to Toshio Fukuyama, probably to the mid-eighth century. His conviction is based on the accidental discovery of a document from the Shōsō-in archives,[7] a repository for textual and other precious items from all over Asia dating from the seventh to eighth centuries. On the back of the document in question was a list of decorative metal fittings ordered for Ise, whose date corresponds roughly to the year 762, or perhaps even earlier. Furthermore, an early ninth-century document, "The Ritual Notes of *Kōtai Jingū* [another name for the inner shrine at Ise]," contains a description of the buildings themselves.

As for its basic form, the main precinct in those very early days consisted of an elevated (*takayuka*) log house (*azekura-zukuri*) structure with two columns supporting a ridge pole (*mune-mochi-bashira*). That these aspects were remnants of an older form is now known from the engraving on a bronze mirror-back of the Kofun period (late third to seventh centuries C.E.). The ninth-century document indicates that by this time a balustrade was also already installed on all four sides of the main building. The handrail of the balustrade, as well as the flammule finial (*giboshi*), derive obviously from China; the selfsame motifs are still in use on Japanese Noh stages today. They were perhaps also in use in court architecture of the period: namely, at *daigoku-den* where the emperor attended to government affairs. The color combinations of the ornamental finials, though arranged differently in the inner and outer shrines, unquestionably relate to Chinese Taoism. Appended to the archaic elevated, log-cabin-style building, therefore, was a Taoist element of alien lineage.

What is more, the inspiration of the metal fittings listed in the Shōsō-in document was not necessarily Japanese either. It is more likely that these derive from details of Buddhist and court architecture both imported from China. It is not impossible that such elements accumulated gradually in the half century after the shrine's initial installation in 690. What interests us here above all is the fact that at Ise both inner and outer shrines exhibit the *hira-iri*, or entrance to one side of the sloping roof, whereas Izumo Taisha, Sumiyoshi Jinja, and Kasuga Taisha—those ancient shrines supposed to maintain an older form—all exhibit the *tsuma-iri* structure, where entry is beneath the gable. *Hira-iri* style has not been found among any of the older elevated structures excavated in ruins from the Kofun age. Therefore, it has long been surmised that these buildings at Ise must represent modification of a style imported from the continent in a more recent past.

It is likely that during the half century after establishment of the periodic alteration of sites, the eastern and western treasure houses of the inner shrine came to be placed behind the main structure (Shōden) with its balustrade, while in the outer shrine they remained in front. If so, the latter arrangement with its emphasis on symmetry is certain to have been based on Chinese cosmology. Not only in the configuration of the precincts, but also in terms of ritual instruments and ceremonial forms, there are numerous traces of Taoism (yin-yang patterns) and the Five Natural Elements (fire, wood, earth, metal, and water).[8]

The crossed beams (called *kagami-kata-gi*—mirrored timbers) along the gable (*tsumakazari*) in the main structure are, like the central column (called *shin-no-mihashira*—heart pillar) (fig. 9.2), considered sacred. In the installation ritual, the master carpenter nails the metal seal to the accompaniment of a spell, attended by

9.2 Detail of "heart pillar," or central column (*shin-no-mihashira*), Ise Shrine.
Photograph by Yasuhiro Ishimoto.

the chief shrine official.[9] I cannot say where this comes from—
Taoism or, perhaps, esoteric Buddhism—because the Imperial
Household Agency has characteristically sought to obscure all of
these elements. There may, indeed, be a confusion of sources concealed behind this doctrinal cover-up.

Something essential is veiled, or so we feel. When you visit
Ise, you experience the true object as blocked and invisible. It
is forbidden to scrutinize even the most minor elements of the
metal fittings, the only emblematic images of the entire structure.
At the headwater of Ise's seduction, we encounter the self-veiling
mechanism.

Whence did the motivation that has driven the Ise system
for thirteen centuries derive? It is scarcely a clear or controlled discipline of any kind. Isn't it rather a sort of elasticity that, throughout the ages, has introduced and synthesized new elements while
sometimes discarding an older one? The earliest known example is
the introduction of the Taoist oriflamme finial already mentioned

during the formative years of the late seventh and eighth centuries. The historian Shunpei Kamiyama argues that one detects the presence of many elements deriving from Tang dynasty China in the various documents concerning Ise's rituals.[10] Finally, although Ise's Shintōism shuns blood as impure, from time to time elements such as chickens (remnants of sacrifice) or dolls (Taoist fetishes) are included in its rituals.

Thus Ise's buildings as well as its rituals were in part influenced by Taoist elements. This suggests an innate idea of gods (*kami*) that permitted Taoist elements to be arranged around it. But this notion of *kami* is not anything solid or constant, but was originally an invisible presence invited from somewhere. The objective locus of festival and ritual is just a device for their advent. Thus the *kami* never manifests itself and can easily depart. The place to invite such *kami* may be essentially void—a "central nothing." Being void, it can also absorb. Being amorphous, its notional manifestation can last forever. Such a central void calls not only for *kami*, but also for a different value system.

In 1186 (the second year of Emperor Bunchi), the priest Chōgen (our protagonist in part III) was canvassing for funds to rebuild Tōdai-ji at Nara. While dozing one day near the sacred hedge of Ise's outer shrine, he received a vision:

> On February 23, the third day of his nocturnal pilgrimage, the great god of Ise manifested itself all of a sudden. *The Record of the Construction of Tōdai-ji* describes that while Chōgen was half asleep, a secular figure in official costume stood in front of the Treasure House, and an infant appeared in Chōgen's bosom and greeted him. Chōgen said to the great god: "These days I am getting tired and feeling powerless, and the task may not be accomplished." The great god replied: "If you really want to accomplish the task, feed me well."[11]

This vision at once prompted Chōgen's brethren at Tōdai-ji to undertake a pilgrimage to Ise, stimulating in large part the transformation of the doctrine of Ise Shrine into a syncretic fusion of Shintōism and Buddhism in the ensuing medieval period. The architectural historian Teiji Itō surmises that we may view the oracle as a strategic maneuver on Chōgen's part to jumpstart his stalled fundraising effort. However, what interests us more here is the similarity of the above narrative to the history of the ritual invitation at Ise of the outer shrine's great god Toyuke.

According to *Notes of Toyuke Shrine's Rituals* (807), Princess Yamato (Empress Yūryaku) had once received a similar oracle to Chōgen's.

> In the era of Emperor Sujin, Amaterasu, the Sun Goddess, had been enshrined upstream in Isuzu river at Ise. She manifested herself in one of Empress Yūryaku's dreams and said: "I am quietly sitting in Takamagahara—the land in heaven—but being alone is inconvenient. Even the food is insufficient. So please bring to me the food god, Toyuke, who is in Manaki in Tanba country." Empress Yūryaku was deeply impressed, and constructed a big sanctuary and invited the god to it. In the shrine, she made a dining hall [*mikeden*] for Amaterasu to be nourished morning and evening.

Chōgen's oracle was similar to this earlier myth in the aspect of both gods being hungry and requesting food. In Chōgen's day, the history of Toyuke Shrine was still well known, and Chōgen may simply have adopted it. The logic of each oracle is also consistent: the empress as *itsukino-miya* (shaman) and the priest are in different situations yet both mediate the voice of an invisible god. In both oracles, the deities show humanlike characteristics of being hungry and wanting food, but it was likewise expected that gods should display uncontrollable, supernatural power. In Japanese history, it was always believed that national crises could be solved by the intervention of a divine wind (*kamikaze*) through prayer to Ise's god, at least until the surrender that ended World War II.

But what was implied by Chōgen's pilgrimage to Ise? As earlier noted, it involved Ise Shrine in the broad trend of the syncretic fusion of Shintōism and Buddhism characteristic of the medieval period. In the first place, Buddhism possessed an intricate theological structure that could be called metaphysical. Borrowing this structure, the Japanese evolved a cosmology for their own gods in Shintōism. As a result, at last a doctrine appeared proclaiming Shintōist and Buddhist deities identical—*shinbutsu-dotai-setsu*. For instance, as applied to Ise, the relationship between inner and outer shrines was paired with that between the Buddhist deities Vajradhatu (*kongō-kai*) and Garbhakosadhatu (*taizō-kai*). Its central deity,

Amaterasu, occupied the center of the mandala, as Mahavairocana. This so-called *honchi-zuiseki-setsu* insisted literally that the Japanese gods were originally Buddhist deities: once in Japan, they merely came to be called by different names. Remarkable at Ise was the establishment of Watarai-shintō, a doctrine *inverting* this narrative. It recounted that Japanese gods had gone to Tenjiku (India) where they became Buddhist deities, thus appropriating the Buddhist doctrine and turning it on its head. Like the drive to restore an original form to architectural production, a strong centripetal force was also at work in the myth-producing domain. The same pattern may be observed once again in the early Meiji period in the form of a move to inspire the modern nation-state to destroy all Buddhist temples—*haibutsu-kishaku*—and reorganize every religious function as part of state Shintōism centered on Ise Jingū. In that context Taoism was employed for the establishment of ritual, Buddhism for its doctrinal aspects, and the ideal of the modern state itself for the propagation of the newly inclusive state religious ideology.

Nonetheless, Ise has never lost its own identity, for the mechanism sustaining it was constantly at work, at the core of which stands the *shikinen-zōkan*, or periodic rebuilding. The architectural historian Eizō Inagaki has enlarged on the significance of this:

> So long as the [rebuilding] ceremony continues to take place, the beginning is never lost but repeated each time. This is exactly what the individual who founded this institution required. The periodic relocation [*shikinen-sengū*] in the autumn of 1973 was the sixtieth, taking that of the era of Empress Jitō to be the first. The sixtieth [act of refounding] entailed exact repetition of the religious ritual. Not only did the ritual itself not disappear after the ancient state system collapsed, but with the advent of modern times it has been refurbished and handed down to the present. Participation in the periodic relocation repeated in every age is an escape from time proper to a particular epoch. As Mircea Eliade points out, this act is a refusal of history as well as a rejection of creative freedom. In fact, the constructional efforts of each age that have upheld the periodic relocation leave little or no creative trace in the actual form of the shrine. The history of its construction does not crystallize as form, but disappears into the void in an effort of sheer continuity. We are entitled to believe that, in the

history of this repetition, we envision the universal structure of a culture beyond history.[12]

Indeed, all the efforts accumulated in Ise's architectural configuration are steered toward repetition in an effort to sustain identity. By contrast, an architecture of stone, such as the Great Pyramids, relies on the enduring physical power of a mineral substance; monumental form is impressed into it, rebelling against the march of time, and seeking eternity through the endurance of material. In the details of Egyptian and Greek temples, we observe traces of that process by which it is believed wooden buildings were transubstantiated as stone over the ages. In the Semperian architectural doctrine of the nineteenth century on which Chūta Itō relied, the progress of architectural form and technique was stressed. We may also discover a Darwinist influence at work here, and Bruno Taut's reference to the Parthenon stood clearly within such a paradigm. In the tradition persisting since classicism, positing the Parthenon as a convenient standard for measuring architectural progress had become commonplace. For instance, the lithic column with its entasis is said to preserve the trace of its having been made from a bundle of plants. This form then crystallized as a mass of stone, as an immutable emblem of progress as well as a means of achieving timelessness.

At Ise, transubstantiation is omitted. Instead, the rebuilding-and-relocation scheme of twenty-year cycles embraces a biological model of regeneration. In order to preserve life, forms are generated and regenerate isomorphically. In this manner, Ise ensures a replica of itself, daring to retain those impermanent elements such as *hottate-bashira* (massive bearing columns without stone bases) and a thatch of miscanthus. In the process, architectural and ritual impetus strive to preserve identity through maintenance of an archetypal form. In their shared will to embody permanence, Ise and the Parthenon are alike, but the paths to attainment are opposed. Stone structures weather over time. Wooden structures are less characteristically able to withstand alterity (changes in social systems and the style and taste of each age) yet better able to respond flexibly to the spirit of the age by way of a naturally restorative and self-regulating impulse. The sole requirement is that invisible mechanism for preserving and sustaining identity which we have explored.

To me it seems that Ise's mechanism in that respect is completely different from the architectonic will toward an everlasting presence that monumental masonry architecture attains in its very essence. Yet the Ise stratagem hardly pertains to a unique Japanese stance rooted in a passive awe of nature. For here, too, is a powerful constructive will that works toward maintenance and even restoration. As Eizō Inagaki argues, the repetition of relocation and rebuilding repels the blind progress of history in order to preserve an identity over time. This consistent will to create an eternity, a different eternity to be sure, is something like what the philosopher Heidegger calls "temporality of falling," or the temporal mode of a vertical fall into the present.[13] Each repetition is the repetition of a beginning compelled to similitude. We are forever being lured toward whatever may be lurking in a beginning endlessly repeated.

Originally Japanese shrines were not buildings. For instance, it is claimed that Miwa Jinja in Yamato in Nara prefecture, said to be one of the oldest shrines in Japan, had no buildings at all. The mountain—called Miwa—was itself the object of worship; at its foot was established a ritual site where a simple threshold (*iwasaka*) had been set up, and, at its center, a sacred enclosure (*himorogi*) erected. Furthermore, on Mount Miwa many *iwakura*—the rocks upon which gods are thought to repose—have been identified. It is uncertain whether these rocks were perfectly natural or artificially crafted, but all look as if they were quite natural, with hollows where the gods might sit. Such is the prototype of the shrine in Japan.

Visiting Ise Shrine today, we encounter next to each active sanctuary a large geometric space that intrudes upon the view, encompassed by the dense green of the surrounding forest. This is *kodenchi*—the old, unoccupied site of each dismantled twin structure. The site has been leveled, a broad rectangle covered by pebbles. In the center is a small fenced-in space with a roof, indicating the presence of a sacred column, *shin-no-mihashira* (heart pillar)—originally set under the floor of the main structure, yet detached from it (fig. 10.2). This scene without architecture may teach us even more about the elemental form of Ise than would the actual site in use. Let us imagine how the Ise sanctuary began. First one takes stock of the vast forest and demarcates a sacred domain; if we set simple hedges or fences around it, the place would become *iwasaka*; with the addition of a sacred central column it would be more properly *himorogi*. To achieve the prototypical status or archi-image of "shrine," these minimal acts—siting and demarcation—suffice. It might even be that the architecture that takes

内宮

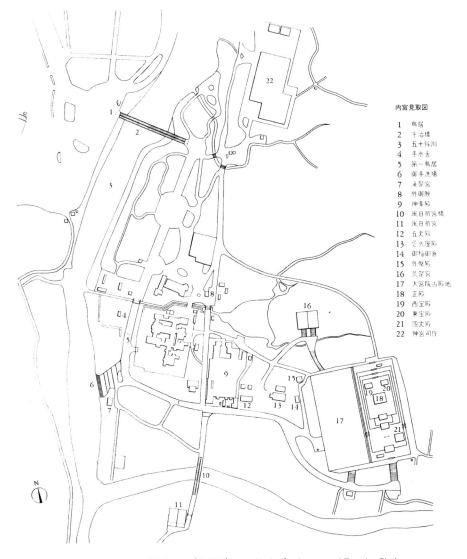

内宮見取図

1 鳥居
2 宇治橋
3 五十鈴川
4 手水舎
5 第一鳥居
6 御手洗場
7 瀧祭宮
8 外御厩
9 神楽殿
10 風日祈宮橋
11 風日祈宮
12 五丈殿
13 忌火屋殿
14 御稲御倉
15 外幣殿
16 荒祭宮
17 大宮院古殿地
18 正殿
19 西宝殿
20 東宝殿
21 四丈殿
22 神宮司庁

10.1 Ise Shrine: Imperial Shrine (Naikū/Inner Shrine), above, and Toyuke Shrine (Gekū/Outer Shrine), opposite, site plans.

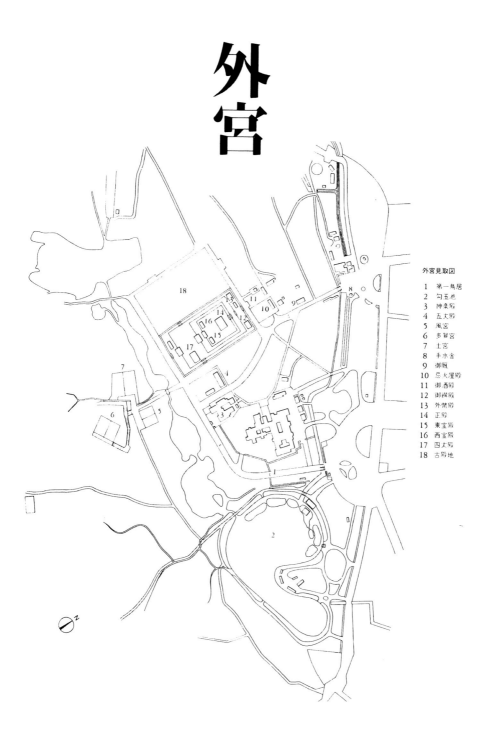

外宮

外宮見取図

1　第一鳥居
2　勾玉池
3　神楽殿
4　五丈殿
5　風宮
6　多賀宮
7　土宮
8　手水舎
9　御厩
10　忌火屋殿
11　御酒殿
12　御饌殿
13　外幣殿
14　正殿
15　東宝殿
16　西宝殿
17　四丈殿
18　古殿地

10.2 Ise Shrine: *kodenchi*, the old, unused site of the dismantled twin. Photograph by Yasuhiro Ishimoto.

form above ground is just an appendage. But at the same time, some sort of structure is requisite to mark and embellish the sacred invited being—the god's body as void—precisely by veiling and distancing it from the spectator's gaze.

By the time of the first recorded installation of the Ise apparatus in 690, it is certain that a shrine structure already existed—this can be inferred from the element *zōkan* (meaning rebuilding) of *shikinen-zōkan*. There are different conjectures about the initial state: Kawazoe believes that there was only the sacred central column at first, while Horiguchi maintains that simpler, more primitive versions of today's treasure houses had already been built, such as *takayuka* (elevated)- or even *azekura* (log)-style buildings. But neither conjecture can be proven. Because the origin itself is hidden, it is impossible to speak of any pre-seventh-century state. More to the point, it might be said, the buildings of Ise were constructed precisely in order to conceal the origin, or the state before the *beginning* in the seventh century. Thus, the veiling of the origin was itself intended. Above all, the gods enshrined therein needed to be veiled. Thus the whole architectural scheme at Ise was designed as an obscuring mechanism.

Each main precinct of the present-day version has four layers of hedge. In contrast to the example of Ise, however, the demarcation of any sanctuary has by and large been left minimal in the Japanese tradition. This lightness of touch is exemplified by the Shintō notion of *iwasaka* as well as the Buddhist *kekkai*, literally meaning demarcation. In *kekkai*, either four poles installed at the corners of a square of ground or a mere rope stretched between two points suffices to indicate a sacred site or enclosure. Or to take an extreme example, the invisible *kehai*—or atmospheric indication of sacredness that the lay of the land itself might express—was deemed sufficient, such as when the locus of a spirit was discovered in a mountain fastness. In accordance with these traditional methods of demarcation, concealment was quite uncalled for. At Ise, as well, there are many such lightly marked yet conspicuous demarcations: for example, on the bridge over the Isuzu River, around the *torii* (gateway), and along the zigzagging approaches to the main precinct. The obvious exception is the main precinct in its deep seclusion.

There are notable efforts to conceal in this architecture. If the use of hedges was intended solely to block the visitor's gaze, one layer of some solid material would have been sufficient. But the layer was doubled at some juncture, and then quadrupled. I believe such layering is nothing short of a symbolic gesture and, in fact, also has a hierarchical aspect. The gates of the four-layered hedges are capable of being opened, from one to all four, according to the rank and permission accorded the visitor. This is clearly a hierarchy of concealment. And finally, even hidden by the building itself, is the sacred heart pillar—*shin-no-mihashira*—placed under the floor of the main precinct, and detached from it. The ritual concerning this central pillar is also performed beneath the floor—a fact reminding us that the derivation of the column is not one with the structure above it. We can no longer tell whence it derived (or whether phylogeny or ontogeny was implicated). For instance, Izumo Taisha in Shimane prefecture was built prior to 550 (well before Ise), and its style, so-called *taisha-zukuri*, is considered one of the earliest shrine prototypes. It also has a central pillar like Ise's, except that at Izumo it penetrates the roof. In other words, it is possible to assume that in the beginning there was a huge column, then the skeletal structure was constructed around it, and finally the shrine superstructure was completed. The altar is not located above the central column, but rather behind a wall next to it, as seen from the entrance; so the central column is part and parcel of the architecture. In Ise, as has been repeatedly stressed, the pillar is structurally detached from the fabric of the building. Thus it is not difficult to imagine that Ise's main structure was built above a sacred central column that had once stood independently, in order symbolically to cover it.

The interior of this main structure is completely veiled (fig. 10.3). The climax of the ritual of rebuilding and relocation takes place within this cell. It is not only performed in darkness, but it is performed in secret—a ceremony transmitted directly from one *tennō* to another. But something is known about the interior space: a belief at least that the four surrounding walls and the ceiling are covered with silk, and that within is a stool—*minashiro*[1]—for the god to sit on; a quantity of daily utensils for the god (naturally, treated as holy treasures) are arranged around it. If this is the case, it would mean that, here inside, even for an invisible god, practical daily utensils, clothing, and food are all provided. Yet the ritual of offering these items would be sheer pantomime, a mimicry (*modoki*). The form itself is traceable to the core and origin of

10.3 Ise Shrine, frontal view of one end of the Shōden (main sanctuary), inner precinct, detailing roof construction and balustrade. Photograph by Yasuhiro Ishimoto.

Japanese traditional performing arts, where the ritual of offering to an invisible god was performed before an audience. For instance, in both Kabuki and Noh, actors appear to be performing for the audience, but it is also obvious at times that they are rendering this mime to the god's host (*yorishiro*) as represented, for example, by the familiar "mirror board" (*kagami-ita*)—a wooden wall on which a Japanese pine tree is depicted life-size—as background to the Noh stage, or to the festival scaffold (*yagura*) behind the audience seating in the Kabuki theater; and that the audience attends the ritual in the role of observer. Acting in Japan is always, thus, a consecration ritual of sorts.

Inviting the invisible god, talking to the god as if it were present, and offering daily utensils and food—such sublime mimicry persists. And at Ise, the invisible god is transposed from the *yorishiro* in the old main building to that of the new one. While what is hidden is nonetheless illuminated by this train of mimicries and seems as though it were about to be revealed, it never is nor will it be.

The architectural prototype of the main building is that of an ancient-style storage house: an elevated-floor (*taka-yuka*), log-cabin-style (*azekura*) building. If one thinks about it, the notion of storage already contains a sense of hiding and would be the perfect model for Ise's architecture. The word *kura* (storage) functions here in diverse aspects. *Iwa-kura* (rock-storage) affords a host for gods, and *taka-kura* (high-storage) is a prototype for a structure that enshrines the host. The primary meaning of *kura* is storage, but a secondary one is darkness, and a third is position or seat. There is an implication here that the important gods used to be hidden behind rocks (*iwa*) or in a storage (*kura*) receptacle without windows. Yet the gods always reveal themselves at the invitation of mimicry.

In the mythology of the origins of Japan—whether *Kojiki* or *Nihongi*—narratives of beginning inscribe the repetition of *modoki*, the mimetic ritual practice of inviting the presence of the gods. This thematic is inspired by the rhythms of day and night, of sun and moon, the yearly return of the four seasons, and the process of harvest. Marking each year's completion is the major annual celebration of *Kan-name-sai*—Ise's festival of offering the new harvest to the Sun Goddess;[2] and the same logic also extends to the succession of *tennō*, marked once in each reign by the festival of *Ō-name-sai* (cf. ch. 8, n. 21). One assumes that the twenty-year term of Ise's *shikinen-zōkan* also results from a similar rhythm of repetition applied to the shrine buildings themselves. But, according to recent excavation, it is now known that the *shikinen-zōkan* did not start at Ise, but already existed elsewhere in the fourth to fifth centuries. According to the architectural historian Kazuhiro Tatsumi, in this earlier period the residences of baronial families (*gōzoku*) had two categories of buildings: sacred space (*hare-no-kūkan*) where festivals and policy-making took place, and profane space (*ke-no-kūkan*) where the activities of daily life were carried on. It is likely that in the eastern region of Japan, a one-storied building was used for sacred space, while in the west, for example in Yamato and Izumo, a raised structure was common.[3]

An example of the western type is provided by the Nagase Takahama ruins located at the foot of Mount Daisen in present-day Tottori prefecture facing the Sea of Japan, where traces of three different types of buildings for festivals and rituals were discovered. What is more, it seems that these were rebuilt at twenty-year intervals. The oldest is in raised style (*takayuka shiki*), and the roof ridge runs north to south supported by thick columns (*mune-mochi-bashira*). Under the floor is a rectangular hole. Tatsumi suggests this may represent the most sacred place in the household, where ritual utensils were stored or in which an equivalent of the heart pillar (*shin-no-mihashira*) was installed.[4]

A building that seems to have been built after this one is also in raised style and had outside steps. But, interestingly, the whole space under the floor seems to have been dug out and hedged by lath, suggesting the existence of a sacred space veiled to the external gaze. The most recent building in date was also raised with four large holes for columns, and it was also surrounded by fences. Estimating from the span and thickness of the remains of the columns, its total elevation may have been more than fifteen meters, and even the floor height could well have been more than six meters above grade.

This proves that already two centuries before Ise's initial rebuilding and relocation, structures sharing the basic characteristics of those at Ise had existed as festival sites amidst sacred space. It is tempting to ascribe the fact that these also seem to have been constructed at twenty-year intervals as the basis for Ise's rebuilding schedule. But this is far from clear. It is claimed that the sovereigns who oversaw the festival events in the sacred space may have coincidentally changed over twenty-year intervals, and that new structures were built each time this occurred.

In terms of both location and cultural proximity, the Nagase Takahama ruins are relatively close to Izumo. The last of the three buildings exhibits a tendency toward mammoth proportions, echoing Izumo's own legend of giant gods.[5] But what draws our attention in this context, more than any other feature of the buildings, are those devices for obscuring the gaze and barring access: for example, the oddly located gateway in the surrounding enclosure, and the interior altar placed around the corner from the central pillar. This last derives from the main feature of *taisha-zukuri*. Namely, because of the gable-side entry (*tsuma-iri*) and the central column supporting the ridge (*mune-mochi-bashira*), entrance and stairs are both decentered, that is placed on the right side (fig. 10.4). Furthermore, the altar is set behind the wall next to the central column. These make for zigzagging axes that prevent sacred objects from being gazed upon easily and directly.

At Ise, in contrast to the *taisha-zukuri*, the concealment devices are minimal or very specific. This speaks to yet another aspect of Ise. For instance, there are no intentional zigzag paths except for the main approach itself. Once we confront the main building, we note a central axis that penetrates the whole composition from north to south. What is more, the entrance itself is likewise on center, *hira-iri*, beneath the eave ledge of the sloping roof, unlike the gable-side entry in *taisha-zukuri*. At Ise, both the main building as well as the east and west treasure houses have three bays, and in the central one of each is an entrance. The avoidance of a central column is normal to China as well as the West, while the *taisha-zukuri* is an exception.[6] In any event, the formal zigzagging devices in *taisha-zukuri* are consistent in obscuring the gaze and approach to the altar. At Ise, these somewhat ad hoc devices known from Izumo were reorganized into a firm architectural rhetoric of concealment.

Concealment was itself the origin. However, unlike *taisha-zukuri*, Ise embraces the form of the central axis—the sacred object at the center was inevitably open to view, so that, paradoxically, a

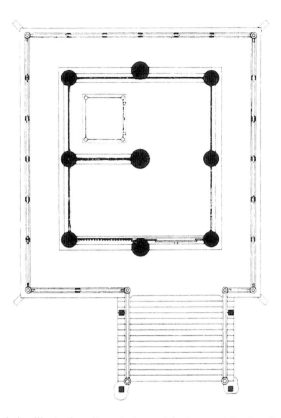

10.4 Typical plan illustrating alternate *tsuma-iri* entrance style of ancient Japanese shrine architecture (cf. fig. 8.2) on displaced axis.

number of layers capable of obscuring it had to be introduced. Ise thus exhibits conflicting tendencies toward transparency and opacity. All those elements making for transparency—the enclosure gate, the central portal, the sacred central pillar under the floor, and the stool for the god (*minashiro*)—are cut off from our gaze by a well-defined series of interventions. The notion of transparency was newly derived in Japan from the urban planning of ancient China centered on the position of the emperor. Backed by the polar star, the son of Heaven was enthroned on a central axis, facing south. From this position, he was believed to be able to see the whole world that was his to rule. This logic was imagined as a perfect, transparent, hierarchical space without obstacle. Japanese ancient capitals adopted both the ideology and the formal layout it implies; and so did Ise. This tends to support other evidence that Ise was designed after the introduction of temple and palace prototypes from the continent. Owing to this untoward degree of spatial transparency, the architecture at Ise had deliberately to introduce a means of closing itself off: the hedges that surround it, the gates that close, and the doors kept firmly shut. Things may be "open" only in darkness and obscurity.

A Fabricated Origin: Ise and the Jinshin Disturbance

In *Nihongi*, the origin of Ise's annual *Kan-name-sai* observance is narrated in several places.

In the record of Emperor Sujin:

> In the 6th year, the people took to wandering, and there was re-bellion, the violence of which was such that by worth alone (i.e., by the virtues of the Sovereign commanding the respect and obe-dience of the people) it could not be assuaged.
>
> Therefore, rising early in the morning and being full of awe until the evening, the Emperor prayed to the Gods of Heaven and Earth.
>
> Before this the two Gods Ama-terasu-ō-mikami [the Sun God-dess] and Yamato-no-ō-kuni-tama [the domestic god of Yamato] were worshiped together within the Imperial Palace [in accor-dance with the Chinese notion that national calamites are owing to the faults of the Emperor]. He dreaded, however, the power of these Gods, and did not feel secure in their dwelling together. Therefore he entrusted Ama-terasu-ō-mikami to the shaman princess Toyosuki-iri-hime No Mikoto to be worshipped at the village of Kasanui in Yamato, where he constructed a strong *himorogi* with stones. Moreover, he entrusted Yamato-no-ō-kuni-tama to the shaman princess Nunaki-iri-hime No Mikoto to be worshiped. But the shaman princess became bald and lean, and therefore unable to perform the rites of worship.[1]

In the record of Emperor Sunin:

> Third month, 10th day. Ama-terasu-no-ō-mikami was taken from Toyosuki-iri-hime No Mikoto and entrusted to the shaman

princess, Yamato-hime No Mikoto. Now Yamato-hime No Mikoto sought for a place where she might enshrine the Great Goddess. So she proceeded to Sasahata in Uda. Then turning back from thence, she entered the land of Ōmi, and went round eastwards to Mino, whence she arrived in the province of Ise.

Now Ama-terasu-no-ō-mikami instructed her, saying: "The province of Ise, of the divine wind, is the land whither repair the waves from the eternal world, the successive waves. It is a secluded and pleasant land. In this land I wish to dwell." In compliance, therefore, with the instruction of the Great Goddess, a shrine was erected to her in the province of Ise. Accordingly a shaman's palace was built by the Isuzu river. This was called the palace of Ise. It was there that Ama-terasu-no-ō-mikami first descended from Heaven.[2]

It is possible from these accounts to deduce certain items of historical background regarding the foundation of Ise Jingū. The text explains that the Sun Goddess—divine ancestress of the *tennō* family—used to be enshrined in the same palace in Yamato where *tennō* resided, along with various domestic gods (*kunitsu-kami*). It seems that the gods were enshrined within the actual living quarters. So when the reign became unstable, it was thought that this was because the gods had been enshrined in the palace. Thus the imperial princess became a shaman (*yorishiro*, or host) for these gods and moved out of the palace. First she prepared *iwakura* on Mount Miwa to accept the gods. Later, her younger sister, Princess Yamato, also became a shaman, traveled to various regions, and finally settled at Ise.

It is said that Princess Yamato had a portable *himorogi* with her and was accompanied by armed retainers when she arrived at Ise. For some reason, she had gone northward from Yamato first, passing the regions of Iga, Ōmi, and Mino, but came at last to Ise. And in the place now known as the site of *itsuki-no-miya* (shrine of the shaman), the princess hosting the Sun Goddess resided. On a map, this spot is located due east of Mount Miwa, her point of departure. Land surveying techniques being already well developed at this time, it is likely that the princess's ultimate arrival at Ise, far from being accidental, had been determined beforehand.

The idea of composing *Nihongi* was first put forward by Emperor Tenmu (r. 673–686), and the project was continued by his wife, Empress Jitō (r. 686–697); as there was an interruption of about 30 years, the project was only completed in 720. Meanwhile, *Kojiki* had been completed eight years earlier, in 712. *Nihongi* was considered to be a synthesis of the records kept by baronial families of the different regions. But the view today holds the content to be heavily biased by the political agenda of Emperor Tenmu and Empress Jitō. *Nihongi* describes the Jinshin Disturbance (672) in detail, especially the episode in which (the future) Emperor Tenmu kills his nephew, Crown Prince Ōtomo, and seizes power by a coup. His reign initiated the so-called ancient legislative constitution, or centralized patrimonial rule inspired by Chinese precedent (*ritsuryō-sei*); the insurrection of local powers that led to civil war began in Yoshino, and passed through various places (Iga, Ise, Mino) until the new emperor came to occupy the palace of Ōtsu in Ōmi. Interestingly, this itinerary is essentially the same as Princess Yamato's, except for minor differences in the order of imperial progress. Moreover, during his campaign, the future emperor also visited and worshipped Ise's god, suggesting that this deity was already regarded as a powerful guardian god. The ancient poet Kakinomoto Hitomaro sang of the great battle for succession in a poem from *The Ten Thousand Leaves* (*Man'yōshu*):

> As they [the enemy soldiers] struggled
>   like zooming birds,
>   the divine wind [*kamikaze*]
>   from the Shrine of our offerings [*itsuki-no-miya*]
>   at Ise in Watarai
>   blew confusion upon them,
>   hiding the very light of day
>   as clouds blanketed the heavens
>   in eternal darkness.[3]

This is the origin of the so-called *kamikaze* (divine wind) that blew from where the shaman Princess resided in Ise and which for centuries was relied upon to save Japan at moments of crisis.

For some unknown reason, it was unconventional for a *tennō* himself to visit Ise. It is said that this convention was violated only when Emperor Meiji visited the shrine over a millennium later, in 1871. The only other exception was the pilgrimage of Empress Jitō. A record of the empress in *Nihongi* says that she insisted on visiting Ise despite the warning of her politico-religious advisor.[4] What was the cause of this exceptional pilgrimage? One possibility is the empress's desire to commemorate the war, and another is faith that her husband Emperor Tenmu's spirit would reside at Ise.

In the elegy section of the second volume of *Man'yōshu*, we have a poem from Empress Jitō addressed to her husband.

On the ninth day of the ninth month in the eighth year after the Emperor's death (694), a feast was held in his memory. That night the following poem came to the Empress in a dream.

Our Lord, sovereign
of the earth's eight corners,
who ruled the realm under heaven
from the Kiyomihara Palace
   in Asuka,
child of the high-shining sun—
what could have been in his mind?
The land of Ise,
   of the divine wind,
is a land of brine-smacking waves
where toss the seaweed of the offing.
O so well did I love
the child of the high-shining sun![5]

Nihongi ends with this brief record of Empress Jitō. But, in fact, late in life the empress undertook another trip to the east. She once more visited Iga, Ise, Mino, and Owari to commemorate battle sites. As indicated, *Nihongi* was composed through the collaborative efforts of emperor and empress, written as an official record of the civil insurrection that marked the beginning of their reign. This took place just fifty years before the completion of *Nihongi*, so the data concerning battle sites was still fresh and precise. The journey must also have been partly motivated by her desire symbolically to embrace Ise Jingū and the Sun Goddess, who the empress believed had sanctioned the victory. Furthermore, she was at the same time no doubt reenacting the narrative of Princess Yamato's voyage, the myth of origin for her clan, by means of her own performative itinerary.

Itsukino-miko indicates literally a shaman who hosts the Sun Goddess, and this would allude to Princess Yamato herself. Empress Jitō may also have been such a shaman—or at least desired to be. Throughout her reign she made erratically timed trips to the Yoshino region as well as performing her pilgrimage to Ise Jingū. Her behavior, it is said, may be explained by the Chinese principles of yin and yang and the five elements (fire, wood, earth, metal, and water).[6] As contrasted with the primitive shamanism of the fourth and fifth centuries (Kofun period)—the age of *taisha-zukuri* shrines already noted—Empress Jitō's reign boasted a properly developed system of magic (*jujutsu*). As *Nihongi* records, yin-and-yang diviners accompanied her to Ise, but it is also quite possible that the empress herself possessed those abilities. For, as I have explained, when a *tennō* is enthroned, the body itself becomes host to the imperial spirit, namely in the ritual of *Ō-name-sai*. I imagine, therefore, Empress Jitō to have been a shaman. With the aim of securing the new patrimonial state (*ritsuryō-sei*), she must have sought to become host to the Sun Goddess. In this effort, she will certainly have called upon the newfangled techniques of Taoism (including the principles of yin and yang) derived from the continent.

In the fourth year of the reign of Empress Jitō (690), the first rebuilding and relocation of the inner shrine (*naikū*) of Ise took place. I consider this an expression of her firm will to institutionalize the politico-religious complex of the new centralized state. Then, she herself insisted on undertaking the trip to Ise against the warnings of her close advisors, two years after the relocation and rebuilding of the inner shrine, in the year of the first rebuilding and relocation of the outer shrine (*gekū*). (At this time, rebuilding and relocation occurred in different years for the two parts.) Thus, this inspection must have been to confirm the new system with her own presence on site.

It was at this point that Ise as we know it was "fabricated," so to say invented. Yet there had long been a tradition of worshipping the Sun Goddess along with the local gods of Ise, and of making the imperial princess shaman. Meanwhile, the previous emperor Tenji (r. 668–671) had established his capital in Ōtsu in Ōmi, in anticipation of a feared invasion by the combined forces of Tang China and the Silla kingdom of Korea. In the Jinshin Disturbance precipitated by the death of Emperor Tenji, his brother the future emperor Tenmu started his rebellion against Ōtsu from the east. In this campaign, Ise evolved as the most important strategic base. As all these examples show, the problematic system of "Ise"—its *beginning*—is then reset to the late seventh century. At this time, existing ritual and festival sites were reconfigured by a whole new gamut of institutions, new forms of ritual and festival were devised, and the architectural nature of the whole complex was imbued with a flavor of the new reactionary and defensive political scheme, and thereby radically updated.

The most common consensus is that the rebuilding and relocation were institutionalized in the fourteenth year of Emperor Tenmu. In that same year, the titles of peerages were changed from the Tang-style Chinese to a native designation. According to the historian Isezō Umezawa, "this change speaks to the fact that, at that time of Emperor Tenmu, a nationalist consciousness had arisen through an interest in Japanese, the native language. Many historians claim that the age of Emperor Tenmu was one of conservative nationalism. That is not altogether clear. But, at least, a new regard for the Japanese language definitely began to surface over against the more dominant current of imitating mainland cultures initiated in Empress Suiko's reign (592–628)."[7]

In the reign of Emperor Tenmu many individuals from the Korean peninsula were employed at the Japanese imperial court. They brought with them advanced forms of knowledge and technology that must have required the most precise Chinese writing. On the other hand, the Japanese language, too, was certainly much in evidence. It is likely that these Korean emissaries and their Japanese hosts spoke in Japanese while writing in Chinese —a bilingual culture with a gap between *écriture* and *parole*. This gap also affected the recent constitution. All legislative and constitutional notions had necessarily been imported from the continent, including official titles—yet now an important revision in the era of Emperor Tenmu was to change the latter into Japanese. This involved a certain national consciousness. The same bilingual culture influenced the writing of history. In the event, *Nihongi* was conceived as a formal Chinese narrative, while *Kojiki* was a direct transcription, using a mixed script—*kanji* (Chinese characters) and *kana* (the simplified syllabary for phonetic notation).[8] I would say that it is this same duality that underlay the changes in Ise's architectural scheme.

By this time, more than a century and a half had passed since Buddhism had penetrated Japan. Temples such as Shitennō-ji in Osaka (ca. 623) and Hōryū-ji now stood in the new continental style. But meanwhile, the ancient elevated architecture of *taisha-zukuri*—what Chūta Itō referred to as a "southern aboriginal" style—was preserved in older cultural regions, such as Izumo and Sumiyoshi. In contradistinction to the new imported culture—the Chinese writing system, the legislative constitution (*ritsuryō-sei*), and numerous Buddhist temples and monasteries—was a broad substratum of native culture: Yamato language, shamanism, elevated buildings raised on heavy columns without stone bases, and even dugout housing. What Emperor Tenmu intended late in life, I imagine, was to revitalize this native culture by strengthening and enriching it, in order that it might compete on more equal terms with the new foreign importations.

Such a cultural strategy was also a requisite of the prevailing international political situation. In 663 (between the eras of Empress Saimei and Emperor Tenji), the Yamato court had sent troops to the Korean peninsula to support the Paekche dynasty against the allied forces of Tang and Silla, but the battle was lost. In consequence, a strong line of defense was built in northern Kyushu island, facing the Korean peninsula, with the help of Paekche technology. Thus Emperor Tenji's transfer of the capital to his Ōtsu palace in Ōmi was prompted by fears of an invasion from the west. Thanks to a break in relations between Tang and Silla, however, that invasion never took place, though tensions in the international political arena persisted.

In times such as these the overarching aim was to demonstrate the achievements of Japanese culture, in the event by constructing a comprehensive network of Buddhist temples up and down the country. But it was felt that if the style of these were merely to imitate Chinese models (even with a certain Japanization [*wayō-ka*], as at Hōryū-ji), the scheme would be ineffective. Architecture would incur the same dependency on Chinese prototypes as the now hybridized writing system. Although the Yamato court had struggled to introduce Buddhism a century before (against the Mononobe clan, who had opposed the new religion), now, in the late seventh century, the court felt a more urgent need to create a culture of its own. The nationalist ambitions of Emperor Tenmu constituted not only a domestic policy but also, and crucially, a countermeasure to international threats. As part of the strategy, *Kojiki* was conceived and produced—in addition to *Nihongi*—and in a similar vein, it was essential that the design of Ise be unique.

As I have said, *Kojiki* became a transcription of the ancient Japanese oral tradition, creating the mixed writing system of *kanji* and *kana* still in use today. The new and far-reaching nationalization of culture also devised a method of transliterating Chinese into Japanese. I believe the cultural matrix of Ise to have been similar to *Kojiki*, in the sense that Ise was intended to be Japanese while retaining diverse elements of imported culture. My point is that Ise was not the result of any natural development of a particular archetype, but rather the conscious result of a fictive eclecticism dictating what "Japanese" design should be like.

The characteristics of Ise's main building (Shōden) that distinguish it from imported Buddhist structures are that columns do not have bases (*hottate-bashira*); two great columns (*mune-mochi-bashira*) support the roof; four rafter ends protrude diagonally from the roof ridge providing a flamboyant decorative element (*chigi*); on top of the ridge ten cylindrical poles are posed horizontally to provide decoration (*katsuo-gi*)—and the whole is made of wood left with its natural finish, hence unpainted. Basically we find only straight linear elements, none curved, with the sole exception of the *katsuo-gi*, which exhibit a slight entasis. The roof of the Shōden is thatched and, finally, although the whole fabric consists of horizontal layers of squared logs, a number of pillars are also visible, in order to stress the vertical element. Each individual member may derive from such and such a prototype, but it is unproductive to set forth a precise genealogy. The way they were assembled is Ise's own—its narrative of origin. Without a doubt, people of the time were able to recognize these elements of Ise as the novel expression of a native culture that they were.

Who, then, was the designer? There can be no answer to this question. Unlike for the construction of Tōdai-ji (745), we have no record of any participants in Ise's construction. At the time, virtually all Buddhist temples would have been designed and erected by foreign technicians. But there are no records about the sort of individuals who participated at Ise. In this light we should recall the recorded fact that, up until sometime in the Muromachi period (1392–1573), Ise preserved a gable decoration similar to that of the Kondō (main hall) at Hōryū-ji. More than anything else, it has also been noted that the elevated floor and the columns supporting the roof ridge—remnants of the ancient gable entry style—were at some time altered at Ise in the direction of the continental court style, and accordingly, there is no reason to deny the intervention of foreign technicians. But the crucial point is the taste that originally selected all the above non-Buddhist and thus native elements—the will that determined to furnish a native scheme for the main building of Ise. Such was what I would call the design ideology of the project. After all, the native elements enumerated above had for some time been considered inferior to the newly imported ones, yet someone dared to select them anyway in order to combat the foreign style.

This will corresponded to the production of *Kojiki*. First of all, the very notion and form of setting forth a mythology was imported. The writing of *Kojiki* entailed the process of appropriating the genre itself, then using Chinese ideograms and transforming these somewhat, and realizing an appropriate Japanese linguistic format. The design of Ise's main building reinterprets, in a certain sense, the ancient forms of *iwakura* (seats of the gods), *himorogi* (the tree designated to host gods), and *takayuka* (raised building style) and integrates these into a new design paradigm, all in making use of imported technical and formal means. Therefore, I would stamp Ise as a fiction motivated by a strong will to design, which any historical view of it based merely upon a theory of *un*motivated evolution can never fully explain. What brought Ise into being was hardly an evolutionary trend but rather an urgent political necessity, provoked once more from beyond Japan's borders.

It must be stressed that the core element in the production of this new nationalist phenomenon was the tension of international politics. In the due process of internalizing an advanced and imported culture, all of a sudden contradictory aspects of the Other came to be recognized, whereby the alterity of the Other's culture and technology were set in perspective and native culture reevaluated and reinstated. Ise has long occupied such a frame of cultural perception within Japanese history. The way in which Bruno Taut triggered a renewal of appreciation of it in the 1930s was not irrelevant. Taut's intervention, as we have seen, was itself a function of external pressure and, therefore, immediately subsumed in the problematic of Japan-ness.

Japanese history repeats this pattern over and over: first external pressure strikes Japan; triggered by it, social turmoil occurs and brings civil disturbance in its wake; and, finally, society is restabilized by a cultural Japanization. The return to a Saigyōesque awe of nature is one of the most typical modes of this Japanization process. The seventh, twelfth, sixteenth, and nineteenth centuries in Japan all experienced social turmoil, followed by such periods of Japanization. Ise was the earliest symptom of Japanization after the seventh-century wave of political struggles: the lost battle against the Tang and Silla allied forces in the Korean peninsula and the consequent Jinshin Disturbance at home. Therefore, the problematic of Japan-ness in the 1930s was simply a distant echo, a mere repetition of all this. Why, indeed, this act of repetition? Is it something Japan harbors as a cultural gene? We cannot know for certain. However, this mechanism is dramatically objectified and reinforced by Ise's perpetuation of *shiki-nen-zōkan* (periodic rebuilding and relocation), in which the beginning—mere fabricated origin—is repeated over and over. There should be neither deviation nor development nor progress in the repetition. The beginning form is simply traced by a reenactment. What is required is an exact repetition of the prototype. The meaning of the beginning is never questioned, but is forever concealed.

The *shiki-nen-zōkan* that has been repeated for a long, long time contains, after all, this tireless repetition of beginning. It is not hard to associate such a phenomenon with the way the text of *Kojiki* was revisited and scrutinized by the well-known Edo scholar Motoori Norinaga (revealed by the modern scholar Hideo Kobayashi only in the post-World War II era, as I have touched upon at the end of chapter 7). Likewise, Nobukuni Koyasu has recently stressed how Motoori's textual critique was in effect a "renarration" of *Kojiki* as a narrational beginning.

> The essential element that [Motoori] Norinaga retold is the narrative concerning *Kojiki*'s own production. And if Norinaga's most important renarration of *Kojiki* is about its beginning, then the rediscovery of *Kojiki* by Norinaga is equal to *Kojiki* itself being [re]presented to the [Japanese] by way of his own recomposition.

Therefore, since Norinaga, the significance of *Kojiki* is subsumed by [that] of the narrative of *Kojiki*'s own beginning.[9]

Motoori's renarration strongly parallels the repeated rebuilding and relocation of Ise. Both trace a beginning—or fabricated origin—in the seventh century. The tectonic qualities and decorative features of Ise, as listed above, were perpetuated and preserved and, before anyone was aware of it, had turned into the crux of Japan-ness.

In certain rebuildings and relocations of Ise, as we have seen, there were revisions, which were however always re-revised in order to recapture the "pure" form, or archetype. Lurking behind the Ise system is the original command code of the genome: "recover the beginning." But the beginning harbors a fiction in that it is motivated by the fiction of origin itself. The beginning entices us with the ruse that there must be an origin behind it. And this non-existent origin is always veiled in gesture. The repeated gesture of beginning casts the absent origin into relief, miragelike. Here the allure begins. This is the stratagem of "Ise," preserved as an exquisite cultural mechanism that subsumes everything within the force of the *tennō* system.

Construction of the Pure Land (*Jōdo*): Chōgen's Rebuilding of Tōdai-ji

The Swiss architectural historian Adolf Max Vogt points out that frequently before a revolution, or in its early stages, architects fixated on pure geometric form emerge.[1] The schemes they propose are autonomous and can seem divorced from any external context. Momentarily they produce a radical influence on a certain social stratum, but once the revolutionary instant has passed and the new state is secured, such schemes are thrown out and forgotten. For some time I have been fascinated by the mechanism of rejection whereby the bold, Platonic forms of Etienne-Louis Boullée and Claude-Nicolas Ledoux (prior to the French Revolution), and Kazimir Malevich or Ivan Ilich Leonidov (on the eve of the Russian Revolution) were hastily buried as passé, even within the lifetime of the artists themselves. Such architects were cast as cultural scapegoats of a social process focused on constitutional change. After trashing such "revolutionaries," the new French constitution of the late eighteenth century adopted a more docile neo-classicism; likewise the Soviet state of the mid-twentieth century enforced a policy of pseudo-classicism. Both styles, though sharing a geometrical bias, were deviations from the heroic mainstream of classicism.

Long before their embrace by architects, pure geometric forms had, of course, been employed to decipher the cosmos. In *Timaeus*, Plato paired the four cosmic elements fire, earth, air, and water, respectively, with the unchanging forms of the tetrahedron, hexahedron, octahedron, and icosahedron. The cosmos itself, Plato thought, was modeled on the form of a regular dodecahedron. Eastern culture, too, grasped the composite elements of the cosmos in terms of geometry. The Chinese creation myth features the basic elements of heaven = circle and earth = rectangle. The great Temple of Heaven expressed heaven by its circular roof, and earth in a square base. The Indian "five major elements," air (*akasa*), wind (*vayu*), fire (*tejas*), water (*apas*), and earth (*prthiv*), were identified with the sphere, semicircle, triangle, circle, and rectangle, respectively—and in this manner geometric forms also came to permeate Buddhist iconography.

Francesco di Giorgio Martini in his celebrated drawing of the human figure made during the Renaissance inscribed it in a circle inscribed, in turn, within a square, thus linking human proportions to an ideal geometry. Leonardo da Vinci owned the book containing this diagram and made copious notes in its margins. Ever since, artistic discourse on anthropomorphism has converged on this scheme. And it should be noted that Francesco, in laying the groundwork for this idea, took circle and square to be the compositional principles of classicism—the selfsame shapes that make up the Chinese cosmic cypher.

Such speculation must have influenced the mathematician Johannes Kepler's early ideas. As is well known, Kepler later established his theory of elliptic orbital path, where the gravitational attraction of two heavenly bodies determines their movement. But, before reaching this conclusion, he had tried to calculate distances between planetary orbits and claimed to detect the orbital scheme of Mercury as an icosahedron, of Venus as an octahedron, of Earth as a dodecahedron, and so forth. He even went so far as to construct a model.

These orbits were believed to give rise to a "music of the spheres." In ancient Greece, it was held that the path to truth was via geometry and music, since the principles of harmony were tantamount to geometry itself and could be applied to the cosmic model. Classicism absorbed this principle, and approaches such as Kepler's were widely studied and even applied to excess in diverse architectural schemes of the seventeenth century, so that the notion of the architectural project was resolved in the most archaic, fundamental forms. Manfredo Tafuri sees a foretoken of this tendency in Piranesi's main altar in the priory church of the Knights of Malta, Santa Maria del Priorato on the Aventine, designed and built in the early eighteenth century.[2] Seen from the front, his altar expresses the complicated interaction of flowing shapes typical of the late baroque, yet in drawings and from the back, the basic form of the pure sphere is explicit, in a manner proper to the age of Enlightenment. In Piranesi's time, when the applications of the ellipse were already well understood, the notion of such forms as the sphere was certainly more sophisticated than in the age of the Renaissance. As Karl Marx's *The Eighteenth Brumaire of Louis Bonaparte* has it, at the moment of social overturn aspects of antiquity often reappear: "At the very time when men appear engaged in revolutionising things and themselves, in bringing about what never was before … they anxiously conjure into their service the spirits of the past, assume their names, their battle cries, their costumes, to enact a new historic scene in such time-honoured disguise and with such borrowed language."[3] In quoting this passage, Tafuri points to the mechanism of historical repetition, whereby in times of revolution elements of the immediate past are displaced in favor of purer forms that seem to belong to a more ancient time. And, according to Emil Kaufmann, it was in just this way that an autonomous, hence modern, architecture first came into existence.[4] Though these pure elements appear estranged, or even irrational, and unsuited to the routine of daily life, precisely for that reason they possess a power to impress change upon the status quo.

With hindsight it might be imagined that Boullée, Ledoux, Malevich, and Leonidov with their autonomous forms would have become the pioneers of a new state art or architecture. Instead, all of them failed. As is well known, both the French and Russian revolutions ended in the establishment of aggressively nationalist states. After the revolutionary stage had passed, when Napoleon, and later Stalin, sought to construct a solid state apparatus, the first thing they banished was revolutionary design. The pretexts for this dismissal were issues of personal temperament or behavior. Ledoux had been a royal architect who conceived monuments and unpopular new tollgates for Paris, as well as a significant complex for a state monopoly enterprise, the saltworks at Chaux. He was thus marked as a counterrevolutionary, then mistaken for a criminal of the same name and thrown into jail. Thus, it was his disciples that ended up working on important facilities and, with their less emphatic classicism, designing a tamer species of public monument for the new state.

Leonidov was attacked by the Soviet bureaucracy as a petit bourgeois adventurist. The period in which he had been truly obsessed with pure geometric form was limited to several years during and after the completion of his graduation project. By the time he was actually invited to enter his first competition for a state facility—the Ministry of Heavy Industry located near Red Square—he had already begun to introduce historical and cultural references to native Russian forms that foretold his later historicist manner. So his was a willed, and not a forced, conversion. Nevertheless, this design language, which was never smooth and somewhat contorted, was eventually pushed aside by the bland and tasteful pseudo-classicist designs of his contemporaries.

Both Ledoux and Leonidov had nonetheless dared to inject pure geometric forms into architecture—a radicalism eschewed by successive "revolutionary" regimes. In both cases, it is possible to point out who the villains were that misjudged their designs. But fast-forwarding to today's situation, the face of the individual or even the collective apparatus that renders such decisions has become invisible. For the decision no longer rests with an individual or even a committee, but instead with the media as approximative sum total of current discourse on art and architecture, a power exercised at random. Notwithstanding the seeming randomness, however, motives accumulate over time to render rejection or acceptance, thus all the same producing a hierarchy. In such an ambiance, being a radical or a revolutionary seems downright impossible. Any reduction to pure form is no longer so labeled. In place of the state's clear-cut "yes" or "no," the media as an assemblage of public opinion hands down its judgment ex post facto. Donald Judd, for instance, wanting to escape this mechanism and hoping to persist in the radical conditions of modernity, which he imagined his pure forms might still confront, was unable to let go of the concept of "art" that objects used to embody in an age of modernity. Thus he constructed a singular environment for his purely formal projects in a remote Texas desert, realizing that his concept of art could never be a popular one. This speaks clearly to the destiny of radical forms in an age without revolution.

At some long past stage in human history, pure geometric forms must have been regarded as part of nature, if only because certain minerals crystallize in such manner. But despite that coincidence, the four cosmic elements of Western alchemy as well as the Chinese five major elements were artificially introduced in order to decode Nature, since the pure geometric forms referred to by such theories belonged to a category totally different from those that occur in Nature herself. Both Eastern and Western schemas were attempts to construct a metaphysics, made up of forms tentatively assigned to each element. Nevertheless, the question of why radical forms return in ages of revolutionary displacement has never been given a satisfying answer, whether in the West or the East. The issue arises not only in abstraction and symbolism but also in living architectural design. In Japan as well, at the beginning of the medieval age, a powerful attempt to assign pride of place to pure architectonic form was made and just as quickly forgotten or suppressed—this is the story of Chōgen and his legacy.

Chōgen's Constructivism

In medieval Japan there existed a system of building once known as *tenjiku-yō* (the Indian style), a term since replaced by *daibutsu-yō* (Big Buddha style). The latter has come to indicate the architectural projects conducted by the monk Chōgen in the twelfth century, as epitomized by the imposing Nandai-mon (Great South Gate, or Southern Gatehouse) of the great Tōdai-ji in Nara, as well as the Jōdo-dō (Pure Land Pavilion) of Jōdo-ji (one of Tōdai-ji's branches) in then-distant Hyōgo prefecture.[1] Subsequently, the preeminence of this style was eclipsed by that of the *zenshu-yō* (Zen sect style). Meanwhile, the more generalized wave of Japanization, referred to as *wayō* style, continued apace. Eventually, *zenshu-yō* and *wayō* coalesced to form the so-called *secchu-yō* (eclectic style). Such is a simplified outline of the architectural history of medieval Japan. But I would like to make clear how different this *yō*-suffix is from the term "style" in Western art and architectural history. The Western term brings together details and the whole, décor and its arrangement. But *yō* basically means "like" something, or "modeled after" something: it may point to architectural examples from the past as well as those from foreign countries. The *yō* convention was useful in a building tradition where clients proposed certain models or images to master carpenters, who (without architects) proceeded to realize the desired structure based on their own store of historical knowledge and technique.

To Japanese, both *daibutsu-yō* and *zenshu-yō* were foreign styles that had flourished in Sung dynasty China. Meanwhile, *wayō* meant the style that developed within the Japanese building community, though its seeds had been disseminated from the continent at some point in the past. The *yō* terminology was first used in painting, calligraphy, and poetry. In architecture it appeared only much later on, in a secret book of carpentry techniques dating to the seventeenth century.[2] While *zenshu-yō*, *wayō*, and *secchu-yō* coexisted even into the early modern period, *daibutsu-yō* for the most part disappeared (except for a few technical innovations) after a brief lifespan of only twenty-five years. This was exactly the period during which Chōgen was director of the reconstruction project at Tōdai-ji. He assumed this position in 1180, immediately after the temple burned down; he served until his death in 1206 at the age of eighty-five. His "style" lasted, therefore, for only one generation. Nobody succeeded him, rather like Ledoux or Leonidov. What is more, Chōgen's method of design was similar to these Western architects in that it referred back, in radical fashion, to a range of primary geometric forms. And, in all three cases, seemingly because of this, it had no successors. The line was cruelly severed.

Chōgen used wood—Ledoux worked in stone and Leonidov in metal, thus their architectonic and materials varied. But the general reduction—or I would call it a gravitational descent, or "fall"—into pure forms was shared. The French and Soviet architects failed from the very start to harness their architectural representations to the will of the state. Chōgen, on the other hand, succeeded in forging a link between the growing power of the *samurai* class and state religious aims, thus bringing into being at Tōdai-ji one of the most dramatic architectural complexes in all Japanese history. Unlike Ledoux or Leonidov he was lucky in being granted a powerful position; he was able to pursue the work at hand with a fullness of novelty, device, leap, and "estrangement," as the Russian formalists would have said. Nonetheless, though Chōgen was personally successful, the *daibutsu-yō* was discontinued. In contrast, *zenshu-yō* survived and flourished. But why? Because the latter was easily integrated with the current of Japanesque *wayō*, or more precisely, it could be easily Japanized as *wayō-ka*. Which is to say, *daibutsu-yō* had something that all too obviously resisted what I have been calling Japanization, possessing as it now seems elements that could never be assimilated into any other *yō* or manner.

I would judge Chōgen's manner to be the raw embodiment of a material imagination exceeding any species of familiar, or merely humane, vision. Once this imagination began its *vertical* descent into archetypical form and in so doing was empowered to full expression, Japanese insularity could no longer tolerate it. In other words, when the lucid yet radically idealistic equation—cosmic force = unadorned geometry—materialized as pure architectural form, the community needed to transform and acclimate it into the familiar landscape of style but could not find a way. This excess of objective imagination on the part of Chōgen was neutralized precisely by the *wayō-ka* mechanism—Japanizing or Japanesquization, as we might call it.

Jōdo-dō of Jōdo-ji enshrines a strange object, about 40 centimeters high, made of gilt bronze (fig. 14.1). This is of the monk Chōgen's design and making. It is the kind of structure usually called a "five-ring pagoda [*gorin-tō*]." As contrasted to other examples, it looks unrefined, almost like an accumulation of toy blocks. The five geometric forms from bottom to top are cube, ellipsoid, tetrahedron, hemisphere, and sphere. Emblematic of Mahavairocana—the central source of light that illuminates every corner of the universe in esoteric Buddhism—the diminutive sculpture represents the five major cosmic elements: earth, water, fire, air, and wind. The same kind of miniature, in stone, is often seen in tombs, as well as in small altars. But Chōgen's example is of the gilt bronze used for reliquaries that enshrine a fragment of the Buddha's bones (*Busshari*), where the cubic base would be hollowed out to contain a spherical crystal ossuary.

Commonly this kind of object was a small pagoda replete with realistic architectural detail. But Chōgen's version refuses any easy association with an actual building. What distinguishes his from others is also that the midmost stage corresponding to the element of fire is a regular tetrahedron, while the more common type employs a pyramid with a square base given that shape's more direct visual association with a roof. Chōgen's is indeed more faithful, too faithful perhaps, to the geometric idea of the five elements. The underside of the triangular pyramid lends the whole a sense of instability, since from a certain angle it recalls a slanted, irregular roof.

This odd imbalance is found only in Chōgen's model. He founded seven branch temples of Tōdai-ji, supplying the identical object for each. The majority have been lost, but records indicate

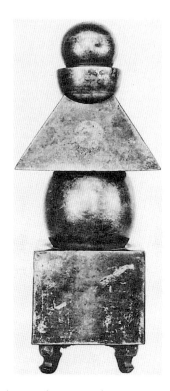

14.1 Five Ring Pagoda (Gorin-tō) of Jōdo-ji. (From *Kokuhō Jōdo-ji, Jōdo-dō Shūri-kōji Hōkoku Sho, Zuhan-hen* [Report on the Repair of National Treasures, Jōdo-dō of Jōdo-ji].)

that all had the regular tetrahedron substituted for the usual square-based pyramidal fire element. Refusing the more obvious reference to building practice and leaving the form as an archetype, Chōgen was faithful to the logic of ritual at the cost of offending tectonic perception. Even if the object shows no sophistication, it strikes us with the peculiar power that only pure Platonic forms can exert. Hand in hand with the weight of gilt bronze, the pagoda miniature impresses us with an overwhelming sense of its material being.

How did such an anomaly in design come about? As I have already suggested, one clue lies in the fact that Chōgen (like his later Western counterparts) lived a moment of revolutionary diastrophism. Chōgen directed the Tōdai-ji reconstruction project for the last two decades of the twelfth century, a moment in Japanese political history when the head of the *samurai* clan of Genji,

Minamoto Yoritomo, took up arms against the opposing Heike clan then in power, eventually installing a new government in east Japan at Kamakura. After Yoritomo's uprising, the head of the Heike clan, Taira Shigehira, attacked Nara in 1180 and in the ensuing turmoil, both Tōdai-ji and Kōfuku-ji[1] were burnt down. Because Kōfuku-ji was the family temple of the aristocratic Fujiwara family (nominally chief advisors to the emperor), a rebuilding was quickly undertaken. On the other hand, Tōdai-ji had been in conflict with the Heike clan and was therefore deprived of its manors and domains; so there remained no endowment for reconstruction. Then, the idea of raising funds from all over Japan took hold, and Chōgen was appointed director of this project—that is how he first appeared on the historical scene.

Although the rebuilding of Tōdai-ji was ostensibly supported by the *tennō* as well as by many of the families in power, their support was not substantial. Monies had to be raised by the temple organization itself. Chōgen's position was building commissioner, but he was also de facto fundraiser-in-chief. Born a *samurai* in 1121, he became a priest when he was thirteen (a choice of many *samurai* children other than the first son and heir). The famous traveler-poet-monk Saigyō (whose awe before Ise Jingū figures in part I) was just three years older than Chōgen. They were friends. Saigyō's trip to eastern Japan was in fact owing to Chōgen. Asked to act as an envoy, Saigyō visited Yoritomo in Kamakura to beg for support, and then went further north to Hiraizumi in Ōshu (Iwate prefecture), a country rich in gold mines, to ask the local branch of the Fujiwara clan for their support. While Saigyō left important poems, about Chōgen we have only a handful of anecdotes expressed as epithets. Among these, what interests us most here is the fact that Chōgen was called "the priest who went to Tang three times" and "a most clever priest for [building] planning." According to this tradition, he had obviously acquainted himself with continental culture and acquired skills in managing building production. He was also known as "the great priest-fundraiser." Clearly, he was clever at persuading those in power.

At that time, ordinary people's faith in reconstructing the Big Buddha (*daibutsu shinkō*) at Tōdai-ji was fervent, but it was also necessary to be assured of the support of the authorities. The obstacle for Chōgen in the 1180s was that the political climate was in total disarray, it being difficult to tell who might seize power next or who might become whose ally. For instance, in August 1185 the ritual of Opening the Eyes of the Big Buddha (*daibutsu kaigan*) was due to be celebrated. Though Yoritomo had already annihilated the entire Heike clan at the bay of Dan-no-ura near Shimonoseki in Yamaguchi prefecture, his relationship with his own brother Yoshitsune had worsened. In other words, after the main political conflict had been resolved, a more minor issue threatened.[2] What is more, one month before that ceremony was to take place, nearby Kyoto was devasted by a strong earthquake, recalling the disastrous scenes depicted in *Hōjō-ki* (Notes from a Four-and-a-Half-*Tatami* Room) by Kamo no Chōmei: "The world became unworldly: mountains collapsed and buried rivers; the ocean tilted and immersed the land."[3] On the day of the ceremony, Goshirakawa Hō-ō (a former emperor retired to the priesthood, but still politically influential) attended, while the man in power—Yoritomo—was still on his way back from eastern Japan. Afterward, it turned out that an imperial edict to hunt down Yoritomo had been issued, but within a month the order had been rescinded and another issued to kill the chief of the opposite force, Yoritomo's brother Yoshitsune, instead. Everything was in flux.

In such a situation, Chōgen had now to do anything and everything to further the reconstruction of Tōdai-ji. Certainly he had to approach Yoritomo, who had survived as victor. But that was not enough. In order to break the deadlock, a half year after the Opening the Eyes of the Big Buddha ceremony, Chōgen organized a bombastic performance with himself as protagonist, namely his pilgrimage to Ise Jingū. His retinue numbered over sixty, while six hundred volumes of hand-written sutra were dedicated at Ise's Inner and Outer Shrines. All this was in aid of the fundraising for Tōdai-ji.

In several senses, Chōgen indeed belonged to the age of the Genji, especially that of Yoritomo. Not only did his activities coincide with the foundation of *samurai* power, but also his "design" corresponded to the simple but powerful aesthetic of burgeoning *samurai* culture. His *daibutsu-yō*, along with the *Kei-ha* school of Buddhist sculpture,[4] embodied the new zeitgeist. By contrast, the elegance of the rival Heike clan, though also of *samurai* inspiration, leaned toward the aristocratic tone of the Heian court of the Fujiwara family at Kyoto, who had ruled Japan for the previous four hundred years.[5] By way of example, the Heike clan likewise dedicated scrolls of handwritten sutra, but at Itsukushima Jinja in Hiroshima.[6] Having been prepared in Kyoto, they were incomparably richer than Chōgen's.

Chōgen's humility was evinced not only in his sutras but above all by his unassuming five-ring pagoda design. Chōgen's style was a reflection of the spirit of the *samurai* regime in the east (read the *opposite* of Kyoto). But this would be a restricted interpretation, for his obsession sprang from elsewhere and went much deeper than the embodiment of any "humble" aesthetic. His design completely undercuts the ostentation of the court style, and diverged insofar as possible from the trend toward Japanesquization, or *wayō-ka*. I imagine thus that when he went to Sung, what he had grasped there was not this or that aesthetic sense with which to replace the court style, but rather a pure ideal. That was all. Upon his return, Chōgen simply sought to transpose this fervor to Japan irrespective of any reigning Japanesque sense of harmony or décor. This was how a frightful apparition of pure form suddenly reached the island nation.

In terms of straightforward application of geometry, there was in Europe one figure: the great man of letters Johann Wolfgang von Goethe. On a similar impulse he designed the "Good Luck Stone (or Altar of Agathe Tyche)" (1777) at his home in Weimar. Like the bottom two levels of Chōgen's five-ring pagoda, it sets a sphere atop a cube. In his youth, it seems that Goethe had interpreted the combination of sphere and cube as the essence of that classicizing spirit already noted in the iconography of Francesco di Giorgio and Leonardo da Vinci during the Renaissance. Sphere-and-cube are circle-and-square rendered three-dimensional. Classicism was grounded in this pair of archetypal forms. In the *Italian Journey* written and published later in life, Goethe recalls this altar. He undertook the trip to Italy in order to reconsider and learn more about the classical spirit—after having been initially attracted by the Gothic, praising it as pure Germanic essence.[7]

In cases of radical discontinuity and groping for new beginnings, what first appear on the blank sheet of paper are those irreducible forms like circle and square. Considering the advent of primary form throughout the ages, I detect the same impulse in response to deep crises. After reduction, excision, and abandon, a certain state of apathy sets in exposing thing-ness (*Sachlichkeit*), and in the end, for reasons unexplained, we confront pure form. It would be easy to cite the lineage of Brunelleschi, Ledoux, Loos, Leonidov, and Buckminster Fuller and to interpret such a pantheon from the vantage point of Platonism, *Timaeus* in particular.

I would hazard that the obsession with primary form underlying our concept of Architecture simply bursts forth spontaneously in moments of crisis. Mutual influence being out of the question, such singularities nonetheless bear a certain correspondence. Therefore Chōgen's work might be compared to that of Brunelleschi, who was himself obsessed with technological innovation. He shook off the bonds of the Gothic by appealing to a rigorous system of primary forms, yet his radicalism was likewise cut off. Time chose Alberti and his more orthodox and articulated version of classicism, just as time also chose *zenshu-yō* in Japan over the Big Buddha style originated by Chōgen two and a half centuries earlier.

The site plan of Jōdo-ji in Hyōgo prefecture, a subtemple of the Pure Land sect, displays certain oddities (fig. 15.1). Toward the flat fields spreading to the west is a tongue-shaped table of higher land that is the site of the complex. The hall of Bhechadjaguru (Physician of Souls) is on the eastern side, while most importantly on the west is Jōdo-dō (Pure Land Pavilion). These two main halls face each other determining an east-west axis. But between them, at the meeting point with the north-south axis, are two ponds shaped like a pair of giant footprints facing south. They are called *Soku-sen-ike* (foot-washing ponds). To the north is a shrine to the god of war (Hachiman)—a god[1] of Japanese origin—comprising a pavilion for prayer, facing the ponds, and a smaller main shrine behind it. Directly east of this Hachiman Jinja is a repository where several related minor shrines once stood. At the termination of the south axis, facing the ponds, used to be a hall for Manjushiri, the bodhisattva of wisdom and intellect, but now instead there is a dining hall. The buildings define a perfect crossing of north-south and east-west axes, centered on the giant-foot ponds. What is unusual about the layout is not the placement of these four structures, but the approaches, which are all set off-axis. And what is more, there are no gates, as at other temples.

Authentic Buddhist temples, especially those built on flat land, were inevitably laid out following Chinese convention: a central axis designates the approach to the main temple. Tōdai-ji, too, the parent temple of Jōdo-ji, is set on an axis in regular fashion; the approach leads us directly from the Nandai-mon (Southern Gatehouse), to the Central Gate, and finally to the Pavilion of the Big Buddha (Daibutsu-den)—all facing south. In the case of temples of esoteric Buddhism built in mountainous terrain, approaches

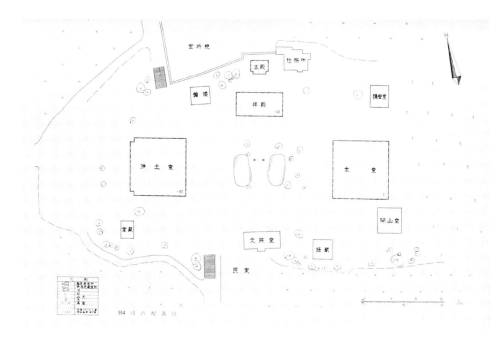

15.1 Schematic site plan of Jōdo-ji, Ono city, Hyōgo prefecture. (From *Kokuhō Jōdo-ji, Jōdo-dō Shūrikōji Hōkoku Sho, Zuhan-hen* [Report on the Repair of National Treasures, Jōdo-dō of Jōdo-ji].) Jōdo-dō at left of Buddha's footprints (center).

tend to twist or curve owing to exigencies of the topography, yet even there efforts are made to sustain a regular relationship of approaches and buildings for the sake of visual alignment, deviating only when necessary. Taking all this into consideration, the approaches at Jōdo-ji appear haphazard. While the buildings are centered more or less symmetrically on the foot ponds, their approaches are hardly more than an assortment of stone stairways that lead from outside the spit of raised land to the interstices *between* the buildings. In other words, at this temple complex, the conventions of alignment and access are ignored altogether.

The impression gleaned from the site plan is that of a standard scheme projected onto an actual terrain, but with little adjustment. First of all, the high spit of table land is inexorably closed to the open fields outside, more like a fortress rather than a temple. Here one conjectures that the intention of the builders was to connect an isolated site directly to the Pure Land existing in heaven, as it were, rather than to the secular world. Standing at the crossing of the axes, surrounded by the four principal buildings, we sense this clearly. At the crossing are the foot ponds, the trace of the Big Buddha of Tōdai-ji standing. The whole arrangement can be interpreted as a mandala: the deity Vairocana (the source of omnipresent light) as the center of the universe (Mahavairocana) stands at the center; the hall of Bhechadjaguru (Physician of Souls), the Pure Land pavilion for Amitabha, the shrine of the god of war (Hachiman), and the hall of the bodhisattva of wisdom and intellect (Manjusri) lay to the north, south, east, and west, respectively, all facing the center.

The monk Kūkai (774–835), founder of Shingon sect Buddhism in Japan, went to Tang China in 804 and brought back a knowledge of the cosmology of esoteric Buddhism as contained in the *ryō-kai* mandala (the mandala of two domains).[2] This is essentially the mandala of Tibetan esoteric Buddhism, and has a basic structure of nine squares arranged in grid form. In such a cosmic diagram the nine-grid structure provides a matrix for recreating a model of the universe. Each of the bodhisattvas depicted in the mandala is an embodiment, or sign, of one of the cosmic elements. In the pictorial version of the mandala, they are depicted as fiercely anthropomorphized, but in another kind of mandala these may only be expressed abstractly as Sanskrit characters. In either case, the cosmology needs no reference to any existing terrain. In the same way that Chōgen's five-ring pagoda was the expression of pure idea, the mandala at this stage should be understood all as a pure geometric schema.

In Japan, as faith in Amitabha as the savior of living things (*Amida shinkō*) quite soon gained a tremendous following, the mandala was gradually transformed from an abstract schema to a more pictorial representation. In one of the oldest examples, the mandala of Taima-ji (made in the eighth century), Amitabha as a gently anthropomorphized deity—surrounded by other gods— had already replaced the more awesome and remote concept of Mahavairocana (abstract center of the universe). This mandala depicts a great temple with ranks of bodhisattvas set in position; it thus approaches the scene of an actual temple hall with its many sculpted representations. The change was obviously undertaken in order to render the abstract cosmology accessible. In the pictorial representations of "the coming down of Amitabha to welcome the spirit of his believers [*raigō-zu*]" that began to be produced in the mid-Heian period and later flourished throughout medieval Japan, Amitabha appears from behind a western mountainside, accompanied by a multitude of other bodhisattvas. Only the Pure Land believed to exist at the western end of the world is not visible here, since the earlier idealistic scheme was transformed into an actual landscape—this being another inevitable aspect of *wayō-ka*.

This latter transformation entailed a substantial shift of viewpoint. As can still be seen in the ritual crafting of the Tibetan mandala today with its many-colored sands, the older schematic mandalas we possess present a view directly from above, with all figures flattened and abstracted. The mandala of Taima temple just referred to, then, embodies the midpoint in this representational shift. The scene is now set in perspective, in such a way that buildings and figures come to be depicted three-dimensionally. In the mandalas that narrate the origins of Kasuga Jinja and Kumano Jinja, dating to the fourteenth century,[3] the pilgrims themselves appear at the front of the picture, beyond which we can see the temple pavilions and the sacred mountain behind these. The gaze is pulled down to the level of the viewer, that is, the worshippers themselves. Finally, in *raigō-zu*, the gaze is perfectly horizontal and the viewer observes the strings of five colors offered directly by the hands of Amitabha to those who earnestly desire the Pure Land—a pictorial device that tends to pull the Pure Land so close that the believer can almost feel and touch it.

In this sense the tendency of *wayō-ka* as regards the mandala was to accommodate a shift of viewpoint from above (perpendicular) to frontal (horizontal). One might also see this shift in the directionality of paths within actual temple precincts. In that context, the change in approach could be attributed to the same process of secularization at work in the pictorial arts. The esoteric *ryō-kai* mandala does not even display an entrance, so to speak, not to mention an approach. The Pure Land, set forth via pure ideation, does not provide a direct access from the daily world. Meanwhile, the approach to the real-life Pure Land temple slowly developed in accordance with the requirements of a multitude of worshippers, like the viewpoint presupposed in the later mandalas, all in still maintaining the notion of axes plotted from above. By a reversion, it is possible to interpret the unusual site plan of Jōdo-ji as a return to the more idealistic scheme of the *ryō-kai* mandala and its severing of ties with the everyday world.

In terms of historical origin, what is customarily referred to as the Jōdo-do (Pavilion of the Pure Land) was the equivalent of the Amitabha Hall of earlier Heian-period Buddhism. Halls for Amitabha came to be built in the *shinden-zukuri*-style mansion of aristocrats and retired emperors as private sanctuaries for worship. These were commonly sited facing the main house (*shinden*) across a pond. According to convention, the hall of Amitabha had been situated on the west side of the pond, facing east (like the later Jōdo-dō). Finally this Amitabha hall was absorbed as a conventional feature of Pure Land sect temples, but in many cases even afterward the principal edifice of the temple still enshrined the "center of the universe," Mahavairocana; importantly, it was placed east of the pond, in the same relative location as the living area of the former mansion. It is said that, beginning with Byōdō-in in Uji built in 1052, the hall of Amitabha, which had been in a minor position, came to have a central role; but even there, a *smaller* main hall nevertheless enshrined Mahavairocana.

The Pure Land Pavilion of Jōdo-ji grew out of this complicated history of the evolution of temple sites. The center shifted from the hall of Mahavairocana, that remote idealist concept, to the Amitabha hall of the beneficent, anthropomorphized deity. At the same time the temple complex absorbed various local deities (such as Hachiman, the god of war). Before Chōgen's intervention, the building styles had varied, too, including both *shinden-zukuri* and *wayō-zukuri*. Chōgen forcibly reorganized all this. For example, we can observe traces of his efforts to undo the asymmetrical arrangement of *shinden-zukuri* structures surrounding their irregularly shaped ponds. Despite the natural irregularity of uneven terrain, where it was tempting to pursue an asymmetrical site arrangement, Chōgen restored the basic structure of the mandala. In terms of building styles, he followed existing types with minor revisions. But inside the least demonstrative building pushed to the west of Jōdo-ji, the square hall of the Pure Land, the monk Chōgen contributed a surprising device.

The Architectonics of the Jōdo-dō (Pure Land Pavilion) at Jōdo-ji

I shall first describe the architecture of the small but celebrated and unique Pure Land Pavilion in its present state. The plan is an absolute square divided into nine square bays by sixteen columns raised at six-meter intervals (fig. 16.1). The four central columns, referred to as *shi-ten-chū* (four divine columns), mark out a core area inscribed with a circular pedestal surmounted by a statue of Amitabha some five meters high, with two smaller attendant bodhisattvas on either side. The floor is wooden. There is no décor except for the statues. The entire roof structure is exposed to view from below, without any concealment or overlay.

The roof is pyramidal and tiled. An open veranda one and a half meters wide surrounds the front and sides. Cut stone steps lead to the middle bay in each of these three principal façades. The eaves extend two and a half meters over the verandas, protruding slightly beyond them. Fascia board is attached vertically at the outer edge of the eaves and there is a slight curvature to the roof just sufficient to correct any optical distortion. The pitch is about six to ten (fig. 16.2).

The supporting structure is distinguished by an overall use of braces. These penetrate the columns and rafter ends to support the cantilevered eaves. Furthermore, due to the broad six-meter spans, a kind of rafter is inserted between columns, to balance and support a system of tiered horizontal members. In the roof structure above the area of the eight peripheral bays, decorative beams with a curved chamfer, or *kō-ryō* (rainbow beam), bridge from columns to eaves, diminishing in three stages by length. It bears repeating that these structural elements are all exposed to view, unconcealed by any ceiling.

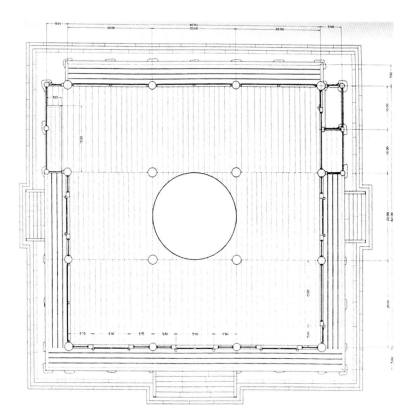

16.1 Plan of Jōdo-dō, Jōdo-ji. (From *Kokuhō Jōdo-ji, Jōdo-dō Shūrikōji Hōkoku Sho, Zuhan-hen* [Report on the Repair of National Treasures, Jōdo-dō of Jōdo-ji].)

On the eastern façade, a sort of paneled door fills each of the three spans. The central one opens all the way to the top, but the upper part is of lattice that introduces light. The western façade is distinguished by an old-fashioned top-hinged, latticed shutter called *shitomi-do*, typical of the Heian period, the exceptional *wayō* element in this structure.

The appearance of Jōdo-dō has been described variously in different periods. A text written in 1192 describes it as "one space [*ken*] with four sides [*men*]" that is "three spans [*ken*] square [*ho*]." A text from 1197 mentions a "tiled hall," "square-structured, [of] three spans [*ken*]." In a 1203 text, it is called as a "single-roofed hall of the Pure Land," having "one space [*ken*] with four sides [*men*]." A 1242 text refers to "a tiled one-roof building," and again

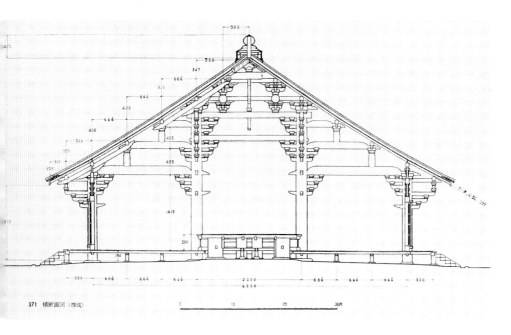

371 橫斷面図 (complex)

16.2 Section of Jōdo-dō, Jōdo-ji. (From *Kokuhō Jōdo-ji, Jōdo-dō Shūrikōji Hōkoku Sho, Zuhan-hen* [Report on the Repair of National Treasures, Jōdo-dō of Jōdo-ji].) Supplementary rafters visible at left.

"one space [*ken*] with four sides [*men*]." During the Edo period in 1687, it was described as "nine spaces [*ken*] with four sides [*men*]."

In sum, we have three different characterizations: "one space [*ken*—間] with four sides [*men*—面]," "three spans [*ken*—間] square [*ho*—方]," and "nine spaces [*ken*—間] with four sides [*men*—面]." They all point to the same facts, in other words the differences in terminology indicate various interpretations of the same "tiled single-roof building." For one thing, the character *ma*—間 (or space in between), has diverse meanings. In the present structural context it is read phonetically as *ken* instead of *ma*. *Ken* can mean either: (1) a unit of length, (2) the number of spans, or (3) one whole building. Likewise, *men* translates as: (1) the four sides of a building, (2) the number of eaves in a buildings, or (3) chamfer.

The final description "nine spaces with four sides" from the Edo period is at odds with all the others, partly because of a confusion in terminology that began to occur at this time. There are two possible interpretations for "nine spaces with four sides": either that each of the four sides is eighteen meters (nine *ken*) in length, or that a square plan is divided into nine sections. I would choose the first. The phrase cited seems to me to be dealing with actual measurement, instead of just describing a shape or form. Then, what about the difference between "one space with four sides" and "three spans square"?

Hirotarō Ōta examined this confused use of *ken* and *men*, observable in particular during the Meiji period, and hit upon a new interpretation: *ken* may indicate the number of spans, while *men* denotes the number of eaves (possibly either on all four sides, or just the two in front and back). "This definition not only recontextualizes supposed mistakes in conventional notation, but also poses a new interpretation regarding the architectural consciousness of premodern Japanese, namely that they expressed the space of the main structure [*omoya*] as a unity and the space under the surrounding eaves or lean-tos [*hisashi*] by the number of their orientations. With reference to the Buddha hall in general, the *omoya* area was reserved for the image of Buddha, while *hisashi* designated spaces for human worshippers. Even when no physical barriers were present except for columns, a strict articulation was maintained, indicated architecturally by columns."[1]

Accordingly, "one space with four sides" comes to mean a building whose *omoya* is of a single span and on whose four sides eaves are appended. This is consistent with the Jōdo-dō at Jōdo-ji: the four central columns delineate the core area (*omoya*) where the large statue of Amitabha stands, and the surrounding area, with its quadruple orientation, is structured, as it were, under the eaves, and affords a broad expanse of wooden floor. What about "three spans square" in this context? A square building that has three spans on every side ought nevertheless to afford one continuous space 間 for the Buddha image.

Logically, the Pavilion of the Pure Land can be interpreted either way. I can imagine that when the descriptions were composed the writers had a hard time choosing their viewpoint. The structure entails an ambiguity, especially in the interior. According to the point of observation chosen—whether floor or roof structure—the interpretation would vary. The core space inside the four central columns can be interpreted as *omoya* (a sacred space), and the outside (under the eaves) belongs to a secular world, but the space

16.3 Ceiling detail of Jōdo-dō, Jōdo-ji. Photograph by Shinchōsha Press, Tokyo.

may also be sensed as a huge continuous edifice beneath a pyramidal roof (fig. 16.3). The complete exposure of the roof structure
distinguishes this pavilion from others (especially Tōshō-dai-ji's
Kondō—Golden Pavilion—built in 759 in Nara by a monk from
Tang China), where the sacred space (*omoya*) and secular space
(under the eaves) are distinguished by the placement of ceiling
boards.

The general articulation between *omoya* and *hisashi* in Buddhist
halls is expressed most distinctively by the construction of the roof.
Up until the eighth century, the technology and style of major
architectural undertakings had relied mostly on ideas imported
from the continent. After that, in the wave of *wayō-ka*, the spatial
articulation of *omoya* and *hisashi* began to develop in its own fashion. In the late ninth century in particular, after the Japanese envoy
to the Tang court was recalled as a consequence of a new nationalist direction in policy, a more distinctive cultural style may be
noted. In roof construction, it was expressed by the advent of a doubled rafter structure—*no-yane*—that enabled the roof to slope flexibly, since it was now increasingly detached from the underlying
framework.

Even prior to the eighth century, Japan possessed a native style of wooden housing types, quite apart from the imported Chinese styles used for temples. Its basic attribute was the construction of the roof in such a way that superstructure and base were separate. Already in *tateana jūkyo* (pit dwellings), the base was embedded, below grade, under an elevated roof truss. More simply, four or six columns formed a basic frame along with connecting beams, so that an umbrella-like roof covered the whole. In *azekura-zukuri* (log-cabin-style) buildings, a floor was elevated above the ground, and the roof truss was set on top of the layered logs. Even the architecture of Ise Jingū can be seen as a layered assemblage of floor framing, wall, and roof, all of which had once been discrete elements. The divided and assembled structure is consistent with the much later *minka* (vernacular housing): for example, in *gasshō-zukuri*,[2] a bamboo roof truss is laid on top of a stout interior frame.

The domestic *no-yane* structure is clearly different from the roof structure of Chinese temples. In the latter, the roof truss is a continuation of the basic frame and the two form a unity. It naturally possesses greater stablity in terms of structure, but likewise required a more advanced calculation. Its joinery techniques—needed to assemble columns, beams, and girders—are far more complex. In consequence, everything—including the roof truss, *omoya*, and roof sheathing—remains exposed to view. When the *no-yane* structure, as an aspect of *wayō-ka*, was called into service, the roof truss and adjunct framing (and thus, by analogy, *omoya* and eaves) were separated by the insertion of ceiling boards.

Briefly, in Tang China's temple interiors roof trusses and attics were always exposed, while by contrast, in Japan since ancient times, ceiling boards had concealed the roof truss structure, partly owing to local framing techniques. Although in both traditions of temple architecture, the space of the core area rose higher than the surrounding space, Chinese builders were inclined to expose the structure, while Japanese carpenters were motivated to articulate the space under the roof by means of a ceiling or other partitioning devices. This difference in technical traditions may also be viewed as reflecting different cultural propensities: the Chinese tradition grasped building conceptually and structurally, while the Japanese tradition has tended toward a certain spatial sensuality. This same quality is also expressed in the development of the Japanese wooden floor. The Japanese architectonic sought to articulate interior space into top and bottom—ceiling and floor—irrespective of the underlying structural basis. In addition, it opted for lighter, more temporary partitioning devices. While the growth of a Japanese tradition was reducing built form to what is perceived sensually, the older constructive impulse took second place or was lost altogether.

In the Jōdo-dō (Pure Land Pavilion) of Jōdo-ji, however, there is no ceiling whatsoever separating *omoya* and *hisashi* to conceal the roof truss. The structural form is distinctively Sung through and through. Because there is no ceiling partitioning, that epitome of *wayō-ka*, the expression "three spans square," perfectly matches the structurally continuous single space. Nonetheless, if we attend instead to the hierarchical articulation of the pavilion's interior space—the Buddha's domain at the core and the secular space that surrounds it—we ought to employ the expression "one space with four eaves." In fact there was yet another and substantial reason for this articulation. It is said that monks as well as worshippers circled the surrounding space while chanting scripture, paying homage to the statues of Amitabha and the two guardians standing within the domain inscribed by the four central columns. This performative style of worship (*yu-gyō*) spread quickly in the late Heian period (beginning of the twelfth century) and soon became a driving force in transforming the institution of Japanese Buddhism itself.

This type of Amitabha hall was called *jokō-zanmai-dō* (hall for achieving *Samadhi*), and it called for a square plan for the encircling and chanting performance. This form (especially in Chōgen's version) represented a radical break from the previous Amitabha halls mentioned as having been built by Heian aristocrats between the tenth and twelfth centuries. The earlier type is referred to as *kutai-amida-dō* (nine-Amitabha-statues hall). In the unique surviving example of this style—the main hall of Jōruri-ji near Kyoto, built in 1107—nine statues of Amitabha are aligned frontally in a row: the central Amitabha, with four attendant Amitabhas on either side. In front of these statues is the secondary space, the part under the *hisashi*, reserved for worshippers. An extreme instance of this style is Sanjūsan-gen-dō (Thirty-three-Span Hall) of Renge-ō-in in Kyoto, built in 1167, a hall with an unusually wide span, where worshippers are presented with one thousand and one aligned statues of Kannon (goddess of mercy). Later in the century, and until

Chōgen's intervention, the *jokō-zanmai-dō* for the encircling and chanting ritual was put on the defensive: reduced from "five spans square" to "three spans square." But in Jōdo-dō at Jōdo-ji, the performative encircling and chanting was given preeminence over an assembly of quietly respectful worshippers. The space became, as it were, a disco rather than a concert hall.

Chōgen seems to have preferred the simple and dramatic, even if less refined, architectural gesture to any intricate manipulations of space. He kept the three-span-square style for performative worship, but greatly enlarged the scale of the span itself. He daringly rendered the prevailing three-and-a-half-to-four meters as six. Moreover, the span of Daibutsu-den (Big Buddha Pavilion) that he built first at Nara was incomparably greater than that of the provincial Jōdo-dō. For Japanese carpenters of that era, the calculations required to enlarge the span beyond the standard width called forth a certain technical bravado. This effort may have been even greater than that needed to cast the giant Buddha itself.

The three-staged decorative beams and the peculiar combination of joints and rafters framing the outer eaves were all required by the broadening of the bay and its span. All were techniques imported from Sung China. What is remarkable is the extent to which any sophisticated Japanesque manipulations were decisively rejected. If one compares the innovations of Chōgen with the Amitabha hall of Byōdō-in in Uji, Kyoto (built about a century earlier, in 1053), which epitomizes the sophisticated, aristocratic *wayō* style of its time, one may be able to grasp how radically constructivist such innovations at Jōdo-ji were. In the hall at Byōdō-in, a benign statue of a seated Buddha by Jōchō (d. 1057)[3] is embellished with so-called *shōgon* ornament[4] and surrounded by murals in which heavenly maidens flit to and fro. By contrast with this picturesque ensemble, the interior of Jōdo-dō contains only three statues of Amitabha by Kaikei (1183-1236), a Buddhist sculptor of the Kei-ha school, whose work offered a paradigm for the new *samurai* age—a sophisticated yet realistic style, with no ornament whatsoever. Because the space under the outer eaves is so extensive, Chōgen's hall feels empty to the casual observer. Moreover, any inclination to portray the Pure Land by pictorial means is resisted. The focal point is the triad of Amitabha statues on their cloud-shaped pedestal. A band of chanting monks would have encircled the nakedly exposed presence of the divinity. Chōgen must have conceived the scale of the hall to accommodate a larger-than-ever crowd, a louder-than-ever chorus of voices. He must have believed the chanting would overcome the sophisticated music of the court, amid a unison of footfalls emanating from the dynamic encircling rhythm of a great crowd. The central images are thus not merely confronted, but surrounded. The architecture of the great hall yielded a rough if purified shelter for the three Amitabhas having just alighted from the Pure Land, as it were. The hall's structure could remain exposed, for it, at least, belongs unabashedly to this world in contrast with the heavenly visitors.

We sense the radical avoidance of contemporary *shōgon* ornamentation or any other imaging suggestive of the Pure Land. The Pure Land is to be grasped by the performative invocation (*nenbutsu*) to Amitabha alone. The welcoming Amitabha triad (*raigōbutsu*) is a living embassy from the Pure Land present to our gaze, such that any further imaginative faculty on our part would be redundant. Thus the vast overarching structure is raised solely to shelter the newly descended guides.

For a building framed in wood, the six-meter eave span is so great that a beam with bowed chamfer called *kō-ryō* had to be extended outward in three tiers, from all four central columns in three directions. Such a number of mortise holes were bored into the upper reaches of each column in order to support these that the body of each column barely seems to remain intact. This assemblage has a truly unusual appearance: looking up inside the roof, we see innumerable rugged beams piled high into the air. The whole candid structure is at odds with the sophisticated image of Amitabha at the center. This statue appears on the muscular side of Kaikei's stylistic inventory; nonetheless it can barely hold its own under the tension of all these exposed beams. And taking into account the dimensioning of the structure, the whole is simply in a different class and there almost seems a kind of mismatch. Only the breadth and scale of the enormous seated Buddha at Tōdai-ji could hope to compete with the constructivist power of the exposed framework at Jōdo-ji. Although the five-meter standing Amitabha almost overpowers the interior space in terms of mere height, its delicate articulation of linear elements, such as the striations used to form the halo behind the image, impede any overall competition with the architectonic ensemble. This potential imbalance explains the will to suppress the delicate conventions of *shō-gon* ornament. For we gradually apprehend a tension suffusing this openhandedly structured interior, which is nothing less than the quintessential constructive power that Japanese building practice had relinquished during five centuries of *wayō-ka*. Was this effect deliberate on Chōgen's part? Or was it merely a result of his single-minded importation at this time of the robust Sung style of Chinese mainland builders?

Today Jōdo-dō at Jōdo-ji is the only existing example of a *daibutsu-yō* temple hall in complete form. Only here is it possible to feel how the dynamism and tension of this constructivist style yielded a decisive break with the delicate ministrations of a nationalist culture, such as had been percolating along with *wayō-ka*. But how much greater, then, must have been the impact of the vast Daibutsu-den of Tōdai-ji as reconstructed by Chōgen at Nara? To comprehend its scale, the extant Nandai-mon (Southern Gatehouse, built in 1199) offers the ideal point of reference, yet the height of the gate would have to be doubled, its frontage tripled, and its depth quintupled. Imagine the effect if such a massive structure sheltered a huge seated Buddha of a size the same as today's. The present Daibutsu-den was reconstructed only in 1705 (mid-Edo period), after having burned down over a century earlier in 1567. By comparison with today's building, the volume of Chōgen's structure would have been more than double. What is more, unlike in today's version, the superstructure was open to view precisely as at Jōdo-dō, where each structural element is apparent. Thus the overall interior was more than triple. Even at its present reduced scale, the existing pavilion holds claim to be the world's largest wooden edifice. How, then, would Chōgen's structure at Nara have appeared? Chōgen built his giant in only ten years, at the end of the twelfth century.

If one undertakes to compare working drawings reconstructed from the original Daibutsu-den begun in 745 (Tenpyō era) with those of the one Chōgen built (Kamakura period) (fig. 17.1), it is possible to feel the revolutionary aspect of Chōgen's style.[1] This appears most of all in the scale of his work, influenced by the introduction of the new building engineering methods imported

17.1 Frontal section of Daibutsu-den, Tōdai-ji, Nara, as reconstructed in Kamakura period in *daibutsu-yō* by Chōgen (conception by Minoru Ō-oka).

from Sung China. By looking beyond *wayō* elements, what Chōgen learned from Sung technicians was an innovative manner of framing very close to the semi-rigid joint of today's wooden construction, if not the actual rigid joint of a modern steel frame.

First was the great seated Buddha. It is not known how its size was determined, but the height to the top of the head of the present reconstruction is some sixteen meters, not including the massive halo. The hall of the Big Buddha had to shelter a slightly larger image even than this. The frontage of the original building was seven bays, and the depth three. Eaves were to be extended on all sides with additional, lean-to construction planned all around. Through excavation, we have learned that the Kamakura period reconstruction reused the original column foundations. No longer a structural articulation into eaves and lean-to appendages, the whole façade of the new building would have spanned eleven bays (with twelve columns), seven bays (with eight columns) in depth. To accommodate the seated Buddha, twelve interior columns were removed from the central area; thus there remained eighty-four columns in total. The span of this core area was as great as nine meters (frontal dimension) by eight meters (in depth), taking into account the extraction of the twelve columns. Inevitably, the overall structure was weakened, so that within twenty years reinforcement was needed. Weakness induced by great size also affected the cast Buddha image itself, since during the earthquake of 855 the head had toppled, the damage taking six years to repair.

In Chōgen's time (four and a half centuries having elapsed since original completion in the Tenpyō era), both the seated Buddha and the great hall itself were in perilous condition. Chōgen's first job as building commissioner was to repair the Buddha by means of partial recasting and reinforcement. In the most recent fire (1180), the head had fallen again, and the body now slanted backward. Chōgen stabilized the position of the huge image by setting up a mound of earth in back and began to recast. But Japanese artisans, though having worked for the imperial court for generations, found this unaccustomed casting job virtually impossible. In line with the trend of *wayō-ka*, techniques had become ever more delicate and sophisticated, so that basic knowledge of casting large forms deteriorated. Here, too, the engineering skills of Sung were needed, and somewhat miraculously an enigmatic figure, Chin Nakei, appeared on the scene. Chin, apparently an engineer, had happened to be in Japan transacting business of some sort. Hearing of this, Chōgen bade him take the role of general technical consultant.

The record concerning Chin is mostly unofficial, but his involvement was fraught with accusations: sabotaging of Japanese casters, failure to deliver large logs from Suō in Yamaguchi prefecture, and the covert building of a ship for his own return to China. In surviving records and anecdotes, Chin's behavior often appears contradictory: on the one hand, he is depicted as a self-motivated profiteer, yet on the other, he settled his landed domain, which was originally attached to Jōdo-ji but was then awarded him by the state, on Tōdai-ji (leading to Jōdo-ji's eventually becoming a branch of Tōdai-ji). In contrast to Chin-the-trickster, history has painted Chōgen as a great and self-sacrificing leader. Owing to his job, the record of Chōgen's life is officially without reproach; however, his behavior likewise may be read as contradictory in both personal and political terms. He must have encountered endless trouble and failure, but these negative aspects of the saga of Tōdai-ji's rebuilding were all charged to Chin. In this sense, Chin, the scapegoat, looms as Chōgen's shadow.

After the recasting accomplished in patchwork fashion had succeeded, the great Buddha, still with the mound of earth at its back, was left exposed to the weather, except for the shelter of a huge temporary shed. In these circumstances, Chōgen undertook to design a more orthodox refuge. Simple reuse of all existing foundations would have been the most efficient procedure; but Chōgen determined to add eight more columns as buttressing to the original. In the event, it turned out that some of the new columns intruded upon the circular base of the image, and the total number of columns had to be reduced to ninety-two.

The reconstructed and original versions of the hall were similar in plan, but the styles employed were fundamentally different. The *daibutsu-yō* of the reconstruction was once commonly spoken of in terms of detail: ancones, or elbow-shaped consoles (*hijiki*), *tokyō* (a structure connecting ancones and eaves), and decorative beams with curved chamfer (*kō-ryō*). It is easier, instead, to characterize the style in terms of its overall visible form. However, what most distinguishes the *wayō* and Sung styles (read *daibutsu-yō*) is the difference by which *omoya* and *hisashi* are rendered structurally, affording distinct spatial articulations. Chōgen's purpose in introducing Sung building and engineering practices through the agency of Chin was to realize a style in complete contrast to the dominant *wayō*. In such a context, different cultures were bound to collide— especially in such an outsized architectural undertaking.

Chōgen, who visited China in both the Tang and Sung reigns, must have had a clear knowledge of the ways in which Chinese and Japanese temples were different from one another. Still there is no record of his having brought back any architectural sketches or plans, nor is there any evidence that Chin did so. It is known, however, that they procured sculptors having the requisite technique to fashion Chinese marble for images of the minor Bodhisattvas in Daibutsu-den. Thus, it can be assumed that they invited skilled carpenters as well, notably from Wutaishan, one of the highest sacred mountains in China. In this way, Chōgen came to realize a vast interior space—one without any traditional partitioning of *omoya* and *hisashi* in the Japanese fashion.

How in such a long-ago age did one conceive of a structure with an eleven-bay frontage, and a depth of seven bays? This time there were no longer *hisashi* or lean-tos, so even peripheral columns rose full height, exactly like those of the extant Nandaimon gatehouse (fig. 24.1). As they stand today, the Nandai-mon columns penetrate both tiers of the double roof structure, and the so-called lantern roof of the lower component rather looks as if it were somehow coiled about these columns. Looking up at the interior of the Nandai-mon, we see uncountable ranks of ancones protruding in different directions, moreover the entire roof truss is visible from below. Imagining the interior of Chōgen's Daibutsu-den by analogy, it must have been a huge empty space articulated by a crisscrossing lattice of structure. As mentioned, its volume was three times that of today's pavilion. Nor did it simply shelter the huge sculpture. More than enveloping the Big Buddha, the great hall would have impressed the beholder with its own vast scale. The interior must, therefore, have surpassed even the image itself. This relationship is best grasped today by focusing on the relation achieved between statues and interior structure at Jōdo-dō, as described in the previous chapter. That is, in Chōgen's Daibutsu-den, one must have been thoroughly aware of the existence of a sweeping tectonic force.

In the twelfth century it was easier to obtain wood for building in Japan than in China. Reports assert that in order to mold enough bricks for its Great Wall, northern China was largely deforested and desertified. In any event, it seems true that wood for building, especially for any structure of surpassing size, was lacking there. Therefore, both Chōgen and his successor Eisai[2] contributed to Sung any large timber left over from the reconstruction effort at Nara. Furthermore, in China, cutting wood into square-sectioned timbers was considered wasteful, so that raw tree trunks were used there as much as possible. In Japan, by contrast, while round logs might be used as monumental elements in shrine buildings, they were more often shaped into rectangular units. The *wayō-ka* aesthetic dictated that structural and decorative elements be merged as nearly as possible, so that Chōgen's approach presented an anomaly. For instance, the *kō-ryō* beams installed in three tiers in the Pure Land Pavilion at Jōdo-ji have curved chamfers, a technique that would have appeared rough and curious to sophisticated and delicate *wayō* taste. The roughness of *daibutsu-yō* in no way accorded with the prevailing *wayō* aesthetic. This was possibly the main reason why *daibutsu-yō* was set aside and abandoned so quickly. Moreover, the tendency of a return to *wayō-ka* is already present in certain elements that almost appear as a *wayō* revival internal to Chōgen's endeavor, and these are especially noticeable in the Nandai-mon built seven years after the Great Hall. Although there the basic framework is clearly Sung, certain details are touched by a *wayō* aesthetic, producing a whiff of eclecticism: for instance while making general use of the round column, as in established Sung style, the entablature of ancones that support the eaves of the gate consists of squared units. After the experience of rupture produced by the sudden advent of *daibutsu-yō*, this reversion might be deemed the beginning of an even more academic *wayō-ka*, in which revision focuses on a treatment of details in order to induce a sense of visual balance.

After the conflagration of 1180, the order of reconstruction of the Tōdai-ji-related series of works that have come down to us was as follows: Daibutsu-den (1190), Jōdo-dō (1192), and Nandai-mon (1199). The initial reconstruction of Daibutsu-den seems an attempt to wipe out any trace of *wayō-ka* entirely. Indeed it is common that the first building project in a revolutionary new style embodies its purest essence. And up until the Jōdo-dō, the imported Sung style was more or less sustained—the only exception there being that the performative worship of the *raigō* Amida necessitated an unobstructed expanse of wooden floor. Also *wayō*-esque latticed shutters (*shitomi-do*) had to be introduced anew on the western façade in order to provide sufficient illumination. By the time Chōgen began to build Nandai-mon, however, a touch of explicit *wayō-ka* made its appearance, and the seeds of eclecticism were thus replanted.

My discussion has centered on the figure of Chōgen, but the name to me is little more than a marker for the issues he confronted. In the reconstruction of Tōdai-ji one observes, by way of an inversion, the mechanism of *wayō-ka* that had for so long assimilated everything into a national aesthetic. Seen thus, Chōgen's last endeavor, Nandai-mon, may be regarded as a miracle of equilibrium: on the one hand, radical constructivism as alterity, and the drive toward assimilation on the other. But this tightrope act could not be sustained as a style. The incipient eclecticism of the Southern Gatehouse appears as the beginning of the end of *daibutsu-yō*.

The next building to be reconstructed at Tōdai-ji itself was the seven-storied pagoda. If Chōgen had lived long enough to complete it, an idiosyncratic balance between Chinese and Japanese elements might have been the result. But he died, and his successor, Eisai, produced only a strange belfry with a Chinese silhouette and Japanesque details. The second successor, Gyōyū,[3] finally completed the pagoda in 1227. There are no records of it, but it is likely that by such a late date the Sung elements would have been mostly eliminated. Fifteen years after this, a Big Buddha pavilion was erected in Kamakura, but there is no evidence that *daibutsu-yō* was employed there.

In Daibutsu-den the introduction of Sung building techniques to raise aloft a massive frame structure had—if only briefly—erased the carefully Japanesquized, or *wayō*, forms of the prior edifice, and the result was a giant wooden hall of a sort never before seen. Chōgen's Daibutsu-den, lost to fire in 1567, was thoroughly comparable to Chartres cathedral (thirteenth century) or the Duomo at Florence (fifteenth century) in magnificence as well as scale. All three structures were first and foremost applications of technology and engineering. The Duomo was a product of what in a subsequent chapter I shall call Brunelleschi's techno-nihilism, and in such terms Chōgen and Brunelleschi may be regarded as peers. Both men were demiurges of sorts, and their lives recall a time when construction touched upon the social realm in exemplary fashion. Both appear to repeat the myth of Daidalos. Brunelleschi's drama unfolded via his invention of an aerial, or mobile, scaffold, while Chōgen regales us with his anecdotes of how he went about obtaining the raw materials for his mammoth construction, as we shall hear in the following chapter.

Chōgen visited the burned-down Daibutsu-den right after the fire in 1180. The head of the Big Buddha had fallen and the body was buried under rubble and once again thrust off balance. After having become a priest and undergone further training at Shimo-daigo in Kyoto, Chōgen took up his vocation as fundraiser and construction commissioner for temple buildings. Around this time, he also moved to the famous center for ascetic Buddhism founded by Kūkai atop Mount Kōya. Senpuku-ji, near the mountain, preserves a copper bell often cited as proof of both Chōgen's China connection and his talent as a fundraiser. The inscriptions I quoted earlier, "the priest who went to Tang three times" and "a most clever priest for planning [building]," are from this bell. Perhaps those achievements enabled him to assume the position of fundraiser and architectural commissioner for the Tōdai-ji reconstruction project. He was already 60 years old in 1180. Other candidates included Hōnen[1] and Eisai, who had both been working to establish new sects of Buddhism. Chōgen belonged to a minor faction of a much older school that had existed for four centuries: Jōdo-mon. In contrast to his rivals, he was less concerned with the foundation of a Buddhist sect than with actual temple construction. Now before his eyes was the rubble of the Big Buddha and its hall—and beyond, the whole burned-out precinct that surrounded them. Chōgen's time was one of civil disturbance and war. Did he really have hopes of reconstructing this huge edifice after his inspection tour of the vast burned-out domain?

I myself cleave to a memory of a similar scene in a Japanese city, exactly 765 years after Chōgen's experience. I was much younger than Chōgen, and even less an architect than he. But now that I have passed his age, I am able to affirm that the initial feeling at witnessing a scene of total disappearance is a sensation of vast emptiness. Thus, one might easily imagine that seeing the burned-down Big Buddha fired Chōgen's immense passion to reconstruct it. Speaking of his success after the fact, one could easily employ such logic. Based on my own experience, however, I would testify instead that Chōgen probably had little confidence in a successful outcome. The original construction completed in 751 was driven by the slogan *chingo-kokka*: "ensuring the peace of the state through Buddhism." What Chōgen saw was the collapse of this ideal that had lasted for four and a half centuries. He was perhaps simply witnessing the end of an age but without any active notion of reconstruction.

Already about 130 years before Chōgen's epiphany, the Japanese public imagination had been captured by the end of the Law (*mappō-shisō*), an apocalyptic view of the world linked to Mahayana Buddhist belief. A deep pessimism took hold of people's minds at that time and they seemed to be awaiting some radical breakthrough. In such an age, the last thing to appeal to the human mind would be a solemn, gorgeous, and grandiose religious edifice; instead, an amorphous vision of infinite emptiness would probably take root. Chōgen, I believe, sought something to fill this emptiness. The vision conjured up in his mind, as he persisted, determined his eventual position in history. I believe this vision was based on three main aims: (1) to construct an unimaginably vast building, (2) to break with all familiar cultural tradition, and (3) to set in motion an unparalleled mise-en-scène.

At times when a great emptiness prevails, the equilibrium of the status quo may be disturbed. Disequilibrium then provokes excess, deviance, and a certain *salto mortale*. It is at such moments that the spirit of the demiurge pushes us to an achievement beyond human scale. The image of the gigantic inspires a sublime excitement. In consequence, the bizarre, unsound, and wondrous are welcomed. Chōgen's leap into the void entailed the construction of a volume of untoward proportions, importation of unfamiliar Sung building techniques, the accomplishment of pure form, and the grandeur of a new and overwhelming spatial setting. It goes without saying that each and every element was the opposite of *wayō* tendencies.

Only when a fervor attacks people can a fundraising campaign fully succeed. An enormous quantity of energy must be consumed for the production of an image of the sublime at a never-before-imagined scale. In an aura of mass excitement, bigger is better, and a potlatch frame of mind prevails.

Each of the columns of Chōgen's Daibutsu-den was some one and a half meters in diameter. The eighth-century originals are said to have been only about one meter, so the squared section of Chōgen's would have been more than double. Column height ranged from twenty to thirty meters. Faithful to Sung principles, each column must have been a single trunk. Furthermore, construction dictated the cutting of innumerable mortises for battens and ancones; and still each column had an enormous weight to support, so the section needed to be that large. At the time of the Edo reconstruction in 1708, when it was no longer possible to obtain such huge trees, the builders had instead to assemble a thick laminated pillar fastened together with metallic bands—an engineering technique called *kanawa-zukuri*.

One of Chōgen's hardest tasks had been to find a way to transport the giant trunks from forest to building site. To move a tree of this scale, one thousand men were required. As a means of economizing the labor force, *rokuro*—a kind of roller—was invented and rivers were also dammed so that rafts could be used to transport the wood. Thanks to these means, the record says, seventy porters per tree trunk sufficed. These ideas were all attributed to Chōgen's genius, but I cannot help sensing the presence of Chin as engineering consultant. When Chōgen visited the forest tracts of Suō in Yamaguchi prefecture, he surely took Chin along.

The acquisition and safe delivery of the giant logs generated innumerable stories concerning Chōgen. He organized the transfer of more than a hundred over several hundred kilometers—a formidable job even by today's standards. Meanwhile, strife and accident during this campaign were mostly attributed to his alter ego,

Chin, according to delations on the occasion of the latter's resignation. We need not believe these recriminations.

The true difficulty in all this may have been that Chōgen had to proceed apace while raising funds from a mass of small donors. Although a large part of these were procured with the agreement and support of those in power, Chōgen nevertheless felt that aristocratic believers and the *samurai* classes must also contribute. A special fief was to be allocated for the reconstruction project, yet mass propaganda was needed to cover the deficit. I believe Chōgen sought to provoke momentum and spontaneity among the faithful by mobilizing the incomparable and intangible image of the giant seated Buddha.

An inclination toward giganticism belongs to the overall cultural paradigm of antiquity. The crux of theocracy was materialization of the transcendent in colossal constructions. In the prehistoric Japanese context, a typical Jōmon-period monument such as the tomb of Emperor Nintoku (d. 425) in Osaka affords the epitome of this principle: an artificial mound ninety feet high and 1,620 feet long surrounded by three moats. It has the characteristic archaic keyhole shape of the *zenpō-kōen-fun* (rectangular-front, circular-back tomb) with an arcuated back 816 feet in diameter. More to the point in structural terms, the formal vocabulary of Izumo Shrine (a typical *taisha-zukuri* construction of 550) is a sort of archetype in embryo of Chōgen's giant columns, a reminder of primitive tree worship. Not least at the time Chōgen accepted the position of fundraiser-in-chief, embedded in the rubble at Tōdai-ji the residue of the Big Seated Buddha was symbolic of the impressive state-sponsored effort of 440 years before. All these belong to a lineage of the worship of gigantic form begun in the Jōmon age.

Chōgen's mode of building is grounded in the classicist formal principle that any motif, once determined, should be applied throughout the edifice at different scales. The element of maximal dimension was a thirty-meter beam. But such pieces were not available even in the famous timberlands of Yoshino and had long been consumed in the fief of Tōdai-ji at Iga Ueno. It was acknowledged that only in the timber reserves of Ise Shrine could such trees still be found. Unfortunately, however, at that time Ise Shrine was preparing for its own periodic reconstruction, and it did not therefore seem possible simply to lodge a petition. Thus, the idea of Chōgen's performative pilgrimage to Ise was conceived.

Yielding to the oracle in his dream, Chōgen organized a bombastic and unprecedented performance: with a company of sixty monks he choreographed the skipping of the Mahaprajnaparamita-sutra (Sutra of Great Wisdom) in order to offer as ostentatiously as possible a new hand-copied text of this sutra to the great Ise Shrine. The total aggregation, including servants and porters, amounted to more than seven hundred souls. All this was to serve Chōgen's ulterior motive of attaining the requisite timber from Ise's superb tracts. At another level, his strategy was to syncretise the people's worship of Ise with that of Tōdai-ji in support of his reconstruction of the Daibutsu-den. The pilgrimage to Ise took place one year after the ceremony of the Opening of the Big Buddha's Eyes, which had hardly been all that lively or unusual, but it, too, had been aimed at giving notice of the future completion ceremony of the massive new temple edifice. Politically, the performance of a grand pilgrimage to Ise played the role of a rapprochement between the center of Shintō worship belonging to the imperial household with the more recent center of state Buddhism (koku-bun-ji) that had been organized to stabilize and protect the nation-state.

Ise had long boasted the Jingū-ji, a Buddhist temple that symbolized a conmingling of Shintōism and Buddhism (shin-butsu-konkō). For its part, Tōdai-ji had also been in touch with Tamuke-yama-hachiman, a Shintō shrine deifying the imperial ancestry. So it was that Buddhist temples and Shintō shrines were scarcely in conflict. Indeed, as soon as Buddhism had been introduced to Japan in the sixth century, a certain blurredness (konkō) had transpired, which Chōgen's performance not only stimulated but also placed in a new historical context, all in serving his own ends. Ise's outer shrine (gekū) was at this time becoming the center of the new doctrine insisting that Japanese gods had originally gone to India and become Buddhist bodhisattvas—gyaku-honchi-suien-setsu. This inverted the previous tendency to graft Buddhism onto Shintō (honchi-suien-setsu) and claim that Buddhist bodhisattvas had come to Japan and become Shintō gods. Chōgen appeared at the very juncture when this more nationalist trend was gaining momentum. At all events, Chōgen's fundraising enterprise further eroded the distinct territoriality of Buddhist and Shintō spheres.

Notwithstanding the phenomenal success of his performance that attracted tremendous public attention, Chōgen failed to win the timber from Ise's reserves. Still he was clever enough to have prepared a backup, for he had negotiated to buy the timberlands of Suō (in today's Yamaguchi prefecture) as a fief for Tōdai-ji, and his building materials were secured. The problem remained as to how to transport the giant trees to Nara from that faraway country deep in the mountains. Once cut, they were flushed down the Sawa River for about thirty kilometers, transported by raft via the Seto Inland Sea to the mouth of the Yodo River near Osaka, then guided upstream along the Kizu River, and finally delivered overland through the Narazaka highlands. One record says that 118 temporary dams were set up along the Sawa River. There were yet other obstacles: heavy-duty braided hemp rope for transportation was needed and had to be procured piecemeal from all over the country; and along the way there were frictions with *jitō*—manorial agents appointed by Minamoto Yoritomo, the powerful new ruler at Kamakura.

At the time of the transition of power—when sovereignty began to shift from the aristocracy to the new *samurai* elite—building enterprise still remained under the direction of the imperial household and its aristocratic allies. Chōgen executed his project from a neutral position depending on neither, while asking for donations and support from both as well as from the populace at large. Politically, economically, administratively, and religiously, he had to proceed by the most equitable route. In achieving this balancing act, he discerned a zone of neutrality in which he was able to construct an unprecedented image not easily subsumed by parti-pris. For this to function successfully, the deeper the fissure he carved from the existing paradigm the better, and the unprecedented giganticism projected for Tōdai-ji served this aim well.

These anecdotes surrounding Chōgen's endeavor spread and were passed down on account of the scale of his undertaking that required the superhuman *technē* of Daidalos. Without Sung's magical engineering, there could have been no successful climax and realization. Thereby all institutions, ideas, and technologies having previously contributed to the history of construction in Japan were severed and ravished. Chōgen's essential forte was to have undertaken the project without possessing anything or intending personal gain. The episode that best speaks to this aspect of his character says: "Chōgen tosses away anything, even a slatted bin for rice-bran-paste [*nuka-miso*] for pickling." That is, he placed himself in a position of owning nothing, or in other words, created a void at the center of his own being, so that the void called forth some never-before-heard-of big thing. The notion of giganticism appeared only thanks to that void. The apparition of a colossal space, made of giant trees, was of a sort that had proven particularly effective in ancient times. And, if so, what Chōgen actually faced and drew up against was "antiquity lost." He willed not merely to renovate what had been constructed 440 years before, but more significantly to return to the cultural paradigm of Izumo and the Jōmon age. In that sense, Chōgen embodied the last realization of the idea of "antiquity" in the long history of Japanese material culture.

It is a commonplace of architectural history to begin the description of Renaissance practice with Brunelleschi. The first example usually cited is his colonnade for the Ospedale degli Innocenti (1419) in Florence. But already a year earlier, Brunelleschi had broached his project to construct the cupola of the Duomo—a structure so large that its shadow was said to fall over the whole of Tuscany. The height to the top of the lantern is one hundred meters and it took eighteen years for that lantern itself to be installed. The design for the façade of the Hospital of the Innocents is founded on a systematic schema of pure forms (square and circle), marking a radical break with the older Tuscan Romanesque, as arrayed two-dimensionally in the little façade of San Miniato al Monte. By contrast, the cupola of the Duomo was not based on "pure" geometry. It doesn't describe a perfect hemisphere like the Pantheon in Rome, for the curved surface of double-shelled brick vault surmounts a massive octagon, and its culmination is a discontinuous curve like the silhouette of a Gothic arch. The inspiring sensation insured that this mixed form was preserved in the cupola of the baroque age, after having been reshaped as an oblate ellipsoid. That is to say, the cupola of the Duomo appears imperfect from the vantage point of any Renaissance reduction to pure geometry—in part also because the nave of the Duomo belongs to the Gothic period, and the cupola was designed, in one sense, as a sequel to it. Brunelleschi made his debut with this great project, but the engineering difficulties were of such magnitude that he was forced to prioritize a technical solution over this or that formal scheme. Again, owing to its vast size, the project had at first sounded impossible to everyone.

A fine biography of Brunelleschi attributed to his contemporary Antonio Manetti (1423–1497) describes a number of sly tricks used to realize the project.[1] The architect once disappeared during a crucial period of decision-making, pleading a trip to Rome for technical research. He would never show any of the models he claimed to have produced. His sole point of argument was that he had come up with a device—the aerial, or mobile, scaffold—that would enable him to build such a cupola, and economically at that. In the next century, Vasari spoke again of these episodes but with a certain hyperbole.[2] Anecdotes about the creation of the cupola were fabricated to the extent of making Brunelleschi out to be a magician. As mentioned earlier, Brunelleschi, who stubbornly persisted in his engineering devices rather at the expense of the actual design, was a techno-nihilist.

It is only because of the giganticism of the realized cupola, after all, that these anecdotes had begun to circulate. Like our Chōgen's Daibutsu-den, Brunelleschi's Florentine cupola afforded an apparition of transcendence. While Gothic cathedrals had expressed a sense of the sublime in their forest of verticals, the Duomo produces a similar sensation by its gigantic interior volume. This type of giganticism was first realized in Hagia Sophia at Constantinople, where the dome unifies an entire architectural space through a resolution of centripetal force. That is, the stresses that the dome generates are absorbed via a canted buttressing structure. But such an engineering solution, achieved with influence from the East, was not repeated. In the Gothic age, the earlier style, meant to unify a space by rendering its horizontal depth and thus framing the technically simple basilica, came to be forgotten. The Gothic master builder was interested in making the roof ever higher. Brunelleschi was able to match a cupola to an existing old-fashioned basilical structure, but to succeed the cupola had to become a completely independent structure realized, as it were, in a single breath.

There was no margin to lavish on formal elaboration or sophisticated details, and the aim above all else was to make this giant stand above its springing. The disbelief Brunelleschi faced was the same as Chōgen had confronted at Nara 250 years before. Brunelleschi's solution was to perform an engineering acrobatic: first, he cantilevered the scaffolding, and then he raised the giant dome by leveraging eight segments of a double shell each buttressing the other. In such a way, the incredible interior space we know at

Santa Maria del Fiore came into existence. Interestingly, the interior Chōgen created was of an opposite sort: far from making a pure void like the Duomo, his must have been crammed with floating beams and flying cloud-shaped ancones throughout. Although the roof truss was forged in perfect unity with the columns, the Daibutsu-den was definitely not an empty space, but more indeed like a forest.

I have been treating the figure of Chōgen with a certain looseness, sometimes as if he were the architect and at other times not. In the strictest sense Chōgen was no architect. He managed the carpenters and engineers Chin had assembled from China and was a promoter who exercised remarkable decision-making skills. In the history of Japanese building, "amateurs" like Chōgen were empowered to propose a model for the design of projects. As I have mentioned, the concept of *yō*—the only Japanese equivalent of style—is not really "style" at all in the Western sense. It means "modeled after" something, indicating a precedent or series of previous examples. In this sense, Chōgen instructed his carpenters to build in the Sung manner. In our Japanese cultural tradition, the intellectual as amateur, or connoisseur, was not supposed to make things manually, as craftspeople did. He was not presumed to use his hands. He judged and decided, but expressed himself only by way of words and did not use drawings or models, like Brunelleschi. In the West, architecture as a profession was gradually established from Brunelleschi's time onward. In Japan, the hierarchical break between intellectuals and artisans continued till the late nineteenth century.

Historically it was only after the Meiji Restoration of 1868 that any radical "design" tradition broke through convention and decorum. Meanwhile, a *wayō* culture, nonetheless collectively radical on its own terms, was created by the ripening of national culture during the Heian period. As such, it began basically as a Japanization of Tang culture and was polished endlessly, after having attained formal autonomy over time. Avoiding technological innovation or any sudden renewal of forms, this nationalization of culture was obsessed with details that affected sensual experience of the work. The Sung style introduced by Chōgen ran in the opposite direction by giving precedence to an eidos of structure. Rough as the attempt may have seemed, it fully succeeded in transmitting its new formal intensity.

Both Chōgen and Brunelleschi focused on the distillation of a radical difference by emphasizing structural innovation and a certain idealistic completeness. In both men the force of imagination (*Einbildungskraft*) overwhelmingly lays down a refreshed standard of architectonic form, as well as loudly proclaiming technological prowess. Neither Ledoux in the eighteenth century nor Leonidov in the twentieth is outdone by either Chōgen or Brunelleschi in terms of their imaginative purity, yet their own schemes remained locked at the stage of sketches and plans. This is partly due to the nature of modernity, where procedures of ensuring social consensus are far more complex than in the premodern age, and the chance to realize an imaginative design correspondingly reduced. The respective successes of Chōgen and Brunelleschi had a great deal to do with the role that a colossal architecture still played for the state, or city-state, at their respective moments in history. Even the anomaly that marked each one in terms of his individual appearance on the scene—Brunelleschi's geometry and Chōgen's tectonics—was effective, and to all appearances and however briefly, welcome.

Opinions are divided about whether the advent of Sung style in Japan was truly epitomized by the reconstruction of Tōdai-ji. Architectural historians tend toward caution because of the paucity of existing buildings, but Fumihiko Gomi has suggested that Sung style (redesignated as *daibutsu-yō*) had already reached Japan more than thirty years before the completion of the Daibutsu-den.[1] At that time, after his ordination, Chōgen was still at Daigo-ji in Kyoto. To that temple, Minamoto Moroyuki, later a supporter of Chōgen's and minister of finance, donated two pavilions: an octagonal two-story hall and a square hall that enshrined nine Buddhas. Nobuzō Sugiyama, who excavated the former, wrote that "as compared to the square hall, which was evidently *daibutsu-yō*, the octagonal two-story hall was much more delicate and appeared to me to be *zenshu-yō*."[2]

The two-story hall was in a new style evolved by Zen sect temples in Sung. So at this early stage, *zenshu-yō*, which would later on become the epitome of *wayō* building, represented yet a different aspect of continental style. The square hall was designed for the encircling and chanting ritual, as at Jōdo-dō at Jōdo-ji. These new buildings of 1155 became stylistic examples to be followed in one way or another by generations thereafter. When they were completed at mid-century, Chōgen was already at Daigo-ji as fundraiser in chief. Therefore, this may represent the initial introduction of Sung style by Chōgen. For, as we have seen, Chōgen is said to have visited Tang (*read* China) three times. The only trip that has been documented was one in 1168, according to the record of his successor, Eisai. There are no archival materials to support the two alleged previous trips. Here, however, the sudden appearance of *daibutsu-yō* predicated in the square hall at Daigo-ji allows us to imagine that Chōgen may have brought back Sung innovations from one of his unconfirmed earlier journeys to China.

By the tenth century, the nationalization of culture, *wayō-ka*, was the major trend. But, then in the twelfth century, commerce with Sung had begun to boom. Then came a critical moment that gradually revealed the limits of nationalization. One of the major *samurai* clans, the Heike, stretched its territories along the Seto Inland Sea precisely for the sake of monopolizing and facilitating this commerce. In such a climate, many priests, regardless of sect or status, took ship to Sung. They were looking for a new system of thought with which to oppose the conventional Pure Land worship (*Jōdo shinkō*) that flourished among the aristocrats. Chōgen was active in this general climate, but he never discovered a new doctrinal or disciplinary system (that of Zen, for instance), like Eisai or Dōgen. Rather, it is said that Chōgen's destination was the center of esoteric Buddhism, Wutaishan, which, however, was occupied by the Hsia of Tangut and inaccessible at that time. So he went south, instead, to Sung to visit Tiantaishan in 1168, accompanied by Eisai, then just 27.

Later, in 1187, Eisai returned to Sung shortly before the ceremony of installing and dedicating the columns for the reconstruction of the Daibutsu-den, and he stayed there until 1191. Significantly, to Japan he brought back Zen, as well as the culture of tea. This was a deliberate shift from the model of Chōgen's example. After his return to Japan, Eisai sent some large-scale building timber, left over from the Tōdai-ji reconstruction, to one of the Chinese temples where he had studied, in order to construct a "seven-span, three-story" gatehouse (1193).

Upon Chōgen's death, Eisai took over his position and worked on constructing Tōdai-ji's belfry (1210), the bizarre style of which was claimed at the time to be beyond description. After a short period of office, he was invited to another temple to oversee architectural projects and left Tōdai-ji. After that move, Eisai not only introduced a new sect of Zen Buddhism but also created his own paradigm of temple architecture. He constructed Kennin-ji in Kyoto in 1202. With its orderly Sung site plan, it became a model for Zen sect temple architecture from that time forward. Including his introduction of the tea ritual, Eisai possessed an uncommon aptitude for grounding elements of imported foreign culture and propagating them. The exception to this was the eclecticism of the Tōdai-ji belfry, which was supposedly to have been built according to Chōgen's scheme without further innovation. This unfortunate foray into eclecticism after Chōgen's death only helped to make the tectonic system he had used in *daibutsu-yō* appear more untenable.

To return to the Nandai-mon (Southern Gatehouse, 1199) at Tōdai-ji, it survives as originally built—the model said to have introduced a tinge of *wayō-ka* into Chōgen's work. The gatehouse is transitional and it can be viewed in either of two ways: as a beginning of *wayō-ka* or else as a sign of the dissolution of *daibutsu-yō* (or the Sung tectonic). This depends on which position one takes: that of the twelfth century when *daibutsu-yō* began or that of the thirteenth century when *daibutsu-yō* was being replaced by *zenshu-yō*, an altogether diverse Sung style. In any event, this great edifice offers the rare example of maturation and dissolution of a style in breathtaking tension. Over the following two centuries, *zenshu-yō* cast a dominant shadow upon the overall style of Japanese religious building. Notably, in permitting a compromise with native style, it furthered *wayō-ka*. The founder of this trend was definitely Eisai, and in that sense, Chōgen had contributed unwittingly through his successor toward the end of a style he himself had struggled to introduce.

Oracles received in dreams seem, in Japan, to have been the purview of influential medieval priests. Whenever such individuals took major decisions or acted upon matters of consequence, their motivation was claimed to be oracular. The place of the oracle was crucial, as was the relation to a particular native god, or departed and hallowed spirit. Of course, singularity of both moment and setting was indispensable. Wandering in a sacred domain and finding inspiration in darkness, the priest would later be uncertain if he had been awake or dreaming. Only when oracles have affected the course of actual events are they set down in history. We may suppose there were also many unrecorded ones.

Anecdotes of hierophany were often used to justify, or resolve, a given conflict. Because such messages are extraordinary and recondite, it is difficult to respond to or confirm them. The hierophant (there is usually just one) is a mere recipient, while the sender is invisible. Ancient, highborn shamans were apt to receive oracles when confined in *takadono*, or stately mansions. The form of the magic ritual prescribed by yin-yang specialists was handed down and preserved in secret: even after the legal code of the early Nara period (*ritsuryō-sei*) was created, the hierophantic convention formed a part of it. Dreamt oracles were, one might say, the unofficial version of official magic, and provided an avenue for monks to express momentous or pivotal needs. In both official and unofficial cases, the hierophant was only a medium. Thus, whatever was encoded in the oracle took on the quality of an ultimatum. Some *tennō* (especially the monk-emperor Goshirakawa) made frequent use of oracles as required.

Another device used to sublimate human will is *yōgō*: a pictorial representation of the moment when the god takes over a human body. Many paintings depict a shadow about to possess the body of a monk or infant, thereby turning the person into a proxy of the god. In ancient Japanese, this shadow of the godhead was called *tama*—spirit.

In the famous moss garden at Saihō-ji in Kyoto is a stone with a Shintō rice-straw festoon (*shime-nawa*) tied round it, called the *yōgō* stone. Tradition has it that the celebrated monk Musō-kokushi (1275–1351) built this garden using stones excavated from the ruins of Matsuo Jinja, an event said to be the origin of the dry garden (*kare-sansui*) style. Matsuo Jinja had been used as the local site for worship of the powerful Hata clan ancestors, and the stones from their ancient tomb site were allotted for the new garden design. So it is said that the *yōgō* stone at Saihō-ji still hosts the divinity of Matsuo Jinja. In addition to dream oracles and spirit possession (*yōgō*), a third example of hierophany is *raigō*: reception of Amitabha's blessing by the worshipper's spirit. Depictions of *raigō* portray the instant when Amitabha descends from the Pure Land of the West. Most teaching of the Pure Land sect in Japan sought to represent this presence of Amitabha the Savior as removed from the original context of the sutra and transposed to the everyday world. Aside from pictorial representation, Jōdo-dō itself, as we have seen, was the concrete portrayal of that moment.

Chōgen emphasized all three types of hierophany and continually looked for the opportunity to dramatize the hierophantic instant in real space—the persistent goal of all his work, not least in the reconstruction of Daibutsu-den. I have already recounted Chōgen's dream oracle. As for *yōgō*, it is best exemplified in one seated monk's statue by the sculptor Kaikei enshrined as the central object of worship in Tamuke-yama Hachiman-gū, within the Tōdai-ji precinct. The figure of this monk is possessed by the god, for embedded inside his head is a five-ring pagoda, identical to the one at Jōdo-dō. Although the imperial court forbade all icons—no statues could be erected at shrines—this example stands as if in deliberate violation of the edict.

The sculptor Kaikei, Chōgen's favorite, dared to carve the statue of god in the figure of a monk and then encased the typical container of the Buddha's bone or ashes in the head of the representation to provide a cosmic dimension. Therefore, within the body of the possessing god is inscribed this objectification of the Buddhist world view—and even a trace of reliquary veneration.

Most surprising of all is the fact that such a Buddhist object was fashioned to be worshipped at a shrine. That is to say, the double and triple possession is like a nested box. At a period when the merging of Shintō with Buddhism was encouraged, Chōgen, the Buddhist monk, undertook and completed a pilgrimage to Ise Jingū. He grasped the relationship between the two different faiths as a nested box and thus, so to say, a specular version of possession by the godhead. Such mirroring embodies the long-held supposition in Japan that Buddhism could scarcely be propagated by doctrine alone, and had instead to merge with native convention and belief in order to take root.

Finally, what Jōdo-dō as an edifice leads us to experience is *raigō*. This architectural expression is strikingly different from both the usual pictorial representations and those statues (mostly in seated position) of Amitabha worshipped earlier in aristocratic households. The Amitabha in Jōdo-dō is standing. Hirotarō Ōta, who commonly writes in subdued and cautious tones, became unusually animated when he spoke of it: "as soon as you open the door and enter the hall, an overpowering golden statue five meters high is standing right in front of you. There are no ceiling boards, so the attic is completely revealed to the very peak of the roof. The thick, curved *kō-ryō* beams are cantilevered from the four central columns in eight directions, exposing all the robust beauty of the framework. Taking a look behind the statue, the whole wall can be opened up by means of *shitomi-do* [latticed shutters]. There is no other Buddhist sanctum as unorthodox as this."[1]

Nowadays, these *shitomi-do* are opened only once a year early on an evening in summer. The pavilion is, as I have said, set on the western edge of a tongue-shaped table of land that extends out toward the flat western horizon. When the flooded fields that surround the site at this time of year reflect the late afternoon sunlight, it shines deep into the hall unobstructed by the shutters that have been pushed up under the eaves. Coming thus from below, the light sways to and fro, whenever the surrounding sheets of water are rippled by a current of air. As the whole inner structure including the undersides of the eaves is painted in cinnabar (common in Buddhist architecture), rays of light imbued with cinnabar permeate the hall filling it with radiance. At such times the huge, gilded standing Amitabha appears to float in glowing orange light.

Even in its more usual daily context, the statue overwhelms us with its breathtaking scale. Meanwhile, the tectonic ensemble above it is remarkably straightforward, even to the extent of appearing crude. I have explained how this apparent mismatch was probably a detracting factor that helped confirm the succeeding fashion for *wayō* roof treatment with its inserted ceiling. But when the Pure Land hall is filled with western light, the crudity is transformed into a singular virtue: each column with its struts generates an intense whirlpool of flickering light particles, making the normally dark halo of the Amitabha image shine, a veritable materialization of authority and transcendence. Although the light streams through the open shutters from behind the statue, any simple backlit effect is avoided. Instead, light is cast in all directions from the cinnabar surfaces of the interior and seemingly multiplied to infinity, thus reaching around as well to the front of the great image. This essence of spirit that comes down from the Pure Land (*raigō*) filling the hall is the ultimate embodiment of hierophany.

I had a similar experience in San Vitale in Ravenna, well known for its golden mosaics and once regarded as the most remarkable church in all Italy. When I visited the large sixth-century edifice late of an afternoon, the interior was dark, and though the mosaics were artificially illuminated, the space itself was far from moving. On another occasion I happened to be there when the morning sunlight shone in. Everything was changed. First a ray struck the ambulatory that surrounds the main octagonal hall, the light gradually increasing until the whole hall was filled with it. At this time of day the golden mosaics not only seem to shine spontaneously in the relative darkness but even amplify the flood of light.

Jōdo-dō, then, is filled with a whirlpool of cinnabar-tinted light, surrounding Amitabha on its cloud-shaped pedestal, as if the god had just come flying down. Likewise, when San Vitale is flooded with golden light, the mosaic, usually in shade, comes alive. Simply by introducing natural illumination at different times of day, both buildings dramatize a scene that is, so to speak, invisible much of the time. The most telling feature of San Vitale is perhaps not the famous effect of its chancel mosaics, but rather the device of the ambulatory, and its gallery above, that describe an octagon around the core, a unique Byzantine architectural achievement in the West. In Japan, Jōdo-dō is the unique structure that plays on such an effect of sunlight. Did Chōgen plan this, knowing the result beforehand?

Starting from its present-day condition, we can, to a certain degree, speculate about how such an effect was produced. First of all, Amitabha is supposed to have come from the west and therefore has to face east. Commonly, halls of Pure Land worship have sizable ponds in front of them, but in this case, there are only the two diminutive "foot-shaped" ponds. Thus the light source is bound to come entirely from behind. In terms of architectural style, the construction is basically Sung, with two Japanesquized elements: the raised ambulant wooden floor and the *shitomi-do* shutters behind the statue. The wooden floor is thoroughly Japanese, for Chinese temples inevitably make use of earthen or tiled floors. And later on, *zenshu-yō* returned to the practice of having an earthen floor. The *shitomi-do* shutters were derived from *shinden-zukuri*, the aristocratic Heian-era residential style. The doors that come from China are all vertically hinged and thus cannot open completely across the span. In contrast, the latticed shutters at Jōdo-ji do reveal the whole horizontal opening, to well above the level of the observer's gaze. To introduce light uninterrupted from a lower position the large openings of *shinden-zukuri* are ideal. Therefore, stylistic consistency may have been deliberately sacrificed to the drama of lighting. Could it be that the latticed shutters as well as the wooden floor were adopted as conscious exceptions to the rule of imported construction? If we push our conjecture far enough, we may well conclude that the western sunlit effect as well as the mismatch of flooring type were both crucial elements of Chōgen's "design."

Time and again I have been requested to name one extant master-work of Japanese historical architecture. The choice is difficult, but I inevitably point to the Nandai-mon of Tōdai-ji (fig. 24.1)—not to Ise or Katsura. As the second and final parts of this book prove, both of the latter are equally important buildings for me. But, ever since Bruno Taut praised them, no one has dared to challenge their value. Meanwhile, Nandai-mon remains unknown, despite its breathtaking quality and fascination. This is why I have felt the need to look at Chōgen for, as I have tried to make clear, his "work" displays the universality of a particular architectonic ideal arising in periods of revolutionary diastrophism. Largely because it demonstrates an exceptional and unwonted constructivism in Japanese building history—which neither the category "architecture" by itself nor any other philological dimension of construction accounts for—Nandai-mon has never been accorded much attention. It has been ignored and somehow rejected as foreign. However, cutting to the core of Japanese culture (and able to be ranked against any other), I would posit Nandai-mon as the prime remaining example of Japanese historical architecture with a capital A. That is to say it displays all the uprightness and integrity of a will to construct later nullified by *wayō-ka*.

What has been the critical fortune of Chōgen and his *daibutsu-yō* in modern Japan? First of all, Chōgen's reconstruction of Daibutsu-den has long since disappeared, and there has been no really satisfactory research on the subject. Until its postwar scientific restoration, Jōdo-dō was treated very badly and allowed to fall into disrepair. Once restored, the interior expressed itself dramatically. At the same time, architectural scholarship has helped to shed light on the structure and vocabulary of *daibutsu-yō*. All the same, less

24.1 Nandai-mon, Tōdai-ji at Nara (Kamakura period), by Chōgen. Photograph by Shinchōsha Press, Tokyo.

stress has been laid on the prototypical Sung elements than on the *wayō* devices, namely the wooden floor and *shitomi-do* shutters we have examined. Thus I would emphasize that the only remaining prototype of *daibutsu-yō* architecture is Nandai-mon, notwithstanding an affectation of *wayō-ka* in some of its details. I, therefore, consider Nandai-mon the obvious choice. But, at the same time, I always ask myself: what was Chōgen's Daibutsu-den like? It must have been very near to the prototype of the Sung style, and in Japan it also represents the first time a revolutionary architecture was conceived and realized. The first instance of technical elaboration of a new style tends to maintain a pure form, as seen in Rietveld's Schröder House outside Utrecht or Pierre Chareau's Maison de Verre in Paris. But then, gradually noise infiltrates and opacity increases in the later work of architects like these.

There is no evidence to tell us how much Chōgen stressed consistency of detail in his adoption of *daibutsu-yō*. Even for Jōdo-dō, claimed to present a purer example of *daibutsu-yō*, there is no model with which to compare it, except for certain similarities in a few temples in China. Thus one might imagine that Chōgen freely assembled the necessary elements from different examples of Sung style, and that somehow in this elective process *wayō* elements, such as the wooden floor and latticed shutters, also got mixed in. In Nandai-mon (built seven years after the completion of Jōdo-dō), we see still more *wayō* elements. The unique features of Jōdo-dō notwithstanding, the power of its linear clarity would be humbled if placed in Nara, where gorgeous *wayō* temples are everywhere, and it could be easily ignored. For this very reason a purist approach would not have been suitable in the design of Nandai-mon, situated in front of Daibutsu-den, *the* symbolic locus of the ancient capital. Naturally, then, a slightly more eclectic approach was required, whereby *wayō* elements were applied in a concession toward the standards of Japanese beauty. Regardless of this compromise, to my eyes the crux of Nandai-mon's grandeur is the dynamic of massive columns against the insistent horizontal composition of its layered linear elements—for example the ancones (*sashi-hijiki*)—that could never have been realized in *wayō* terms. A minimum of decoration was applied to the great load-bearing frame: only details such as *tokyō*, the assembly of ancones, that immediately supports the deep cantilever of the roof above the columns. Even with these minor details the foundational ethos of the design remains constructivist.

Returning, for a moment, to Ise Jingū, considered the ultimate prototype of *wayō* building style, its primary feature—as it happens—is also the construction itself. When first built, the design of wooden joints was still underdeveloped, so the wooden structure at Ise was very close to that of monolithic masonry, using quite unnecessarily thick columns. The material sense of plain wood was, however, emphasized, and even today the main expressive feature of the shrine is the magical power of its thick columns. So here, too, the compelling stress is on linear elements.

This is even truer of Katsura, an exemplar of *shoin-zukuri* building. Yasuhiro Ishimoto's photographs famously emphasize the linear elements of Katsura, composing them into Mondrian-like patterns. Despite these shots being a modernist interpretation of Katsura, Ishimoto fully grasped the essential features of the villa's Ko-shoin (Old Shoin), as I shall specify in greater detail in the next part. At any rate, the characteristic feature of the composition is its sense of zero gravity. Columns that support the roof, studs that reinforce the beams, horizontal pieces of timber (*nageshi*) inserted just for the sake of visual balance, frames of apertures— all these thinner timbers that are relatively alike are sensitively arranged to afford a sophisticated compositional beauty.

The sense of great weight in Ise's beams and the quality of zero gravity in Katsura's composition of predominantly nonstructural elements—both produce unidimensional, flat compositions. But the composition of Nandai-mon is quite otherwise. The materials employed remain as close as possible to the nature of their structural function, with dimensions of bare efficiency, even in the ancones that appear to be mere décor. The design of the great gate is, one might say, as "compositional" as Ise or Katsura, yet Nandai-mon is unburdened by any superficial or excessive element. What is visualized is principally the load-bearing system that runs through the whole structure in order to make it stand. It is a constructive system that counters the force of gravity. It is this feature of exposed structure that has gained a hold on me.

Here is the crux of the problematic surrounding Chōgen. Why, then, has not the constructivism of Nandai-mon been more appreciated, as compared with Ise or Katsura? While the latter two are involved with the *tennō* household and suffer from partly restricted public access, Nandai-mon is out on the roadway exposed to the full light of day, perhaps excessively so. Notwithstanding this accessibility, there have been no grounds to appreciate Chōgen's radical constructivism in a Japanesque Japan. Recalling Masao Maruyama's distinction between *sakui* (artifice) and *jinen* (nature) (see chapters 2 and 4), it must be said that, in the process through which the new will to artifice was received in Japan, this inventiveness was gradually reinvaded (*basso ostinato*) by a preference for the natural, and consequently transformed into something else. In such a context, any constructivism will always be marginalized by a too insistent measure of judgment.

In contrast to Ise's magical power driven by redundant intensity and Katsura's elegance as manifested in floating transparency,

Nandai-mon is simply and humbly constructive, composed of just the necessary elements all at perfect scale and imbued with a functional dynamic. In Japan it has neither antecedent nor offspring. Gatehouses have been used not only at temples but also to divide cities and articulate palaces: *torii* gates, for example, in shrines, the gates of tea gardens (*roji-mon*), and purely decorative gateways such as the Higurashi Gate at Nikkō Tōshōgū—all belong to the same architectural type. In contrast to these, only Nandai-mon adopts the form of temple architecture, at the same time standing quite independently like a *torii* gate. It is, indeed, like the design of a *torii* with its simple composition of giant tree trunks, yet permeated by the details of the structural members of temple architecture. In *daibutsu-yō* in general, *tokyō* had originally been conceived of as a secondary structural element to support the cantilevered roof but was gradually transformed into a decorative element, like the form of a column capital in Western classicism. It is possible therefore to say that the *daibutsu-yō* of Nandai-mon was a willed attempt to reduce decorativeness, turning back to a constructivist orientation. It was a resistance against *wayō-ka*, headed in the direction of the natural (*jinen*). This type of rearguard action, radical as it may appear, met all too soon with a dead end.

Let us think again about the year that Nandai-mon was built— 1199, roughly eight hundred years ago. Minamoto Yoritomo, who established the new *samurai* government and was the leader of the newly elevated *samurai* class on whom Chōgen had relied most as patron, died in that year. The Kamakura shōgunate he had initiated established once and for all the rule of the *samurai*, once the Minamoto were succeeded by the Hōjō clan. The first three generations of the Minamoto clan had struggled to bring the government through a moment of transition, but were replaced, as commonly occurs at the beginning of revolutionary periods. They were destined to live out this transitional moment, and, importantly, the period during which Chōgen was in charge of the great Tōdai-ji reconstruction overlapped Minamoto rule.

The Hōjō clan soon enough came to embrace Zen sect Buddhism full-heartedly as the official state religion. In this climate, Eisai, who succeeded Chōgen but was critical of his methods and thought, was invited up to Kamakura. Eisai achieved the support of these new rulers, who favored neither Pure Land worship nor *daibutsu-yō* architecture—but their own Zen sect and its *zenshu-yō* architecture. When Eisai took over the office at Todai-ji, it is likely that the organization of carpenters trained in *daibutsu-yō* was entirely disbanded. *Zenshu-yō* introduced the meticulous and somewhat *faux* treatment of highly detailed structural elements, while becoming ever more assimilated to a revived and strengthened version of the *wayō* aesthetic and, thus, opening the path toward a fully fledged eclecticism.

Part IV

A Diagonal Strategy: Katsura as Envisioned by
"Enshū Taste"

Background

The buildings and garden of Katsura Imperial Villa, as it exists today, were constructed in three main stages, roughly during the middle fifty years of the seventeenth century.[1] The whole was commissioned by the princes of two generations of the Hachijō Imperial Family, Toshihito (1579–1629), and his son, Toshitada (1619–1662). The exact dates of inception and completion are still debated, but it is safe to suggest that the project was first conceived in 1615 when the site came into the family's ownership. The villa had just about reached its present state of completion by the time former Emperor Gomizuno-o (1596–1680), who made a gift of his ninth son to the Hachijō Imperial Family, paid his final visit there in 1663.[2]

The early state of the villa is faithfully represented in *Scenery in and around Kyoto* (panels of a folding screen previously owned by the Ikeda family) that portrays the landscape of Kyoto around the year 1617 (fig. 25.1).[3] In the painting are three small buildings facing a pond and on the opposite shore an arbor in the *sōan* style. In view of the surrounding layout, it can be assumed that the central building with cypress-shingled roof that appears as the main hall is today's Ko-shoin (Old Shoin). At a later stage the villa is seen in another painting: *Katsura no Miya Gobesso Zenzu* (Panoramic View of Prince Katsura's Country House) made in the late seventeenth century. In this painting, a copy of which is in the collection of the National Diet Library, Tokyo, the buildings are set out in the same arrangement as today. However, the transparent *shōji* screens (*akari-shōji*) in both the Chū-shoin (Central Shoin) and the Shin-goten (New Palace) are placed behind the veranda,

25.1 *Scenery in and around Kyoto*, detail of folding screen previously owned by the Ikeda family, collection of National Museum of Japanese History, Sakura city, Chiba prefecture 〈http://www.rekihaku.ac.jp/index.html〉.

as in the Ko-shoin today, exposing the veranda to the open air and allowing views of the garden. That is to say, at some point since the painting, the *shōji* were moved out to the edge of the veranda, thereby enclosing that space. Another difference is that in the painting, the area in front of the Shōkin-tei (pine and *koto* arbor) Teahouse, where there had once been a bridge, is shown connected to the land. The painting also reminds us that the water forming the pond near *Ama-no-hashidate* (Heaven's standing bridge, where there are numerous stone arrangements) came from a different source than it does today. Lastly, as a note in the margin of the painting informs us, there used to be a "big bridge" over the pond with a red-lacquered balustrade.

All in all, these minor alterations attest to the fact that both buildings and garden began to be amended at an early date. The seventh head of the Hachijō Imperial Family, Prince Yakahito (1703–1762), who frequented Katsura, wrote numerous poems in commemoration of the scenery he enjoyed there;[4] he defined it as *Enshū-gonomi*[5]—after the taste (or "style") of Kobori Enshū (1579–1647), the well-known garden designer and tea master of the early Edo period. Thus in Katsura, certain elements at least came to be identified as *Enshū-gonomi*. Yakahito's mention of Enshū helped spread an impression that Enshū had actually designed Katsura Villa. In any event, it is easy to imagine that Prince Yakahito himself may have ordered the refurbishment of certain parts.

Aside from the main *shoin* pavilions, there are several teahouses of different styles at Katsura. The garden, too, is an assemblage of various styles of garden design—an all-inclusive complex of mixed methods. In the end, the building types and styles that compose Katsura are the product of various individuals from several periods. The Kanei era (1624–1643) that overlapped the initial stage of Katsura's development was a period of drastic stylistic shift in Japanese building history. Methods from before and after this shift, with their radical differences, are naturally disseminated—even amalgamated—all over Katsura. Therefore Katsura is a text rich in ambiguity, where architectural languages of quite different formal and temporal inspiration are juxtaposed.

These layers of approach and language have made Katsura an object of incessant new reading strategies. Modernists, especially, have sought to decode the architecture of Katsura in sympathy

25.2 Katsura Imperial Villa, Kyoto (mid-seventeenth century), site plan.

25.3 Detail of stone path, Katsura Villa, Kyoto, 1953. Photograph by Yasuhiro Ishimoto.

with their own design themes, making it a fulcrum for their own tactics. As such, Katsura as a discourse became an almost mythographical entity, irrespective of its existing buildings and gardens. One of my purposes here will be to follow and analyze such modernist readings.

The photographer Yasuhiro Ishimoto published his initial work on Katsura, *Katsura: Tradition and Creation in Japanese Architecture*, in

25.4 Detail of moon-viewing platform, Old Shoin, Katsura Villa, Kyoto, 1954.
Photograph by Yasuhiro Ishimoto.

1960 in collaboration with Kenzō Tange, with a celebrated preface by Walter Gropius (figs. 25.3, 25.4, 25.5).[6] Nearly a quarter century later, he published his second book, *Katsura Villa: Space and Form*, in 1983 (figs. 25.6, 25.7).[7] If we compare the two works, the difference is so radical that it is nearly impossible to believe we are seeing the same Katsura. As I pointed out in part I, the 1960 book virtually decomposed the villa, buildings and gardens alike, into black and white planar patterns. Well acquainted with the soul of monochromatic photographic expression, Ishimoto determined to disassemble Katsura into fragments in order to frame it. Yet, to bring this off, the bulk and density of Katsura, and its dynamism, are omitted. As Tange acknowledged in his textual accompaniment, Ishimoto's omission was perfectly intentional.

25.5 Detail of composite stone walkway, Katsura Villa, Kyoto, 1953. Photograph by Yasuhiro Ishimoto.

The maneuver of exclusion was based upon an aesthetic collusion between Ishimoto and Tange. The items excluded were limited to certain key elements. While many pictures were included of the *shoin*'s façades, omitted altogether were the elegantly cambered roofs integral to Katsura. Instead, the goal was to extract Mondrianesque patterns, such as those created by the lines of the *shōji*, and the supports and beams apparent in the façades beneath

25.6 Detail of New Palace and Middle Shoin façade, Katsura Villa, Kyoto, 1982. Photograph by Yasuhiro Ishimoto.

the elevated floors. Such nonlinear elements as roofs that connoted "excess" were willfully excluded. Any feature with curvilinear movement or rich formal implications was left out: for instance, the famous built-in Katsura desk and the comb-shaped frame of the window above the dais in the Shin-goten's Main Room; or the Mokkō-crest-shaped opening in the *tokonoma* and the transom in the shape of the stylistically deformed "moon" character in the Second Room of the Shin-goten. Also omitted were decorative and gaudy elements refurbished in later renovations, such as the Gobelin dado in the Shōi-ken (laughing mind arbor) Teahouse. In fact the ensemble of elements that were disregarded by Tange and Ishimoto were those that had contributed over time to Katsura's fame as the expression of quintessential *sukiya*-style architecture. The aim of the modernist project forged in the mid-1950s representation was the erasure of such "excessive" elements.

In contrast to the 1960 work, the images produced for Ishimoto's second book, *Katsura Villa: Space and Form*, introduce thoroughly different features of Katsura. The new color shots convey

25.7 Detail of *shoin* interior, Katsura Villa, Kyoto, 1982. Photograph by Yasuhiro Ishimoto.

more data than black and white, but more to the point, Ishimoto sought to construct a totally different device for reading Katsura. This Katsura no longer strikes us with its sense of transparency. On the contrary, it stresses ambiguous and even kitschlike aspects of the ensemble. Though the camera eye still focuses on detail, it is no longer so exclusionary; it pulls back slightly from the motifs in order to encourage a broader interpretation. Objects are now woven into the tissue of a background context. The quarter century between the two books seems to compel the photographer to offer this new interpretation. And, via this emblematic transformation, one can sense a transition within Japanese modernity itself.

To begin, I would like to trace briefly the views of those three architects—Bruno Taut, Sutemi Horiguchi, and Kenzō Tange— for whom the reading of Katsura played a crucial role in their deployment of modernism. It was in 1933 that Taut spoke of Katsura—the first instance of Katsura in modernist discourse. I am tempted to superimpose the first half of the twentieth century, during which these three modernist readings of Katsura were established, upon the fifty years of the seventeenth century during which Katsura was constructed—since the whole of Katsura as we know it today was built mainly in three stages, each introducing new design methods. These heterogeneous layers could scarcely be revealed by a unified interpretation, so it would seem natural, even, that Katsura once more provoked successive interpretations over yet another fifty-year period—that of modernist development.

And now once again a new interpretation must be sought, but without positing Katsura as the point of departure for evolving a present-day design strategy. The myth created by the modernist Katsura discourses is still alive but is now faded, especially in the aftermath of the 1960s, which saw debates on tradition aimed at resolving contradictions between nationalism and modernism at last superseded. Meanwhile, from the 1950s onward a number of discoveries about Katsura were made (especially in the radical restoration between 1976 and 1982), producing new and objective research that permits a fresh contextualization. But it is not my intention to add to this scholarship nor to say anything new about these recent discoveries. My point of view is far from both the older modernist readings and the new historical facts of design and construction. Rather I would prefer to treat Katsura as a textual space in which one may detect a polysemy of architecture. To achieve this, I need to focus on what the modernists shook off and eliminated. I would like, in particular, to take up the flamboyant, not to say acrobatic, tendency of the later premodern renovations. Though anathema to modernists, the elements thus brought to the fore are indispensable to Katsura. But first in the rest of this chapter let us look again at the modernist readings of Taut, Horiguchi, and Tange—this time in some detail.

Bruno Taut's Reading

No Japanese text on Katsura can ignore the importance of Taut's account of it. But what we observe in most books is a touch of resentment on the part of the authors that a foreign architect got the first word. A typical comment runs as follows: "Since the books of Mr. Taut began to be read popularly, appraisal of Katsura Villa has been revised, and its existence recognized not only within the field of art and architectural history but also by the whole nation. Nevertheless, the fact is that an equivalent [revision] had long been spoken of among Japanese architects but not yet made public."[8]

This was indeed likely. But Taut's appraisal of Katsura was also criticized from the point of view of his unfamiliarity with Katsura: for instance, there was some nitpicking regarding his obsessional belief that Katsura had been "designed" by Enshū. Instead, I maintain that Taut's discourse needs to be read in light of the political brief confronting prewar Japanese modernists.

It was in the mid-1920s that the modernist architectural movement began in Japan. Its protagonists sought to import modern design and drafted a number of manifestos based on Western examples. By the beginning of the 1930s, however, there were serious obstacles. One was the association of modernism with the socialist revolutionary movement, which had come under attack by the state. Another was that modernism had a strong adversary in the revived eclecticism based upon imperialist ideology—the so-called *teikan* style (see chapter 1). This recalls the situation in both the Stalinist Soviet Union and Nazi Germany in the 1930s, where an eclectic fusion of certain modernist and neoclassical elements appeared as a symptom of the rapid conservatization of both regimes. In Japan, the mandate for large state-sponsored competitions now all too frequently read: "the style must be Eastern, that is, based upon Japanese taste." Quite soon the *teikan* style had become the sole government-approved manner of design.

Taut arrived in Japan via Siberia in May 1933, a "refugee" from the Soviet Union and unable to return to Germany. On the very day after his arrival, a member of the Japan International Architectural Association, Isaburō Ueno, and the chief executive of Daimaru Department Store, Shōtarō Shimomura, took Taut to see Katsura Villa, which was closed to the general public. The strong impression made by that first visit caused Taut to write about Katsura time and again during his three-and-a-half-year sojourn in Japan. His assessment of Katsura followed a simple and persuasive scheme: Katsura and Ise together were a concretization of *tennō*'s aesthetic, and therefore genuine, while Tōshōgū in Nikkō, the mausolea of the Tokugawa shōguns, was bogus. This created a new understanding of Katsura plainly accessible to the Japanese public.

The Japan International Architectural Association, one branch of the Japanese modernist movement, was already at this time confronting the above-mentioned government-sponsored pressure to conform. On the occasion of the competition for the main building of the National Museum in Tokyo in 1931, it questioned the imposition of Japanese "taste" and declared a boycott. Notwithstanding this action, the competition resulted in the *teikan*-style pavilion that is still to be seen dominating Ueno Park today (cf. fig. 1.2).

Meanwhile a theoretical critique was being launched against this conservative tendency. Sutemi Horiguchi wrote two essays for a so-called *Anthology of Architectural Styles*, published in 1932:[9] "The Ideological Background of the Tearoom and Its Composition," and "On the Japanese Taste Appearing in Contemporary Architecture." The latter was an outright critique of the *teikan* sabotage of Japanese "taste." The former analyzed the tearoom, the very epitome of Japanese tradition, with the intent of appraising it from a modernist stance.

It is easily imaginable that Isaburō Ueno and his associates had pursued similar strategic aims as Horiguchi, culminating in their invitation to the visitor from afar to Katsura. Taut's subsequent behavior seems to have been scripted by the Japanese modernists of the day, and Taut effectively performed his role.

In a number of his writings, Taut defined Katsura as "eternal" (i.e., the soul of Japan) in the context of the nation's building tradition. In his more public appraisals, however, he limited himself to an acute observation of Katsura and its more prominent features as belonging to "Architecture with a capital A." In other words, he mostly avoided associating his observations with the problematic of contemporary design. Should we likewise seek to establish such a link, the following might perhaps be the only relevant commentary.

> "What would you call this architecture in modern terms?" I asked my friends [Ueno and Shimomura]. After some talk we came to the conclusion that it was an architecture of function or, as one might also call it, a motivated architecture. The entire arrangement, from whichever side one might care to look at it, always followed elastically in all its parts the purpose which each one of them, as well as the whole, had to accomplish. The aim could well have been that of a banal and regular utility, or the necessity of more dignified representation, or of a lofty, philosophical spirituality. And the great mystery was that all three purposes had been united into a whole, their boundaries effaced.[10]

Taut's enthusiasm made Katsura's buildings and its garden a new focus of attention, and publications of Katsura began to multiply. But, to the Japanese modernists, Taut's intervention meant even more: it was a symbolic event. Crucial for them was the fact that Bruno Taut was a pioneer of modernist architecture, and above all else, that he had links with the socialist revolution, and had even been invited to Soviet Russia to take part in government-sponsored projects. Taut had left Germany for a Russia well aware of his own anti-Nazi words and deeds, before being forced to emigrate. He did not dare mention this while staying in Japan, another country prey to fascism. But Japanese architects knew who Taut was and used his comments to escape the cul-de-sac they were being herded into. Additionally, for those modernists who upheld pseudo-historicism, Taut's account of Katsura functioned as a battle-cry against their opponent, the nationalist *teikan* style. Confronting this growing radical conservatism, international modernism, alone and unaided, was an insufficient guiding principle. Around the same time, Sutemi Horiguchi, somewhat outside the context of his own design work, thus began to scrutinize Japanese traditional architecture for a point of contact with contemporary architectural methodology.

By the mid-1930s, Japanese architecture had achieved a few isolated examples of pure modernism, but thereafter, architects were compelled to search for a valid conjuncture, if not an actual compromise, between modernism and nationalism. In such a climate, Taut's vision of Katsura became the cornerstone of a new paradigmatic shift. Consequently, it was Horiguchi who, during World War II, worked to transform Taut's observations into the pursuit of a viable design method. In the end, it was the work of Kenzō Tange in the late war and postwar periods that brought this tendency to fruition. Significantly, both also wrote extensively about Katsura. Katsura thus served at this time to leverage the methodology of the handful of productive architects of the period.

Sutemi Horiguchi's Reading

It was Horiguchi who responded most conscientiously to the vagaries and crisis of Japanese architecture in the 1930s. In his book *Japan-ness in Architecture* published in 1934,[11] he directly tackled the problematic of Japan-ness that had come to be widely disseminated by journalists. In this work, he tagged and set aside those elements of Japanese architecture that were directly influenced by the Chinese; he pointed to "Japan-ness" in such buildings as Tōdai-ji, Ise Shrine, and various tea ceremony rooms. For whatever reason, he did not name Katsura.

A closer look at Horiguchi shows he was more or less oscillating between Western modernism and the Japanese *sukiya* style. But this does not mean that he sought to establish a ground for synthesis; instead, he simply juxtaposed these two modes (as happened literally, and somewhat accidentally, in the celebrated design of his Okada House in Tokyo, also of 1934). All the same, he was struggling to construct a theory that would bridge the gap. In this endeavor, his fulcrum was the doctrine of Neue Sachlichkeit. Around 1938, a time when very few genuine modernist buildings were still being built in Japan, he wrote:

> Architecture comes into being when a material need occurs that can be solved and fulfilled by empathy accompanied by engineering. Before designing a building, there is no such thing as style. Yet after erection, the form of a building may be said to have a certain style. In this sense, architecture possesses *style without style*. In other words, this might be a contemporary wooden style, a contemporary reinforced-concrete style, and so on. Style in this sense expresses the whole of contemporary engineering, charged with the nature of epoch, place, and material (whether wood, steel, or concrete).[12]

Here we must attend to Horiguchi's sensitive response at a time when modernism in architecture could no longer be promoted head-on. Notwithstanding, Horiguchi sought to pursue its principles. To bridge this gap, he used the curiously ironical phrase "style without style." Meanwhile, paralleling this line of thought, Horiguchi had been actively investigating the formation of the great tea master Rikyū's *sōan* style, beginning with publication of "The Ideological Background of the Tearoom and Its Composition." The notion of "style without style" was based on his recognition of the historical fact that something like a modernist spatial composition had already been achieved within the Japanese tradition, moving from the *sōan*-style tearoom to later *sukiya*-style buildings, through the unhampered linear articulation of unfinished materials.

It was only after the war, in 1952, that Horiguchi published a version of *Katsura Rikyū*. His text, which he also deployed in captions to the photographs, had been written in wartime, when Horiguchi confined himself to Kyoto and Nara doing research on historical buildings. In the book's epilogue, he offers a telling analysis of the European modernists' appreciation of Katsura.

> Even before Taut, some foreign architects must have seen Katsura. But none had been much impressed, because modern architecture was not yet mature, even in Europe. It was several years after World War I, at the time Gustav Prattz wrote that European modern architecture was derived from Japanese residences and Taut was active as an expressionist architect in Germany, that a modern view of architecture matured and permeated the world.
>
> Only after accustoming oneself to the beauties of asymmetrical composition and the novelty of steel frame and reinforced concrete structure can one be affected by this architecture [of Katsura]. The aesthetic of asymmetry had been mastered in the world of the tea ceremony from early times; therefore, the practitioners of tea must always have understood the beauty of Katsura.[13]

The seemingly simple task of bridging modern and "national" styles had become the overarching objective of Japanese architects during the 1930s and 1940s. While the *teikan* style with its questionable revival of tradition pervaded popular taste in a way that recalled the kitsch of shōgunate *ikamono*, certain modernists believed they had sufficient theoretical grounds to negate it, by employing the aesthetic of *tennō*-esque *honmono*. Thus Katsura surfaced as a new model. Proffering both *tennō*-esque *honmono* and modernist prototypes, no other paragon could match it. So it was that Katsura came to be praised by modernists and conservative *tennō* worshippers alike, regardless of social or political nuance. The name Katsura was floated like a papal indulgence.

Horiguchi's postwar reading of Katsura affords a truly intricate account, rich in reference and resources, that is especially striking if contrasted with Taut's impressionistic observations. For his part, Horiguchi offered a hypothesis capable of rubbing even modernists the wrong way. For the Katsura beloved of modernists was one that had begun to show the material effects of age and weathering—an entity no longer the same as when first constructed. The wooden beams had darkened and, when seen against the constantly renewed white paper *shōji*, permitted an apt comparison with Mondrianesque composition. The modernists thus saw the garden as an abstract space, articulated mainly by rustic stone arrangements and stepping-stones. However, using such venerable documents as *Katsura Gobetsugyō no Ki* (*Record of Katsura Villa*) and the painting *Panoramic View of Prince Katsura's Country House*, Horiguchi was able to assert that there had once been a great bridge with red-lacquered balustrade over the pond in front of the Shōkin-tei Teahouse. He concludes that without this strident element of landscape, certain unusual interior features of the Shōkin-tei—its checkered pattern of white and indigo on the wall and *fusuma* screens—would scarcely have made sense.

> Two great pine trees facing each other across the pond, and a big red-colored bridge connecting these—such used to constitute the dynamic center of the whole span of Katsura's garden. No matter how much the Katsura of today moves us, having lost its center it is a mere ghost of the original as far as the garden is concerned.[14]

In yet another instance Taut believed he had detected a disharmony at the so-called Cycad Hill (*Sotetsu yama*) near the southern end of the waiting-area-with-bench (*o-koshikake*), and wrote: "Unfortunately, palm trees [cycads] had been planted on the charming lawn, a later addition and absolutely inappropriate."[15] To this, Horiguchi retorted:

> In my view, the forcible and violent element was brought into the hectares of tenderly harmonious terrain in order to break it up, precisely because a disharmonious element was wanted at that spot. Modern music came to use dissonance and in so doing achieved a depth not known before. In a similar sense, garden design required dissonance. The existence of Cycad Hill is just that.[16]

For Horiguchi, the garden of Katsura was above all that space referred to in innumerable poems—a tissue of literary allusions. In this precise sense, all those "excesses" detected by the modernists—Cycad Hill, the great red-lacquered bridge, and the checkered pattern of white and indigo—were perfectly necessary to the composition. I shall return to this aspect of Katsura as a tissue of quotations later. For the moment, I primarily wish to point to the existence of an alternative reading to the "abstract space" that the modernists sought to make of Katsura.

Kenzō Tange's Reading

It was Tange near the end of the war who brought closure to the efforts of Horiguchi and others to juxtapose modern and Japanese currents, and in the postwar period melded them into a single strategic approach to contemporary architectural design. In 1942 and 1944, Tange took first place in two official competitions (cf. chapter 1). Both projects evidently seize on *shinden-zukuri* style as the main motif, employing large, Japanese-style roofs with floor plans of classical inspiration. Such an approach may seem to resemble the *teikan* style, but it was different. Neither project displays eclecticist elements like cornice decorations. Tange's approach might rather be defined as a *shinden-zukuri* revival, in direct reference to that classical Japanese style and its considerable sophistication in combining simplified compositional elements.

Ten years had passed, during which Taut had set the revivalist tenor while Horiguchi continuously attempted to refine and theorize it. At last, with the intervention of Tange in the mid-1940s, the cycle seemed closed. After the multifarious, chaotic phases of eclecticism had passed, a style had been designated. This is what Ryūichi Hamaguchi referred to as a Japanese national style (cf. chapter 2). In his closely related essay of similar title, Hamaguchi posits the background of this style in the trabeated construction of wooden column and beam of Japanese tradition, as contrasted with a more constructivist design articulated in masonry by Western architects. But soon afterward came the end of the war, and all nationalist discourse was abruptly discarded—as was Hamaguchi's notion of style.

Despite the sudden change of climate following the war, I believe that Tange's work up until around 1960 (when he wrote on Katsura) was a direct extension of the methodology he established in these prewar competitions. His postwar works, like the Memorial Peace Center in Hiroshima, are no longer equipped with such "symbolic elements rich in implication" as the curved roof. Any stray decorative elements are likewise swept away. To paraphrase Horiguchi's formulation, it was an expression of the native proportions of column and beam by an architect familiar with the novelty of steel frame and reinforced concrete of the modern West.[17] But, on closer inspection, Tange's manner of building differed little from his prewar exercises, except that the roofs are gone. Here let us recall that Tange and Ishimoto's book on Katsura had similarly omitted views of the roofs of the various *shoin*. As he now insisted on flat roofs (*riku-yane*) in his own architecture, this was Tange's reiterated disavowal of the subtly cambered roofs at Katsura.

Tange's work of this period—Hiroshima Peace Memorial Center, Tokyo Municipal Building (1952–1957), and Kagawa Prefecture Municipal Building (1955–1958)—was based upon principles of modern design, as solidly as that of Oscar Niemeyer in Brazil or José Luis Sert then in the United States. But the buildings nevertheless appear Japanese only insofar as within their three-dimensional volume is an inscription of Japanese traditional composition with its exposed columns and beams. Now it was no longer necessary deliberately to superimpose, or layer, these two different orientations. Thanks to the history of struggle and debate since the 1930s, conviction had grown in Japan by the early 1950s that the architectonic of steel and reinforced concrete could be smoothly translated into the proportional system long ago developed in Japanese traditional wooden architecture. Its role was to replay the principles of modern architecture within a space of Japanese origin. Likewise, sliding partitions and curtain walls assume the play of *fusuma* and *shōji* in order to render a transparent Japanese space.

The 1960 *Katsura* book directly reflected the aesthetic of that time now nearly half a century ago. Both Tange's text and Ishimoto's photographs attempted forcibly to discover and express the compositional beauty of contemporary space in the revered buildings of Katsura. The elements for which Taut and Gropius had contempt—the great cycad trees and the stone arrangements near Shōkin-tei teahouse—are reduced to mere detail in order to refabricate Katsura in the modernist taste.

Near the end of the 1950s, after having realized a quintessential modern architecture in reinforced concrete, Tange began to look for a new direction. From the early to mid-1950s, one of the prime models for contemporary architects had been the exposed, untreated steel post-and-beam structure that evolved in Europe and was first brought to America by Gropius and Mies van der Rohe. Next came Le Corbusier's new postwar manner, soon to be labeled new brutalism, where form-faced reinforced concrete was the common marker. This shift had once again to be reinterpreted in Japan's own context. The steel frame could be associated with aristocratic court taste, while unrefined concrete could be deemed to reflect the vitality of the masses (cf. chapter 3). Forced to choose between the two, as it were, near the end of the 1950s, Tange began to seek a new style emphasizing reinforced concrete. His essay in *Katsura*, "Tradition and Creation in Japanese Architecture," downplays an aristocratic Katsura and discovers instead an image of Katsura that belongs to the masses—pointing, unexpectedly, to a domain beyond modernity.

In this long essay there is only the briefest description of Katsura itself. The bulk of the text is dedicated to an analysis of two contradictory phases in ancient Japanese cultural history: the so-called Jōmon and Yayoi. Noting both these conflicting tendencies to be present in Katsura, Tange stresses the requirement of a new dialectical synthesis to lead that tradition to creativity. For him, the significance of Katsura now lies in the very energy generated by such a collision.

Accordingly, *Katsura* stresses two aspects: a flat composition with lightness afforded by the aspect of the *shoin* ensemble, and the broken meter of the rough surface cut out of garden stones. Upon publication, these images appeared to revolutionize all interpretation of Katsura, as well as the domain of architectural photography itself. Meanwhile, Tange was transforming his own work in line with this refreshed representation of Katsura, from the tranquil composition of the court style to a certain dynamic expressionism (which, to me, pertains less to the masses than to the *samurai* class). In retrospect, Tange's new turn seems to prefigure the rapid economic growth of the 1960s and the candidness of its impact on culture.

For a quarter of a century (from the 1930s to the 1960s), Katsura appeared and reappeared in the purview of contemporary architecture at crucial junctures, each time with a changed countenance. For those Osaka architects who had set the stage for Taut's intervention, Katsura had offered a fulcrum to protect modernist design from the onslaught of conservative eclecticism. For Sutemi

Horiguchi, it was an exercise ground upon which to test his logic bridging the gap between the modern and the national, Western and Japanese. For Tange, beginning in the late 1950s, it became a fresh battlefield, where Jōmonesque and Yayoiesque aesthetics collided, empowering a fresh creative moment. Katsura was the same Katsura, but the devices for reading that each architect constructed had functioned differently in diverse contexts.

After the 1960s, research into Katsura became increasingly advanced and sophisticated. But there have been no further accounts by architects. Now that the situation has changed[18] and the character of modernism itself has been transformed, a new interpretation should be attempted. To begin with, I would like to suggest an oddly assorted and perhaps obscure analogy, that of the different styles of the tea ceremony appearing over the history of its evolution. Bruno Taut's reading is like the tea of Murata Jukō (1422–1502), who studied under the Zen monk Ikkyū and intentionally introduced Zen elements into tea. Just as Jukō initiated the so-called *wabi-cha*, the tea ceremony performed in the four-and-a-half-*tatami*-mat room, Taut shed the first light on Katsura. Sutemi Horiguchi's reading is like the tea of Sen no Rikyū (1522–1591). Horiguchi was himself a scholar of Rikyū, in the first place. But, what is more, Rikyū bravely alternated between contradictory aesthetic systems, conceiving both the tea ceremony in a rustic mountain hut and an opposed ritual with gorgeous accouterments, like gold, for Osaka Castle. Horiguchi similarly read and interpreted Katsura as a space where contradictory elements that beggar assimilation cohabit. Finally, Tange's reading is like the tea of Furuta Oribe (1543–1615). As Oribe transformed the ceramic tea vessel by inscribing it with eccentric patterns and pushing it toward varied anomalous forms, Tange considered Katsura to be an example of self-conscious destruction—produced by a collision of contradictory cultural elements—leading paradoxically to creation.

If we extend this line of analogy, the next reading of Katsura should be like the tea of Kobori Enshū (1579–1647). He is our protagonist in the next chapter who, without necessarily discovering anything new, confronted all the techniques and accumulated knowledge of tea, freely selected his favorites (*konomi*), and regrouped these into a rather daring new system, occasionally even risking kitschification. For a new generation, no longer able to behave heroically like Tange, Enshū's tea seems to offer the only viable approach. In my vision of this reading, Katsura would appear a convergence of anagrams, containing infinite possibilities of arrangement. This latter-day Katsura could display as many features as we solicit, in obedience to our choice of conceptual matrix that would cut across the whole. In this textlike space there is no hierarchy, no specifiable order among its terms.

Katsura's Ambiguity

Katsura's main trait is that it has no clearly defined, dominant form or style. As I already explained, a number of design methods are intermingled in both buildings and garden. Thus any discussion of Katsura must face the task of deciphering the ambiguity created by this mix.

In early seventeenth-century Japan, two styles of residential architecture coexisted side by side. One was *shoin-zukuri*, developed since the medieval period—mainly in residences of the *samurai* class and in abbots' living quarters within temples. Since *shoin-zukuri* was based upon the *kiwari* proportional system evolved and perfected by medieval carpenters, it remained under the supervision of the great master carpenters (*dai-tōryō*). Its virile and authoritarian aesthetic matched the taste of those *samurai* who had been eager to display their newly acquired social standing. The ultimate formality of the style might be compared to the refinement of the Western classical orders. The second style of residence was *sukiya-zukuri*, which afforded a less formal and more flexible manner of building, although at first within the *shoin* canon. Unaffected by sumptuary regulations, it came to be used for the residences of commoners and in a more extreme form for *sōan*-style teahouses. This development reflected the personal tastes of each building's owner, or more precisely, the communication between proprietor and carpenter. I would call this a style that exhibits a sense of *ad libitum* or "free-style" classicism. During the seventeenth century, it rapidly spread to townhouses (*machiya*) for merchants as well as to the secondary residences (*betsugyō*) of *samurai*.

Conceived in an epoch when the two styles still overlapped, Katsura shared characteristics of both. Its main buildings are always referred to as such-and-such *shoin*, whose plans exhibit the attributes of *shoin-zukuri*. However, the *kiwari* proportional system is not always the one established by the great medieval carpenters; elevations and ornament lean toward *sukiya-zukuri*—in other words, the subtle combination of both makes it hard to characterize the style precisely. A plethora of discourses has resulted.

Teiji Itō's description of Katsura begins with an authoritative reconsideration of the main architectural categories: *shoin-zukuri* is based upon a module spanning center to center between columns (*shinshin-chūkan-sei*), while the module of *sukiya-zukuri* measures instead the profile-to-profile interval between columns (*uchinori-chūkan-sei*). Thus by definition, components of Katsura that employ the center-to-center system in *shoin* cannot belong categorically to *sukiya-zukuri*. Katsura mostly exhibits the medieval *kiwari* proportional system inherent in the still earlier but now little discussed *shuden-zukuri* (main palace style); but at the same time, certain *sukiya*-like features evoking traits of the much later tearoom are also introduced. Itō then goes on to explain this stylistic cohabitation by way of the political conditions of the time. In the early years of the Tokugawa shōgunate, the de facto government based in Edo, the prince of the Hachijō Imperial Family was one of the members of the imperial court, in Kyoto, who insisted on keeping up an anti-Tokugawa position. The latter was frequently expressed in the prince's dislike of the *samurai* aesthetic and his inclination toward the taste of the urban populace (*machi-shū*), including their residential version of *sukiya-zukuri*.[1]

Itō's view was partly formed by the historian Tatsusaburō Hayashiya's influential thinking on the culture of the Kanei era (1624–1644). Hayashiya paid utmost attention to the design of a famous and large assignation house, Sumiya (Corner House), in the old red-light district of Kyoto, certain rooms of which have affinities with the various teahouses at Katsura.[2] He seized on this rapport between an aristocrat's villa on the outskirts of the capital and the downtown urban entertainment district, a locale where artists and artisans in the regular employ of town dwellers rubbed shoulders with courtiers, themselves in conflict with the shōgunate. These nobles, having once held power in medieval times, then ousted by the shōgunate, now formed a kind of popular front with elements of the urban populace centered on the merchant class, against the ever-expanding power of the *samurai*.

A second line of interpretation is Hirotarō Ōta's. According to him, as long ago as the Nara period (710–784), aristocrats forced to dwell in the capital envisioned construction of rustic villas of unfinished timber (*kuroki-zukuri*) in the surrounding mountain villages. The notional aesthetic of such a dreamt-of lifestyle later served to facilitate an eventual merger between the rustic *sōan*-style teahouse and the rule-bound *shoin-zukuri* of postmedieval times. Accordingly, villa architecture at last began to introduce the features of the *sukiya* taste into actual *shoin-zukuri*. One of the earliest examples of the trend ever realized is believed by Ōta to be the Ko-shoin of Katsura itself.[3]

Akira Naito also stresses this vision of the mountain villa as a cultural production peculiar to aristocrats.[4] In 1615, the Tokugawa shōgunate issued ordinances to the imperial court and the nobility at large with intent to divest the court of all political power, while restricting its activities to mere "arts and sciences." In consequence, the culture of the Kyoto nobility from this time on was pushed toward a fictional elaboration. These aristocrats, who had long been nurturing a passion for rural life, began to concentrate on creating a pseudo-natural, fictive environment in agrarian areas near the capital. Katsura Villa is the epitome of such a culture, consecrated to the production of a fantasy life.

Lastly, Hidetoshi Saitō has pointed to the imprecision of the widely accepted notion of Katsura as "*shoin-zukuri* transformed into *sukiya-zukuri*." Saitō insists that Katsura can hardly be deemed a transformation from one style, like *shoin*, to another, but is instead a pure hybrid. He defines Katsura as a "*so-an*-like *shoin*," in other words a "*handsome* drawing room with *tatami*" (*kirei zashiki*), a characterization that suggests a *shoin* with certain improvised decorative elements.[5]

What is common to these four historical interpretations is that Katsura remains profoundly embedded in complexity—in terms of cultural genealogy, architectural style, political influence, and class-determined relationships—so that it is hard indeed to assign any single identity. Whether you plump for cohabitation, conflict, compromise, reconciliation, or synthesis of styles depends upon the imputed design discourse of the whole. Katsura is indeed charged with contradictory and conflicting codes, all signaling a number of messages. Such is Katsura's innate ambiguity.

The object of what follows is to grasp this expression of ambiguity by wandering through the real Katsura. It is not my purpose either to scrutinize the literature on Katsura in its entirety or to reconstruct the complex of buildings from a historical perspective. As an architect, I would like to intervene in imagination at the point in time when Katsura was conceived, built, and used. I hope thus to reexperience this historical conjuncture and shed light from the vantage point of the present.

The Flying Geese Formation

Through the painstaking disassembly and restoration completed in 1982, we learned that the *shoin* component of Katsura was erected in three different stages: first the Ko-shoin (Old Shoin), then the Chū-shoin (Middle Shoin), and finally the Gakki-no-ma (the Room of Musical Instruments) as well as the Shin-goten (New Palace, or New Shoin). These main elements are all placed facing the garden; there is a hidden route for household circulation behind the various rooms, connecting them to kitchens and servants' quarters at the rear. Each main room and its service spaces were built as a unit—reception room and utilitarian counterpart, a paired relationship constant through all stages of construction. This arrangement reminds one of Hadrian's Villa near Rome, where a circulation corridor along which servants were able to pass without being perceived by guests was hidden behind a colonnade.

The three-stage process is perfectly discernible in the layout of the buildings as they survive. Beginning from the Ko-shoin with its celebrated Moon-Viewing Platform (*tsukimi-dai*) (fig. 25.4) of bamboo, the Chū-shoin and the Gakki-no-ma were added, and finally the Shin-goten. All rooms face the pond at a uniform angle, whilst successively set back from right to left (as viewed from the pond). This layout is known as a flying geese formation (*gan-kō*) (fig. 26.1). Taken as a whole, the extension scheme produces an irregular and asymmetrical rhythm, likewise affording requisite light and ventilation.

But more importantly for our context, such a layout recalls the positioning of tea utensils during the tea ceremony, called *sumi-*

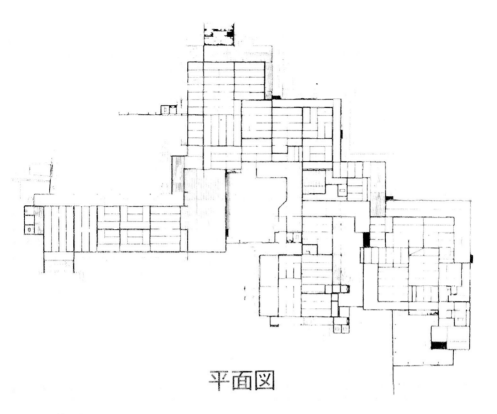

平面図

26.1 Plan of Katsura Villa *shoin*, illustrating diagonal of flying geese formation at top right. Moon-Viewing Platform, top middle.

kake[6] (corner arrangement) or *suji-chigai* (shifting streaks). It was perfected by such tea masters as Oribe and Enshū. Originally the latter expression denoted a way of placing certain utensils (for example, chopsticks) side by side at a uniform angle. Later on, it came to indicate a way of placing multiple objects in parallel on the diagonal.

The dynamism of the flying geese formation allows for a complex of buildings that might easily be aligned according to a more rigid formula to shift off axis by increments, to the eventual point of renouncing all symmetry and centrality. This was the way in which Katsura's varied façade was created. It is also the unique configuration that traditional Japanese builders evolved to express depth—by means of layered planes—in sharp contrast to

Western perspective, which marshaled depth of space toward infinity by taking the human gaze as central.

An example of the flying geese formation may also be seen at Nijō Castle in Kyoto. It is usually claimed that Enshū, as clerk of works, ordered the building of this castle for Emperor Gomizuno-o in 1625. But, in fact, the only parts that Enshū oversaw were the garden and the palace to accommodate the emperor's personal visits (*miyuki goten*). The *shoin* and the Main Hall, set in flying geese formation, were already in place and were just remodeled under Enshū's supervision.[7] The flying geese formation had become a familiar technique by the early seventeenth century. In the Ninomaru Shoin (the *shoin* in the second rampart) at Nijō Castle, the depth created by the flying geese formation objectifies a certain hierarchy, a spatial sine qua non for the military apparatus of *samurai* society. The greater the depth at which rooms were situated, the higher was their status and the more luxurious and elaborate their décor, reflecting restriction of access. From the time of its foundation, the Tokugawa shōgunate made use of a hierarchy of display, and the architectural device of successive setbacks offered an ideal model.

Even though the layout at Katsura reflects this same device, the intent and use were unlike Nijō. To begin with, what the Imperial Prince Toshihito first had in mind was only the Ko-shoin with its service quarters; the pond, too, was much smaller than today, arranged around its central islets referred to as Shinsen-tō (Islands of the Godly Sage), and at the time having the same northwest-southeast orientation as the Katsura River. Expansion began with the addition of the Chū-shoin by Toshihito's son Prince Toshitada. At the beginning he probably did not plan, nor could he have ever imagined, the extent of the present-day flying geese formation. He simply added the Chū-shoin to the Ko-shoin using the *sumi-kake* (corner joint) concept, that is, setting the new construction at right angles. The manner of connecting these two *shoin* reminds me of how the Bōsen Tearoom and the Jikinyū-ken Shoin are connected at the Kohō-an, a minor temple in the vast Daitoku-ji complex in Kyoto (see chapter 27 and fig. 27.1). Extracted from quite different locales, the latter were reassembled by Enshū.[8] In the junction he created, what is remarkable is the articulation of the void of the *fukihanachi-en* (open veranda) by a sash-oriented *shōji* screen inserted in the upper part of its west frontage.

From the outset, the Ko-shoin at Katsura was positioned to face the pond at an angle of 19 degrees to the southeast. Clearly, this orientation was ideal for contemplating the reflection of the mid-autumn moon in the pond—a cultural icon of the Japanese tradition accompanied by festivities.[9] Later, the Chū-shoin was attached at right angles rearward of the older *shoin*, therefore away from the pond. This increased the number of apertures available on the southeast side. Thus both rooms face the garden but with different points of view.

When Prince Toshitada planned the final extension, that is, the addition of the Shin-goten, it is probable that he had the flying geese formation of the *shoin* at Nijō Castle in mind. But, if so, why would a prince of the imperial family incline to the aesthetic of the *samurai* class? His father Toshihito—founder of the family branch—was uncle to Emperor Gomizuno-o, and also his advisor, especially in matters of conflict with the shōgunate. He had, therefore, been entirely on the side of the imperial court and the emperor. But his son, Prince Toshitada, lived in a different climate. His wife Princess Fū was of the powerful Maeda *samurai* clan; furthermore, since childhood, he had been a playmate of the future third shōgun Iemitsu. In this generation, the imperial household and *samurai* society were at last moving closer together. In other words, Toshihito had conceived Katsura as emblematic of the cultural atmosphere of the ancient imperial court, yet the shift of power was suddenly such that Katsura might also be interpreted as evidence of Toshihito's contempt of *samurai* power. The hegemonic tensions between the shōgunate and the court were gradually resolved in a victory for the shōgunate following the death of retired emperor Gomizuno-o. Kyoto was left as capital—no longer of real power, but only of the arts and of learning. Brought up in this climate, Toshitada no longer had to compete with or deny *samurai* power. Rather he began to introduce the *samurai* aesthetic into his own life and was secure in borrowing the device of the flying geese formation, once used as a mark of *samurai* order at Nijō Castle and elsewhere.

The combined length of the extension of the Shin-goten and the Gakki-no-ma together is just about equal to that of the Ko-shoin and the Chū-shoin. In this final phase of expansion, then, the ground plan was doubled. And nothing could have proven more appropriate than the flying geese formation for the extension of the new buildings, since it offered the ideal way to preserve and widen the view of the garden. What is more, looking from the garden side, one does not feel the redoubled size of the ensemble. Drifting over the smooth lawn on the left, our gaze yields to the pleasurable sensation of depth achieved by the successive setbacks. The flying geese formation here was apparently applied in response to the unplanned and evolving nature of the project. The expression of *samurai* hierarchy is here deconstructed to become the expression of a purely aesthetic aim.

The detail of these *shoin* appears particularly elegant and light, owing in part to the fact that each southeast-facing façade conceals a subtle discrepancy. The Ko-shoin is set atop a platform, while the level of the Chū-shoin's floor is raised ever so slightly higher by means of stilts; yet it gives one the impression of being significantly higher on account of the change in support. As for the Shin-goten, the floor level is lowered, but the roof treatment is somewhat different from that of the Chū-shoin: a narrow transom-like wall is interpolated between eaves and *shōji*. Because the incline and camber of all the roofs are uniform, the roof of the Shin-goten, whose area is greater, rises considerably above that of the Chū-shoin. This creates variety in the overall play between the roofs and the façades they surmount. As mentioned earlier (and portrayed in *A Panoramic View of Prince Katsura's Country House*), all verandas were formerly open, with *shōji* set back to the inner edge of the porch. But now, in the Chū-shoin and the Shin-goten, the *shōji* are installed at the outer edge of each veranda, with a consequent emphasis on the volume of their respective façades. Thus, the darkness of the open verandas of the Ko-shoin and Gakki-no-ma and the bright flush surface of *shōji* in the Chū-shoin and Shin-goten sets up an alternating rhythm of contrast— making the component layers of flying geese more intricate and compelling.

The overall diversity of elevation treatments was not altogether intended at the start. For that matter, the Shin-goten was not constructed *ex novo* on site; it was relocated from elsewhere and merely reassembled. As placement of *shōji* screens was altered in later times, the configuration of elevations represents a flexible response to shifting conditions. Plans as well as elevations are full of minute discrepancies that may easily escape attention. All these are embedded in our final impression: a supremely harmonious continuum of raised-floor, one-story buildings. But it is these very discrepancies that undo any impetus toward standardization by their subtle euphony, inducing in the spectator a wave of pleasure.

A Layered Space

From the moment we enter the Ko-shoin, we are impressed by the transparency of its interior. The surrounding *shōji* soften the incoming sunlight, now gently edging its way into all the corners and back rooms of the structure. The Ko-shoin comprises five rooms: a porch called *Okoshiyose* (imperial carriage stop), the Veranda Room, the Room of the Spear (*Yari-no-ma*), a Second Room, and a First Room. These are mostly divided by *fusuma*, on whose gesso-like white surface great paulownia crests embossed in golden mica glisten as they gather light. The indigo lines of the cotton *tatami* edging, the black-lacquered edges of the *fusuma*, and the darkness of the aged columns and lintels crisscross this shining volume. These verticals and horizontals afford modular guidelines that articulate the entire three-dimensional space, creating a sense of infinity. The whole yields something like an impression of the variable space based upon a homogeneous module that modernist architecture took as its premise. It is no surprise that modernists have shown a particular appreciation for the Ko-shoin.

A similar sense of transparency pervades the Chū-shoin. Nonetheless, here we find more colorful and representational elements: India ink paintings on the *fusuma* screens and on the wall in the *tokonoma*, light green edging along the *tatami*, and red-lacquered edges for the sliding *fusuma*. To our eyes that have just absorbed the yellowish earth colors of the Osaka mud wall and the wall of indigo-dyed mulberry paper in the Hearth Room (*irori-no-ma*), these new elements appear natural and mild, and the whole space still feels transparent.

But the Shin-goten offers a quite different impression. There is no longer any systematic division by way of *tatami* mats and *fusuma* screens. Instead, there are a number of original devices for assemblage and display, namely grouped shelves-and-cabinets (*chigaidana*), whose degree of elaboration gradually increases and reaches its zenith at the dais of the First Room. To the right of the comb-shaped *shoin* window are the famous "Katsura shelves" made of precious woods as varied as *kokutan* (ebony), *tagayasan* (Bombay black wood), and *kyara* (aloe wood). In the lateral wall of the *tokonoma* in the Second Room is a lobed opening cut in the shape of the *mokkō* emblem. In the Dressing Room are enclosed Katsura shelves for the storage of clothing. In the Bedchamber is a famous diagonal shelf covered with a fabric of *moji* weave for storing swords. The *tatami* mats of that room are edged in light green silken fabric from the Koryō dynasty of Korea. A particular section of each room, usually a corner area, is decorated in a particular way to specify its use. This series of décors has the effect of grading the rooms, from the Veranda to the Bedchamber and, finally, to the dais of the First Room; however, it is not as systematic a categorization as that used in the *shoin* at Nijō Castle. Although most partitioning is by sliding *fusuma*, there are also some fixed walls here. But thanks to the cutout windows and latticework in the transoms, the entire space feels open, streaming from the outermost rooms to the deepest dais. Like the Ko-shoin, the whole Shin-goten, with its peripheral *shōji*, is pervaded by a filtered light that reaches even the deepest corners, after having been gently reflected innumerable times. All the same, the complex structure of shelves and cabinets manages to create deposits of darkness in certain far corners.

In contrast to the transparency of the Ko-shoin ruled by its unitary system, the main effect of the Shin-goten is a graduated opacity that is articulated by its layers of varied design—although in general both structures obey the formulae of *shoin* architecture. While the Shin-goten exhibits certain deviations from standard *shoin-zukuri*, it should not be blindly categorized as *sukiya-zukuri*, as was sometimes done in the past. Therefore, to describe the heterogeneity, or the transitional nature, of development "from *sōan*-like *shoin* to *sukiya*," it was proper that Hidetoshi Saitō used the unusual term *kirei-zashiki* (*handsome* drawing room with *tatami*) instead. In the strictest sense, the Shin-goten would be a *sōan*-like *shoin* affected by the new decorative quality of *kirei-zashiki*.

In the context of modernist appraisals, the transparency of the Ko-shoin supplied a focal point from the beginning. Its graceful elegance skillfully decomposes the strict *kiwari* proportions of the *buke shoin* (*shoin* appropriate to the *samurai* residence), which are grandiose yet staid. Remarkably, the Ko-shoin can be reckoned both *ōchō-teki* (ancient-court-like) and *sōan-teki* (thatched-cottage-like), thanks to its transparency and basic simplicity. Its pure linear composition without any representational detail must have appeared ideal to modernists, intent on conjuring an abstract space out of mere planes and lines. The glistening décor of the Shin-goten, on the other hand, must have appeared to them excessive and degenerate.

A quarter of a century has passed since this modernist interpretation peaked, and now[10] the complex and opaque design of the Shin-goten is being resurrected—offering in its original splendor a new fascination. During the intervening period, our model of thinking has changed. The shining paradigm of vintage modernism has been challenged, while an atmosphere affirming heterogeneity and its symbiosis of contradictions fills the air. That is to say, ambiguity has returned as a new paradigm. As I mentioned earlier, it is of interest that Katsura, too, required a quarter century, three centuries ago, to achieve its latter phase of extension (from Chū-shoin to Shin-goten). During that time, the inclination of designers must have shifted in a way that parallels our new postmodern zeitgeist.

After the death of the head of the Hachijō Imperial Family, Toshihito, in 1629, Katsura was left intact but deserted. Presumably it was around 1641, the year in which his heir Toshitada became engaged to Princess Fū, that renovation commenced. The Chū-shoin was undertaken first, and, thereafter, reconstruction proceeded quickly. One record states that by 1649, there were five new teahouses.[11] Toshitada ordered this work done when still in his twenties. But it was only in his later years that the construction of the Shin-goten was begun. It is generally assumed that by 1663, when retired Emperor Gomizuno-o visited Katsura, the ensemble was complete—but Toshitada had died a year earlier, at the age of forty-four.

During the interval between these two building campaigns, the taste of the time shifted from clear, simple principles to a preference for more ambiguous space. Enshū had designed a garden retreat (Sendō Palace) for former Emperor Gomizuno-o around 1627–1630. The teahouse there was in the style called cha-zashiki[12]—in whose shoin-style room, not only was the bark of the wood left intact, as in the sōan style, but at the same time a comb-shaped window and complex compositions of shelves appear. It has been said that such a combination already presages the advent of full-blown *sukiya*. At any rate, the most common tendency of this period is an eclectic juxtaposition of forms and styles derived from different sources. The mix is exemplified in Konchi-in at Kyoto, built between 1627 and 1633, with its diverse points of reference—the Tōshōgū mausoleum that enshrines Ieyasu, founder of the Tokugawa shōgunate, a type of abbot's quarters called *hōjō* based upon the orthodox *kiwari* proportion system of *shoin* style, and the so-called *kakoi chaya* (enclosed tearoom) established within a *shoin* by a folding screen (*byōbu*). Moreover, the production of *zashiki* (formal room with *tatami* mats) in *shoin* was henceforth affected and transformed by various elements of the *sōan* (thatched cottage). The same phenomenon has also been called *sukiya-teki-shoin* (*sukiya*-like-*shoin*) or, recently, *kirei-zashiki* (*handsome* drawing room with *tatami*), as defined by Hidetoshi Saitō. This was the trend that came to be favored by nobles of the court centered around former Emperor Gomizuno-o. With its lightness and splendor, far from the *samurai*'s heavy-handed authoritarian style of décor, the Shin-goten of Katsura was its ultimate achievement.

The *sōan* element in Japanese architecture may even be said to correspond to the rustic vogue for cottage-inspired suburban villas during the early industrial age in the West, while we have observed that the *kiwari* proportioning of *shoin* was, in its origins, more like the Western classical orders. The purest example of the classical Renaissance palazzo is the so-called house of Raphael (Palazzo Caprini) in the Borgo at Rome designed by Donato Bramante (1510). The ground floor of the building abutting the street is of courses of rough-hewn stone piled atop one another (the so-called *alla rustica* manner). But the *piano nobile* exhibits evenly spaced, paired Tuscan columns. Here layered and contrasted are the rough and the rustic united in a sophisticated, urbane order. This same juxtaposition eventually achieved a merger in Giulio Romano's Palazzo del Te at Mantua (1526–1533), where a new phantasmagoric order was effected. From the mid-sixteenth century, the order metamorphosed by *rustica* treatment was adopted as a matrix for fantastic architecture throughout the West.

In a way similar to that in which in the West the *rustica* manner had challenged the orders and sublimated them at the level of fantasy, the *sōan* aesthetic helped to realize the fiction of a rustic lifestyle among urban-dwelling aristocrats in Japan. Although it is

possible to point to this as the product of a Kyoto culture surrounding former Emperor Gomizuno-o, it would nevertheless be
inaccurate to call it anti-*samurai*. The related aesthetic known as
kirei-sabi (gorgeous humbleness)—clearly a paradoxical notion—
was created by Enshū, himself born into a *samurai* family. The
kirei-sabi tearoom quickly spread to villas of the *samurai* class and
also to Japanese garden design in general; it eventually took root
even in town dwellings, in the guise of *sukiya-zukuri*. It was the
sōan-style ceremonial tearoom with its thatched roof that triggered
this metamorphosis.

Confronting this tendency, Katsura's position is thoroughly
transitional (or, so to speak, ambiguous). Katsura was almost complete at a moment just prior to the stage when the elements of the
sōan-style tearoom were systematized as *sukiya*. In other words, its
design submitted to the process by which the standard *shoin* style
was being deconstructed using *sōan*-style elements. Thus, Katsura
is Janus-like, and may appear as either *shoin* or *sukiya*, according
to the viewpoint of the observer.

In the Shin-goten (New Shoin) are the shelves, the shaped
windows, and apertures that belong to the *Enshū-gonomi*. These
disjunctive elements are deliberately inserted into that floating
space created by the uniform filtering of daylight through *shōji*, in
order to create wells of darkness here and there. The different systems are superimposed in such a way as to create surprising spatial
relationships. After the final achievement of the *sukiya* style, its
heterogeneity was assimilated as a familiar code (eventually a species of kitsch)—happily at Katsura, contingency still operates at a
level that can still produce actual surprises.

The Touring Gaze

Just as Katsura's array of *shoin* comprises two principal styles, so its
garden involves a shift from one style to another, that is, from a
garden of the ancient imperial court taste used for boating and
other recreation to an early modern garden designed for strolling,
and again boating. In a sense, the flying geese formation has prepared us for this process of outside transformation. In conformity
with the architectural layout, the garden can be divided roughly
into three zones, knit together by garden paths as well as by the
water system.

Until Prince Toshihito first conceived the building project at Katsura sometime after 1615, he seems to have had in mind little more than a simple teahouse in a squash patch located in the mountains outside Kyoto. The Ko-shoin (Old Shoin) we know today seems almost to match this initial plan. The original pond was certainly much smaller than today, containing only the central islets. Still, this area shows vestiges of the front garden inherent in ancient *shinden-zukuri* planning, including the elegantly curved lines of its pond. This kind of garden plan customarily spread white sand in front of a broad veranda, beyond which a pond was excavated. In the pond, a miniature archipelago would be built up with bridges connecting the islands to each other and to the garden beyond. There was a splendid barge—with a bow that joined the shape of a dragon's head and a phoenix's neck (both Chinese mythological creatures)—moored on the pond, and on board banquets were held.

The Katsura property had been the site of a former villa of the aristocrat Fujiwara Michinaga and, in fact, some of the chapters in the *Tale of Genji* are set here. I imagine that Prince Toshihito began his Katsura project in part as a mountain-hut-style villa, but also with the venerable literary association in mind. He was well versed in the *Tale of Genji*, especially those episodes dealing with the former estate. At the time he took it over, the whole must have been dilapidated, but the remains probably still hinted at all the splendors of an ancient garden,[13] and it is likely that Prince Toshihito considered reviving the time-honored court recreation of boating here. In the original form of the Katsura garden produced by Toshihito, there is said to have been a *sōan* hut called *Chiku-rin-tei* (bamboo grove arbor). Sitting in the cottage, one was supposedly able to look out over the Katsura River to the mountains in the distance. This was clearly very different from today's configuration.

Later the garden was extended in two directions: to the northeast, the area that fronts the Shōkin-tei (pine and *koto* arbor) Teahouse, and to the southwest, the zone facing the Shōi-ken (laughing mind arbor) Teahouse. These extensions were executed in different styles, but both must have been overseen by Toshihito. In the northeastern area facing the Shōkin-tei is a narrow promontory known as *Ama-no-hashidate*, arranged using a particular technique of stone placement that recalls an actual site well known since ancient times—the sandbar of the same name near Wakasa Bay in Fukui prefecture, the native country of Prince Toshihito's wife, Joshōin. At the same time elaborate stone arrangements delineate a pathway (*roji-niwa*) from the Waiting Bench (*Okoshikake*) by the Imperial Gate (*Miyuki mon*) to the ceremonial tearoom (*kakoi*) of the Shōkin-tei Teahouse, overlooking the so-called Swastika Arbor (*Manji-tei*) on one side. By contrast, to the southwest, the pond facing the Shōi-ken is shaped into a narrow, almost linear rectangle with cut stones configuring the shorelines, the whole area neatly organized on geometric principles. The Plum Riding Ground (*Ume-no-baba*) in front of the Shin-goten is a wide, open lawn, providing a broad view to the southwest. The entire open, flat, uncluttered zone contrasts sharply with the elaborate construction at the northeast end of the pond.

Diverging from the ancient-court-like (*ōchō-teki*) atmosphere of the area around the central islets, these two garden extensions evoke the first stages of modernity. Here once more, the inspiration may have been borrowed from the "garden of retreat" at Sendō Palace designed by Enshū for retired Emperor Gomizuno-o. The technique of stone arrangement used near *Ama-no-hashidate* is reminiscent of that found in the similar promontory at Sendō Palace and is clearly in *Enshū-gonomi* (Enshū taste). What is more, the rectilinear composition in front of the Shōi-ken Teahouse also recalls the geometrical edging used to protect pond and stream banks at Sendō Palace—it is built of hewn stone. There is no direct evidence of imitation; however, if we consider the fact that the last stage of Katsura's extension was intended for entertaining former Emperor Gomizuno-o, who cherished his life at Sendō Palace, it becomes impossible to ignore these affinities. All in all, the extension of the garden expresses *Enshū-gonomi* as precisely as does the design of the Shin-goten.

As we have seen, the garden consists of elements created at different times and following a variety of design methods. What connects these is our gaze as we stroll through the ensemble. Like our gaze that navigates the flying geese formation of the *shoin*, our gaze in the garden is displaced from the center, at various junctures, before continuing on its way. And it is the stroll route that interweaves these aspects and synthesizes our visual experience.

On March 6, 1663, former Emperor Gomizuno-o paid a visit to Katsura. His itinerary is described as follows: he arrived after early morning rainfall. Having been greeted by members of the household, he took a walk in the garden, during which he visited its teahouses and enjoyed the views of the cherry blossoms as well as rare rocks. After having tea and sweets at the tea ceremony, he went back to the *shoin* and ate *udon* noodles. Next he was invited to go boating on the Katsura River, but the trip was cut short and the group returned to shore, because of difficulty in controlling the barge owing to the surge of current after the rain and a strong wind. It was decided to boat instead on the pond. Here again, tea and sweets were served, and poems presented to the former emperor on board. After returning to shore, dinner was served, and the company spent more time reciting poems and couplets. When the time came for people to go home, torches were lit all around.[14]

Taking the barge, whether in the Katsura River or on the pond, evidently was an important aspect of enjoying the garden. And in the age of the seventh head of the Hachijō Imperial Family, Prince Yakahito, boating was still in vogue.[15] In family records of this period, the land route of the garden tour is also described: guests first came out of the *shoin* and strolled down into the garden. Passing the Plum Riding Ground, they went first to the Shōi-ken Teahouse. Then, from Firefly Valley, they passed the Shōkin-tei Teahouse, crossed over the stone bridge, and went to Cycad Hill. Then they retraced their steps for a short distance back to the Shōka-tei (flower appreciation arbor) Pavilion. Continuing, they went back along the Royal Path (*Miyuki Michi*) as far as the bank of the Katsura River, where they enjoyed a long boating excursion. Returning to the garden, they took a smaller barge out on the pond, where they recited poems, inspired by the two carefully shaped pine trees ashore—named for well-known trees at Takasago Jinja and at Sumiyoshi Jinja. Finally, as dusk was approaching, everyone went up to *Geppa-rō* (Moon Wave Turret) to admire the moon's reflection in the pond.

There are a number of such accounts describing Katsura, and most of them are centered on boating episodes, both in the garden and on the Katsura River. It is likely that the barge was modeled on roofed Tang-style vessels, with short curtains (*noren*) displaying the family crest. The barge was manifestly one of the elements of the scene when viewed from the land. Meanwhile, the garden itself was designed so that it could be viewed from various spots, either on land or from the water, and the touring route marked the ideal positions from which to gaze out upon it. The teahouses also have verandas from which to view the garden. Or, as a name with *rō* indicates, there are turrets from which to overlook the scene.

The site of *Geppa-rō* is a mound on which one can sit and look out at the surface of the pond from a higher position. In contrast to the Bamboo Moon-Viewing Platform of the Ko-shoin, from where the surface of the pond is seen as a horizontal extension, the view from the *Geppa-rō* comprises the central islets and the Shōkin-tei Teahouse in a more dynamic perspective. The difference in viewpoint from these two moon-viewing devices is significant. I have not had the chance to see the reflection of the moon from here, but I once tried to imagine what it might be like when observing the sun's reflection. Although it was a winter's day, a time of year when the sun was low, the light from the pond nevertheless reflected on the intricate structure of the underside of the roof of *Geppa-rō*, so that the roof truss, usually in shadow, was brightly lit. I believe that the moonlight must be reflected in a similar way. The bamboo rafters of the underside of the roof held up by a strange curved kingpin must seem animated in the wavering, eerily bluish moonlight.

The waiting benches and verandas of Katsura are all devices to fix our gaze, which would otherwise continue to drift. From the interior of the Shōkin-tei Teahouse, *Ama-no-hashidate* appears to stretch out horizontally, accentuated by the overhang of heavy eaves that effect a sharp, straight cut across the top of the view. From the Shōka-tei Pavilion, also sometimes called "teahouse on a mountain road," the gaze can follow the silhouette of the trees and enjoy the elegant meandering curve of the shoreline below. After mounting the stone steps at Shōi-ken, one obtains a broad, expansive field of vision from its deep verandas. And so on. By their varying ways of arresting the gaze of the viewer, these techniques of garden design fulfill diverse aims.

If the views from the teahouses are likened to pauses in music, the tour route linking these becomes a device to make us sense the changing scenery in all its continual ebb and flow. The path is made up of a variety of textures that regulate our way of walking and rhythm of breath: gravel, paving stones and stepping-stones laid in a series of patterns (called *shin* [formal], *gyō* [semi-informal], and *sō* [informal] in reference to calligraphy styles), bridges with various degrees of camber, stone stairways, slopes and so on. Such control, or more precisely contextualization, allows visitors to choose their own speed or vary their itinerary, all in determining the general orientation of their gaze.

While the touring route on land is composed in such a way that the gaze is constantly animated, the gaze from the barge moored on the pond is first fixed out over the water, limited to a horizontal span. As the barge proceeds, the scenery itself comes and goes. The guests are mostly still, except for the movements of having tea and sweets as well as writing and reciting poems.

The aim of establishing a tour route is to encourage the visitor to savor the entire garden as fully as possible. In terms of their devices, nearly all other Japanese gardens as well as Katsura are in striking contrast to the formal gardens of Europe. The formal European garden was constructed around a gaze fixed by one or more central axes, assuming the human gaze to rule the world. Scenery was arranged in the same manner as a single-point perspective assumes a central vanishing point. Thus the space unequivocally expands in depth as the visitor proceeds along the axis. In contrast, the gaze of the Japanese tour garden just as consistently refuses the fixation of any axis in space. The gaze is constantly on the move, while scenery is broken down into its parts, yet the tour route comprising both land and water segments deftly recombines these. In the same way that the flying geese formation expresses depth in space by a layering of shifted planes, the touring gaze first breaks down the scenery and then reassembles the parts in layers to reconstitute a complete cycle. Throughout the phases of its development, Katsura has discovered all kinds of ways to manipulate the touring gaze. Therefore, it offers no clear preplanned scheme, as do many other tour gardens. Instead, it is full of unexpected beauties materializing out of the residue of its diachronic composition.

Tissue of Quotation

Yet another essential aspect of Katsura is that in the details of its heterogeneous composition a number of literary allusions are fixed, thanks to Prince Toshihito's noted passion for poetry. He was well acquainted with the world of *waka*, having been initiated into the arcana of the *Kokin waka-shu* (Anthology of Old and New

Waka) by Hosokawa Yūsai (1534–1610), a *samurai* poet and founder of the early modern genre. I can well imagine the passion with which Toshihito intended to reconstruct the legendary site of the Katsura Palace, a principal setting in the *Tale of Genji*. Thus, for example, his own pleasure dome had also to be equipped with a moon-viewing turret.

In China there was a legend of a giant *katsura* (Judas tree) on the moon. It accounts for the pockmark visible on the moon's surface as being the figure of a man named Hshio from Wukang trying to cut down this tree—a legend that reached Japan, as just one of many, in early times. In addition the moon became an established metaphor for the longing for something, or someone, visible yet unobtainable. Book Four of the *Man'yōshu* contains a representative poem by Prince Yuhara:

> What shall I do with this woman
> Like the *katsura* tree in the moon
> That my eyes can see
> But my hands cannot touch?[16]

The moon and the *katsura* tree were thus coupled in the domain of literary allusion.

To take another instance, we still have those two remarkable pine trees, the Takasago and Sumiyoshi pines that once stood facing each other across the pond. The Takasago pine symbolized the *Man'yōshu*, where it is often mentioned, while the Sumiyoshi pine was emblematic of the *Kokin waka-shu*.[17] It is well known that the celebrated Noh play *Takasago* likewise makes mention of the Sumiyoshi pine tree. At Katsura the Sumiyoshi pine tree grows on a mound in the shape of a turtle located at the tip of a promontory, at the side of *Geppa-rō*. Nowadays it is only a small tree, but it used to be a giant. Nor is the present-day Takasago pine the original tree. The simulated beach near *Ama-no-hashidate*, at the end of which is a stone lantern, was once called Takasago beach, where it is thought that the Takasago pine originally stood. Sutemi Horiguchi, who endeavored to reconstruct the original garden at Katsura from its literary associations, wrote that, resembling the old man and the old woman characters in the Noh play *Takasago*, the Takasago and Sumiyoshi pines originally faced each other, with the great red-lacquered bridge between them.

Such literary allusions, however, posit elements that later on were to become clichés of Japanese culture. For example, the Buddhist-inspired central islets of the immortals soon came to be called Crane Island and Turtle Island, recalling the old notion that cranes live ten thousand years while turtles live a thousand, so that the islands are demystified to become mere markers of prosperity and long life. Assigning this simple kind of figuration to garden elements that otherwise might have lacked concrete association was practiced over the years as part of the design strategy. Resources for quotation were not always literary but sometimes had private meanings. *Ama-no-hashidate*, as well as the white-and-indigo checkered pattern on the sliding screens and the back wall of the *tokonoma* in the Shōkin-tei Teahouse, were designated to honor the respective birthplaces of the wives of the first and the second Prince—namely, the Wakasa and Kaga regions of Japan. Other naming devices, for instance in the teahouses, have today become clichéd. The Chinese characters for pine (*matsu/shō*), bamboo (*take/chiku*), and plum (*ume/bai*) are now commonly used to grade the quality of dishes or fixed menu in restaurants. By contrast and far more simply, the Shōkin-tei Teahouse was named specifically in association with a pine (*shō*) tree that once grew near it. The Chikurin-tei Teahouse, no longer extant, used to have a bamboo grove (*chikurin*) nearby. *Geppa-rō*, also called the "moon plum teahouse [*getsu-bai*]," had a plum tree next to it. What is more, the younger sister of Prince Toshitada was named Ume-no-miya, the Plum Princess.

Yet at the same time, all the names of these teahouses were, in the first instance, derived from topographical or literary sources. *Geppa-rō* (moon wave turret) comes from a poem by Po Chu-i, in which the moon figures as "a gem flickering in the heart of the waves." The name Shōkin-tei (pine *koto* arbor) is from the *Tale of Genji*: the chapter "Wind in the Pines," where flute and *koto* music embellish a feast at Katsura itself. Shōka-tei (flower appreciation arbor) displayed the shop curtain of a certain Tatsuta-ya Teahouse at its entrance, because the structure had been relocated from the main house of the Hachijō Imperial Family in northern Kyoto, where it occupied a site next to the well of Tatsuta. The *Onrin-dō* (garden grove mausoleum) is the mausoleum where portraits and ancestor tablets of the successive heads of the family were kept. Its name derives from a line of the Lotus Sutra: "the halls in the garden grove are blessed with many virtues and sublimated." The name Shōi-ken (laughing mind arbor) is associated with an old saying: "the twig, with its overflowing sense of spring, makes me smile," yet is at the same time a quotation from Li Po's *Question and Answers in the Mountains*:

> They ask me for what reason
> I live on Azure mountain,
> I laugh and do not answer
> Here my heart finds rest....

The moon-viewing platform (*tsukimi dai*) of the Old Shoin was also inspired by a line from the above-mentioned "Wind in the Pines" chapter of the *Tale of Genji*: "a village far down the river where the moon is clear, the *katsura* tree's shadow is serene." The designation Autumn Leaves Hill (Kōyō–san) is taken from a line by Po Chu-i: "the wisteria twines around the corridor, and the autumn leaves travel over the parapet." In fact, most names at Katsura are from either the *Tale of Genji* or the *Anthology of Po Chu-i's Poetry*, both being hugely influential in Japan at the time.

In the end, this tradition came to prescribe a set of themes for poetry recitation determined by the seventh head of the family, Yakahito: Katsura's Eight Sights (plum grove [*bai-rin*], flower garden [*ka-rin*], autumn leaves hill [*kōyō-san*], heaven's bridge gate [*Ama-no-hashidate*], pine of looking-back [*mikaeri-no-matsu*], beach stones [*hama-ishi*], streaming water [*ryū-sui*], stone bed [*tatami-ishi*], precious pine [*meishō-matsu*]), and the Katsura Three Windows (window for wind [*sō-fū*], window for moon [*sō-getsu*], window for lantern [*sō-tō*]). In addition were another Eight Sights for river-barge parties (river mist [*ka-sō*], flower appreciation [*shō-ka*], fireflies in the pond [*ike-botaru*], moon on the wave [*ha-getsu*], garden moss [*tei-mō*], snow on the barge [*sen-setsu*], bamboo grove [*chiku-rin*], and pine by the eaves [*ken-shō*]).

In an age when the recitation of poetry was inseparable from any garden outing, every authentic garden had to provide a gamut of themes appropriate to each season. Katsura's ingenious dissemination of such devices made the whole space a complex tissue of quotations. Just as the views from the tour route depend on spatial arrangements to trigger visual pleasure, these literary allusions work to extend this pleasure via the seduction of piecing together their origins. Thanks to such elaborate time/space stratification, the garden and buildings of Katsura are the equivalent of an extensive machine for arousing all our imaginative facilities.

The aim of the current essay is to return Katsura from the transparent and systemic contemplation of the modernists to its original nature as a contingent, confused and ambiguous, overlaid, and opaque composition. To this end, I have emphasized less those parts constructed by Toshihito that provoked nostalgia for the life of the court and an aristocratic aesthetic than the later extensions by Toshitada which more accurately reflect the taste of urban dwellers (whether commoners or *samurai*). This taste, defined as "gorgeous humbleness" in *Enshū-gonomi*, involves those "excessive" elements that in a modern age have frequently yielded to cliché.

All this is perfectly relevant to our current plight [in the mid-1980s] when architects are looking for a new model woven of heterogeneous quotation, a shift in approach that has gained ground by degree over the past quarter century. Meanwhile, the old modernist canon appears increasingly stifled by its tacit laws of exclusion as well as by its rule of composition based on mechanistic repetition. This current critique of modernism seems to hark back to the sixteenth-century Italian mannerists, those artists and architects who were able to create lighter and more heterogeneous designs by decomposing, distorting, and otherwise manipulating the formal principles of the Renaissance. Architecture today seeks to create a model that will recover the maneuvers excluded by modernism: namely, quotation from other domains compounded of heterogeneity, references to past historical styles, and a more decorative playfulness. It seems obvious that the new model has a marked affinity with those design methods employed by Toshitada in his Katsura extensions. By decomposing the rigid rules of *kiwari* proportion as established by master carpenters, his free-style spirit grasped the entire visual domain, so that every element at Katsura was committed to lightheartedness and pleasure.

Over time Katsura held the depth and potency to absorb and integate several changes of style. The clear, transparent composition perceived by modernists and the contradictory and heterogeneous bricollage now reengaging our attention attain a miraculous balance—one might say a mutual harmony—that induces a voluptuous pleasure going beyond, or at times swallowing up, all other discourse. The secret of Katsura's mythical, and myth-provoking, status lies here. In this sense, Katsura is indeed a classic.

Who was the author of Katsura? In fact, the question has long been closed, and that it was not Kobori Enshū is firmly established. More to the point, in premodern Japan, there was never an architectural designer as we understand the term today. For his part, Bruno Taut named Enshū as the designer of Katsura Villa, and until the 1930s that was the most commonly held view. Later scholarship has uncovered circumstantial evidence proving not only that there was no record of Enshū's involvement, but that his authorship would have been impossible. In consequence Taut's authority has been denied. Yet, in my own opinion, the entire issue is built around a blind spot, one concerned with the concept of authorship itself.

According to the scholar Isao Kumakura, during the Kanei era (1624–1644), which overlapped much of the period common to both Katsura's construction and Enshū's activity, Enshū was known solely as a tea ceremony master and as tea instructor to the shōgun (having succeeded Furuta Oribe). Then, some 150 years after Enshū's death, Matsudaira Fumai (1751–1818)[1] revived the so-called *Enshū-gonomi*. By that time, Katsura was already referred to as an example of Enshū's taste, for example, by the seventh head of the Hachijō Imperial Family, Prince Yakahito, in describing the garden. When in 1793 (Kansei 5) the Kohō-an temple and its Bōsen Tearoom were destroyed by fire, Matsudaira dedicated himself to their reconstruction, by which time his discourses on *Enshū-gonomi* were already well known. Much later still, in the 1910s, there was another peak of interest in Enshū's taste; this time the promoter was Masuda Don-no (1847–1938), a modern practitioner of the tea ceremony (*suki-sha*). Thus, by the 1930s, Katsura Villa was popularly revered as the epitome of Enshū's aesthetic.

My point here is that Taut was scarcely to blame for his mistake—he simply took for granted the common assumption of the time. Ultimately the issue is rooted in a discrepancy between the Western concept "architect" and Japanese reality vis-à-vis the concepts of *konomi* (taste), *saku* (making), and *sekkei* (design). In the West, authorship of a painting is founded in traces of the author's hand, whereby signature, writing, personal manner, and the like can all afford a basis for attribution. Customarily, sketches and external evidence also support verification of authorship, but what is at stake is the notion of originality. For Enshū, we recognize his holograph through signatures on wooden boxes containing his calligraphy or on memorial tablets, but this is of little use, since one did not at that time make presentation studies of buildings or gardens. Nevertheless, the National Diet Library owns a document relating to Konchi-in, which is reckoned a notable example of *Enshū-gonomi*. The priest/politician Ishin Sūden (1569–1633), who commissioned the building of this temple (see below), had the following to say about the stand-up plan/model (*tate-okoshiezu*) Enshū caused to be sent to him: "the *Enshū-gonomi* of the *sukiya* and its adjoining anteroom [*kusari-no-ma*] seems remarkably good."[2] While this confirms the document in question as an example of *Enshū-gonomi*, it does nothing to prove Enshū's authorship of it. Similarly, every important tea ceremony held at this time was recorded: namely, by the participants' descriptions and sketches of garden and tearoom, as well as of the arrangement of the tea utensils. There are indeed records of many of the tea ceremonies presided over by Enshū, which were thus not by the tea master but by his guests.

In such a cultural situation, there are no architects or garden designers as *producers* in the Western sense. This is the same problem I attempted to address with respect to the Tōdai-ji reconstruction said to be "by Chōgen." Enshū's official title was the equivalent of clerk of works to the Tokugawa shōgunate. This position would have assured his supervision of the Katsura project, in that he must have determined, or approved, the concept and direction of the design. Moreover, Enshū himself is thought to have been advised by specialists in building and garden design. So it is certainly he who controlled the whole project. But projects were not "designed" by Enshū, nor were the names of executants recorded. At the same time, the term *Enshū-gonomi* was coined and applied to various cultural products.

Taut's misinterpretation may be traced to the Japanese verb *konomaseru* and its derivative *konomi*. The former used to include the meaning "to make or to design," while the latter was equivalent to: "made by or designed by." Yet this was only approximate, since the locution means "in the taste of" or "in the style of." Taut must have taken the term literally as indicative of authorship at a time in Japan when the new concept of architecture was already becoming acclimated, thanks to study in Europe or even America. Thus modernized Japanese themselves had collapsed the idea of *konomi* into the notion of design, two concepts that approximate one another yet are not at all identical. In fact, this cultural difference defies assimilation or transposition.

When Taut wrote that Katsura was "functionalist" or compared Ise Jingū to the Acropolis, he was judging these two Japanese buildings from the vantage point of the Western concept of *architecture* with a capital A. But in Japan where there had been no such term until the modern period, these buildings were mainly respected as religious or cultural sites, being categorized at best according to building type: palace or shrine. They had never been judged as Architecture, for there had never been "architects" who struggled to uphold their work as a transcendental category. There had instead been carpenters who built buildings in accordance with the taste of certain patrons. They did not *design* as such. On the other hand, those who marked a given tendency, or design, as taste or style never used their hands (whether to draw or to build). Nor were they designers, either. In this country, no poetic of *architecture* had evolved out of a synthesis of craft and art. In such a context, Taut's judgment betrayed a quite radical misunderstanding.

Modernized Japanese architects tended to express embarrassment when confronted by Japanese traditional buildings that they felt were mostly wooden shacks. However, thanks to Taut's intervention, this inferiority complex was inverted. They garnered encouragment and then came to feel even a little superior. Thus the claims of Taut's authority spread, accelerated by the chauvinism of the times. Now that we can view this from a distance, we must stress yet again that Taut's intervention was truly epoch-making.

As mentioned earlier, Taut's discourse helped generate a binary opposition: Ise Jingū = *tennō*-esque = *honmono* (the real thing) versus the Tōshōgū in Nikkō = Tokugawa shōgunate = *ikamono* (kitsch). Yet this ended up largely reconfirming, if not actually expanding, the *tennō*-ist ideology first created in the Meiji period. Along with this political thrust, the new valorization of both Ise Jingū and Katsura Villa as Architecture produced a cultural impact both deep as well as lasting in the nation's mind. This resulted in a sort of reversed and belated projection *inherent in the reception of modernity*: a rediscovery that even such buildings as had been produced without any concept of architecture could now be Architecture, and that the Architect could somehow be interpolated, however anachronistically, between patron and master carpenter. This was the paradigm responsible for the illogical jump that in retrospect identified the person whose taste (or style) had influenced the building as its Architect. Thus Enshū became an "architect."

While in the case of paintings, it is possible to locate traces of authorship within the work, architecture has no site where these traces can be inscribed. Instead, *konomi* is identified by the name of its founder: that is, *Enshū-gonomi* or *Rikyū-gonomi*. In this case the proper name is not the author's but that of the inventor of a method or methodology. For instance, in *Matsuya Kaiki* (Record of Matsuya Fêtes)—one of the most elaborate of all documents pertaining to tea ceremonies in Japan between 1533 and 1650 recorded by three generations of the Matsuya family in Nara—we have descriptions such as "the soul of Enshū" or "of Enshū."[3] Osamu Mori claims these expressions as identical to "*Enshū-gonomi*."[4] However, I believe rather that the crux of the issue lies in the expression: "the soul of Enshū." This means that, by imagining and understanding what Enshū had in mind (his *design*), we can determine the form or style Enshū himself would have conceived: this does not require material evidence or the trace of the author's hand. If and only if we were able to identify the system constructed by the tea master's aesthetic or criterion of judgment could this lead us to a proper name. What counts is not the hand but the heart, not material evidence but an aesthetic judgment. The Western concept of "making" is derived from the Greek *technē* modeled upon craft. Opposed to this is the Eastern concept that stresses an aesthetic sense belonging to a cultured individual personality. So in Japan, where there was neither Art nor Architecture, when necessity to identify an author in the Western sense arose, the proper name representing a methodology was misconstrued as the name of the person directly engaged in production of the artifact.

It is perfectly correct to say that Enshū was not the author of Katsura Villa. But it is also correct to say that the *konomi*—the "system" and methods that may be discerned—was indeed Enshū's. This is to claim, in terms of a certain Japanese logic, that the design method that produced Katsura Villa is ultimately attributable to Enshū, therefore it is possible to call it "Enshū's *design*." But according to the Western view, Enshū did not design the architecture and the garden, so Enshū was *not* the designer. Here there is indeed a cultural gap. All of the commentators on Katsura Villa whom I have discussed—Taut, Horiguchi, and Tange—followed the Western procedure that seeks to identify an author by corroborative evidence. And, except for Taut, who paraphrased the commonplace wisdom of his time, Enshū's authorship was denied. For this very reason, no one could produce a context through which to scrutinize *Enshū-gonomi* aspects of Katsura. Belonging as I do, in many ways, to this same modernist mindset, I have nonetheless had to meta-criticique the twentieth-century readings of Katsura, and stress those aspects dropped by modernist readings, the very aspects that overlap those of *Enshū-gonomi*. So I would like here to reconsider these varied *Enshū-gonomi* aspects of Katsura in order to initiate a new reading.

Osamu Mori sets the attributes of *Enshū-gonomi* in different categories.[5] In the context of the teahouse: (1) The room should be a little larger than four *tatami* mats (four regular *tatami* mats and another that is half the regular size)—or else a little more than three *tatami* mats (three regular *tatami* mats and another that is half the regular size); (2) guests should be seated only to the right of the host; (3) there should be an additional room called the *kusari-no-ma* (adjoining anteroom) next to the main tearoom, where guests can enjoy looking at the tea utensils in a relaxed mood; (4) there are to be eight windows; (5) the proportion of a *shōji* grid should be one by two; (6) a picture should be placed at the focal point of the space.

In the context of garden and pathway: (1) The formal garden should use a good deal of cut stone to avoid any mimicry of nature; (2) there should be use of the *shakkei* technique (so-called borrowed landscape); (3) one ought to include symbols for prosperity and long life (such as the crane and turtle); (4) the use of older stone fixtures (such as lanterns) taken from a previous context is advised; (5) the *sumi-kake* technique of corner arrangement should be stressed.

Later on, Toshinori Nakamura redefined the above attributes in somewhat more abstract terms:[6] (1) A mixing of heterogeneous elements: artificial and natural, straight lines and curves, convex and concave, guests and host, and, in general, the use of various materials; (2) a simple and concise arrangement, with concentration at focal points where the gaze rests momentarily, *sukiya-zukuri* style; (3) formalization of floor elements: the *temae-za* (position where the host makes tea) is placed to the middle front of the guest seating, or the *temae-za* and the *tokonoma* may be parallel to each other in front of the seating area for guests, encouraging the host's performance to be read symbolically; (4) articulated composition of the garden, e.g., by planting flowering trees in the *nan-tei* (south garden)—literally, the area in front of the main palace, where white sand would normally have been placed on both sides of the entrance steps.

Perusing lists of *Enshū-gonomi* characteristics can be puzzling. Most of the ideas are nowadays to be found in any teahouse or garden claimed to be authentic. Today these are part of a shared visual language, and may even have become clichés of the teahouse and its garden. In this occurence, everything might be deemed *Enshū-gonomi*. If I may exaggerate for an instant, the concept of *Enshū-gonomi* subsumes all of what is generally referred to as Japanese taste, sensibility, or design. In other words, *Enshū-gonomi* took deep root and was generalized at some point, probably as a result of the boom in *Enshū-gonomi* during the Kansei (1789–1801) and Taisho (1912–1926) eras, pointed out by Isao Kumakura. At such moments, the taste or style was almost deified on the one hand, whilst being selectively polished on the other. It was pushed to an extreme stylization; that is to say, it was vulgarized and kitschified. It may even be more than a little true that at the origin of Japanese kitsch lies *Enshū-gonomi*.

As I mentioned, Hidetoshi Saitō characterized the design of Katsura as *kirei-zashiki*, a notion deriving from the inevitable distinction between *Rikyū-gonomi* and *Enshū-gonomi*. The former was the taste or style of Sen no Rikyū (1522–1591), the founder of ceremonial tea in Japan. *Rikyū-gonomi* was known as *wabi*, denoting the beauty to be found in poverty and simplicity. In contradistinction, *Enshū-gonomi* was called *kirei-sabi*, a conjunction of almost contradictory concepts: gorgeousness and elegant simplicity. What penetrates the whole of Katsura Villa—its garden and buildings constructed in stages—is the somewhat paradoxical concept of *kirei-sabi* (or *Enshū-gonomi*). The spread of this tendency appears in different times and places. For that matter, Enshū was himself a paradox of sorts: born a *samurai*, he studied Zen yet also loved ancient court culture. It may be thought natural that he discovered his *konomi* in diverse methods of garden design. If so, Katsura in the sense of *Enshū-gonomi* may be viewed as an "anthology" of resources, yet ruled by one and the same aesthetic. Indeed, it was verily woven as a tissue of quotation from the final vantage point of *Enshū-gonomi*.

Enshū had been born in the same year, 1579, as Toshihito, founder of the Hachijō branch of the imperial family. Each man began to learn *waka* and tea ceremony in his youth. Enshū served as *kinchū-sakuji* (clerk of works to the imperial court) for a while. It seems that he was fifty years old, around 1630, when he finally got the chance to realize his *konomi* in the construction of the Konchi-in complex at Nanzen-ji, a retreat designed for former Emperor Gomizuno-o. The priest Ishin Sūden, the advisor to the shōgun referred to above, hired Enshū to supervise its construction. By that time, the earlier part of Katsura Villa was already complete, and certain records of garden outings there had even been published. One among these, *Keitei-ki* (Record of the Katsura Residence) by Ishin Sūden himself, was written in a style full of affectation. Becoming somewhat popular, its text is nowadays displayed on the wall of the Ko-shoin, since it contributed to making Katsura known at an early date to the educated public. Support by this priest helped *Enshū-gonomi* to blossom. In other words, even before Enshū undertook the Konchi-in project, Katsura was known thanks to Sūden's writing.

Records tell us that Enshū visited the Hachijō Imperial Family. Admired as a tea master, it was quite natural that he had been invited there. Yet it is not impossible that Enshū was actually probing into the political connections of the various imperial family branches at the request of the anti-shogunate mastermind, former Emperor Gomizuno-o. In any case, it is safe to assume that Enshū did not engage in the design of Katsura. Rather, as I have indicated, after his death, *Enshū-gonomi* began to appear in the

Shin-goten and Gakki-no-ma, under the aegis of its second patron, Toshitada.

Enshū supervised a number of construction projects bridging shōgunate and court; more precisely, he was employed as clerk of works by the shōgunate to vet construction of buildings intended for court use. He worked on the Chamber for the Emperor's Visit (*gyōkō-no-ma*) at Nijō Castle, specifically destined for the unprecedented meeting of the third shōgun Iemitsu and then reigning Emperor Gomizuno-o. Although there are no traces of Enshū's hand, he would definitely have participated in the execution of such a project, owing to his official position and his aesthetic sense. Later, in the eighteenth-century revival of Enshū taste, it was sought to showcase the *Enshū-gonomi* elements throughout Katsura. At that time, it seems, an ideal type of *Enshū-gonomi* was encouraged in the mind of the viewer owing to efforts on the part of the seventh head of the family, Yakahito (see the end of the previous chapter). In other words, *konomi* had become a device for reading, independent of the object itself. The proper name attached to it, Enshū, became a sign, quite independent of the deceased individual. In this way *Enshū-gonomi* took on the character of an autonomous aesthetic.

It has been said that Enshū learned the importance of the *sumi-kake*, or *suji-kake*, method of the placement of tea utensils from Furuta Oribe, his master. Simply said, this means that when we place chopsticks, for instance, on the square hearth or on a dish, we place them diagonally across the corner. This simple maneuver introduces a perceptual shift and creates a dynamic composition. I believe that all the attributes of *Enshū-gonomi* Mori and Nakamura noted above may be summarized by the seemingly simple strategy of this diagonal shift. It comprises two distinct moments: one is the composition itself beyond any gaze consisting, as it does, of a pair of conflicting elements; the other is the advent of a dynamic focus that the body traversing the space discovers sequentially. The latter is the active, strategic aspect.

For instance, the Tai-an Teahouse, built by Rikyū in 1582 within the Myōki-an monastery in Kyoto, is considered the epitome of *Rikyū-gonomi*. It features an enclosed microspace with little margin for the visitor to move. A ghastly darkness hangs over this space, and the consciousness of the visitor drifts out of his body, falling into the netherworld. In contrast to this, the Bōsen Tea-

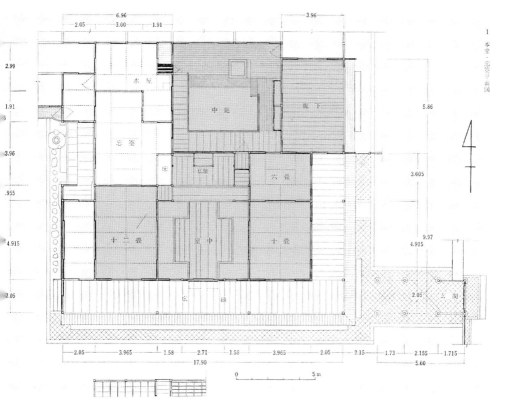

27.1 Bōsen Tearoom (rebuilt 1793), Kohō-an, Daitoku-ji, Kyoto, by Kobori Enshū; irregular twelve-mat area, plus verandah, and adjacencies, left unshaded in plan (mid-seventeenth century). Jikinyū-ken extends at upper left.

room at Kohō-an in the Daitoku-ji complex, which is deemed the epitome of *Enshū-gonomi*, is a diagonally open space (fig. 27.1). Placed at the corner of a passageway, the room is "open" in various manners: the sunlight passes through the *shōji* (fig. 27.2), is reflected from the wood-grained ceiling, and spreads over the narrow *tokonoma* as well as the tea-serving seat (*temae-za*). This event occurs at the very corner where the Kohō-an arbor and the Jikinyū-ken Shoin meet at right angles, where the gaze is directed simultaneously within and without.

The shift from *Rikyū-gonomi* to *Enshū-gonomi* is a transposition between different worlds—from darkness to sunlight, from an enclosed microspace to an open space, from centrality to a diagonal

27.2 View of corner setting of Jikinyū-ken garden from open west wall of Bōsen Tearoom (at middle left in plan, fig. 27.1). Photograph by Shinchōsha Press, Tokyo.

leap. Finally it is a shift from *wabi* (simplicity and poverty) to *kirei-sabi* (gorgeous simplicity). These are examples of *konomi* formalized in accordance with different aesthetic sensibilities. Both the *Rikyū-gonomi* and the *Enshū-gonomi* derive from living personalities, but each later took on a life of its own.

For more than three hundred years after the completion of Katsura Villa, attempts were made to localize *Enshū-gonomi* in both its architecture and garden. These were at the same time efforts to comprehend the formidable new realm of *kirei-sabi*. Incessant attempts at reading produced a mechanism, like an automaton, which moving toward the achievement of pure form or an ideal type subtly replenished the real buildings and gardens. These various Katsura "renovations" localize the process through which successive readings have transformed an ideal.

Konomi is itself an automaton, or self-organizing system. At the core of *Enshū-gonomi* as self-organizing, systematic device is a compendium of all possible diagonal interventions. It is said that the term "mannerism" derives from the Florentine architect and artist Giorgio Vasari's concept of the "*maniera* [method] of the master." In its original meaning, *konomi* is almost indistinguishable from this *maniera*. In particular, such a concept defies any unique origin; instead, it produces and reproduces itself through imitation and repetition. For this reason, it tends to become at first pop and then eventually kitsch.

Kōgetsu Sōgan (1574–1643) was a Zen priest of the early Edo period who established the Ryūkō-in, and employed Enshū as supervisor. The Kohō-an was originally built there, but was later moved to the larger Daitoku-ji complex of temples (whose chief priest at that time was also Sōgan). The Mitsu-tan (secret arbor, or Mittan no Seki) Tearoom (fig. 27.3) was said to be designed by Enshū himself. Nonetheless, even the tireless research of Sutemi Horiguchi was unable to rediscover any hard and fast evidence of this. Sōgan was a son of the tea connoisseur Tsuda Munehisa, in Sakai, and himself became a tea master, so some have attributed the tearoom to him. However in observing the Mitsu-tan's composition of persistent diagonals, I cannot help but confirm the *Enshū-gonomi* thesis. Sitting in the room, one is struck by the overwhelming tension of diagonal shifts. While the dire darkness of Rikyū's Tai-an compels a descent into some interior core, the space of the Mitsu-tan is rent by the diagonal traversing the space. Pairs of contrasting elements are consistently in evidence: (1) the four-*shaku*-long,[7] deep wooden platform alcove (*toko*) at its northwest corner versus the shallower *shoin*-style alcove (*shoin doko*) at its southeast corner; (2) the square shelving versus the deformed hanging shelves above the host's seat (*temae-za*); (3) plain horizontal members (*nageshi*) on two walls versus the *sukiya*-style lintels (*kamoi*) on facing sides; (4) the *shōji* with lacquered frames of gaudy composition versus the *fusuma* with their flat India ink paintings; (5) the false ceiling framed and supported by poles (*sao-buchi-tenjō*) versus the smooth *tatami* floor. Invited into the space as a guest, one is thrown off balance by these contrasting elements, or rather the body is torn between power exerted from different sides. One is, finally, suspended in dynamic equilibrium.

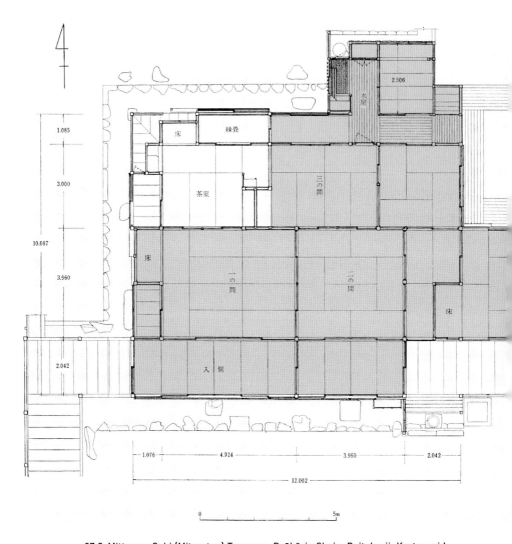

1.085

3.000

10.087

3.960

2.042

1.076 4.924 3.960 2.042

12.002

床　縁畳

茶室

三の間

床

一の間　二の間

床

入側

水屋　2.506

0　　　　　5m

27.3 Mittan no Seki (Mitsu-tan) Tearoom, Ryūkō-in Shoin, Daitoku-ji, Kyoto, said to be by Kobori Enshū; four and a half mats plus *daime*, with two *tokonoma* set at a diagonal to one another (mid-seventeenth century), shown in unshaded portion of plan.

Where does this diagonal strategy originate? Owing to innumerable renovations and relocations, an ethos of contradiction remained: orthodox *shoin* style versus unorthodox *sukiya* style.[8] In the first place, the shelving for the host seat area that is light and shallow had to be in *sukiya* style. This was installed opposite the formal *shoin* shelf—but with the clear intention of creating contrast. From here we can proceed to a number of suppositions with, however, an underlying consistency. In the beginning, the structure was of more or less pure *shoin* style. But, for reasons related to the love of ceremonial tea rather than considerations of the building itself, *sōan*-style and *sukiya*-style elements were added. First, a *sōan*-style tearoom was created in a part of the *shoin*. At that point, the interior space of the tearoom was independent, but this enclosure was later opened up in such a way that new and old elements were allowed to confront each other in a single space. The resulting juxtaposition to be sure deviated from the principles of a certain classicism, but represented an attempt to synthesize contradictory elements by taking an intentionally holistic approach. In the West so-called eclecticism maintains to this day the notion of a stylistic integrity. Heterogeneous elements are introduced, then transformed, and rearranged at the metalevel of one "style." The Mitsu-tan Tearoom, on the other hand, keeps the component forms in play and juxtaposes these in a confrontational mode. This, I submit, is radical eclecticism.

The diagonal impulses attain a dynamic equilibrium, similar to the dynamism of the near contemporary baroque, which created movement by inducing two focal points to draw against one another. But what was intended by such a bold or tricky equilibrium? Previously, Rikyū's classic tearoom model had possessed a consistent centripetal stability, for it was dominated by the existence of the host, Rikyū himself, at the center. What Enshū and later tea masters sought to create, in contrast, was a nonhomogeneous, nonsynthetic space where a plurality of forces pull at one another—a maelstrom of diagonals. There is no dominant center (i.e., subject), for body and gaze are thrust dynamically into tension. Guests feel that from behind someone unknown and invisible is trying to move the whole space without actually being present. This was a clear and evident turn. I imagine that at this time, given the instability of the political atmosphere, cultural producers no longer sensed any reality in a stable composition created in accordance with a unified aesthetic. Their artistic views were metamorphosed by shattered social norms.

In 1628 Kōgetsu Sōgan was implicated in a political conflict known as the Purple Robe Affair (Shi-i Jiken). A purple robe used to be accorded those who performed meritorious services, but only by the emperor's order. However, after the shōgunate took charge, it issued a regulation as a function of its containment policy directed against the court, that approval by the shōgun would henceforth be necessary for the bestowal of the gift. Emperor Gomizuno-o was indicted for authorizing the robe without the shōgun's consent, and three priests of Daitoku-ji signed a petition in protest. Two were sentenced to banishment, but the third, Kōgetsu Sōgan, was allowed to remain if he succeeded to the leadership of the Northern Sect (kita-ha) of Daitoku-ji. It was Ishin Sūden who prosecuted as shōgunal agent.

In the same year, the Konchi-in complex that Sūden had ordered Enshū to oversee (i.e., endow with "taste" or "stylize" [kono-maseru]), was completed. Subsequently, the shōgunate commanded Enshū to work on the buildings and garden of a retreat for Emperor Gomizuno-o, in order to calm the latter's ire from the Purple Robe Affair. I believe that these two projects attained Enshū-gonomi for the first time, as the buildings progressed amid the power struggle between court and shōgunate. And Enshū's clients happened to be on both sides.

His position was thus deeply ambiguous. His personal and professional status set Enshū on the side of samurai society and the shōgunate. But he also practiced Zen meditation at Daitoku-ji, and worked on the building at Ryūkō-in that was later moved to and reconstructed in the Kohō-an—on behalf of individuals affiliated with the court. And the sources of his scholarship and taste were descended from no less than the culture of the imperial court itself. So, Enshū's cultural identity belonged squarely to the court.

In terms of ceramics for the tea ceremony, Rikyū created chō-jirō ware, which is considered the beginning of raku ware and Japanese-type ware (wa-mono) in general, at a time when kara-mono ware (Tang and later Chinese ceramics) was still popular, as it had been ever since the Muromachi period (1392–1573). Then, Furuta Oribe displayed his own konomi inspired by elements of Western taste imported via the southeast Asian countries, so that it might be said that he helped destroy the solid core of Rikyū-

gonomi. Enshū succeeded *Oribe-gonomi* by mediating and attenuating the ancient imperial court taste. He completely decomposed the previous aesthetic and reconstructed it on a teetering tightrope. He had to set himself between the *samurai* culture and that of the imperial court, or rather he may have used the tightrope as the catalyst for his proposed aesthetic deconstruction. I would say that this position underlay all his diagonal strategies. The space wherein the *shoin* aesthetic of *samurai* culture and the proto-*sukiya* elements of the court confronted one another was a neutral zone afforded by the Zen temple. The Mitsu-tan Tearoom is the pinnacle of a perilous equilibrium. In that sense, the diagonal positioning was in the end a product of political tensions. Out of the abyss of the times, when two opposed cultural spheres collided, *Enshū-gonomi* was born.

There exists today a tearoom called San-un-shō (Bed of the Mountain Cloud), next door to the Kohō-an and the Jikinyū-ken—a copy of the Mitsu-tan Tearoom. In plan or in pictures, the two are barely distinguishable. But once seated in the former, we are struck by the difference: an absence of aura. That is not simply to say that the Mitsu-tan is the original and the San-un-shō is a copy. Rather the latter lacks something essential, which, I believe, is the tension inherent in Enshū's diagonal strategy. Is this the difference between a design materialized in political tension and one copied when that tension had already dispersed? I cannot explain in full. Yet, as I have tried to impart, *konomi* itself involves a mechanism of quotation as well as that notion of its reproduction ad infinitum, destined to become cliché or eventual kitsch. And, in Japan, we remain seemingly forever in the grip of this selfsame mechanism of cultural production.

azuma-ya. A pavilion for repose set within a garden. The square-thatched roof of the hut is supported by four columns, and the four sides are open.

Bunri-ha. The earliest Japanese modernist architectural movement, whose name derives from the translation of *Sezession*; it was formed in 1920 by six students (Kikuji Ishimoto, Mayumi Takizawa, Sutemi Horiguchi, Keiichi Mori, Shigeru Yada, and Mamoru Yamada) of Tokyo Imperial University.

chashitsu. A room specifically designed for ceremonial tea. It always contains a *tokonoma*—a recessed section for presenting a scroll painting or a vase with flowers; an *oshi-ita*—a pedestal for displaying objects; and *ro*—a hearth embedded in the floor. It is said that this formula was conceived by Murata Jukō (1422–1502).

Chu Hsi School. Chu Hsi (or Tzu) was a philosopher of the Southern Sung dynasty in China. Based upon a cosmology developed in the Northern Sung period, he grasped the cosmos dualistically, as consisting of *ki* (pneuma) as Being, or Nature, and *ri* (reason) as the law of existence. The goal of his philosophy was to realize *ri* by bringing together Nature and reason. During the Ming and Qing dynasties, it promoted an ideology solidifying and sustaining the feudal class system. It was then introduced, along with this aspect, into Edo-period Japan.

Dōgen (1200–1253). Founder of the Sōdō sect of Japanese Zen Buddhism. The text that descibes Dōgen's experience of Zen discipline, *Shōbō Genzō* ("the right teaching of Buddha sheds light on and includes everything"), remains influential.

Eisai (1141–1215). Founder of one of the major Zen sects, Rinzai-shū. He went to Sung (i.e., China) twice, in 1168 and 1178, and is said to have brought back seeds of the tea bush.

Enshū, Kobori (1579–1647). A celebrated tea specialist and arbiter of taste in the early Edo period, hired by the third shōgun Iemitsu as a teacher of tea and Clerk of Works. His taste is referred to collectively as *Enshū-gonomi*.

Fenollosa, Ernest (1853–1908). American philosopher who came to Japan in 1876 at the invitation of Tokyo Imperial University. While teaching philosophy, he also researched Japanese art and helped his disciple, Tenshin Okakura, to establish an art school. He was later director of the East Asia section of the Museum of Fine Arts in Boston.

gasshō-zukuri. A type of vernacular housing in certain areas of north central Japan, Hida and Shirakawa. The roof rises sharply under a giant truss to accommodate two to three stories of silkworm culture.

Greater East Asia Co-prosperity Sphere. Slogan used during World War II to justify Japan's annexation of much of Asia. The policy, which advocated a Japanese-led liberation of Asia from the colonization of Western nations, originated in a pronouncement by the Minister of Foreign Affairs, Hiroaki Matsuoka.

Gyōyū (1163–1241). A student of doctrines of both exoteric and esoteric Buddhism (*Ken Mitsu*), Gyōyū became priest-in-residence at Hachiman-gū in Kamakura. He later moved to Jufuku-ji, also in Kamakura, where he was Eisai's disciple.

Hachiman. A Japanese native god, but according to the syncretic interpretation that all Japanese gods derive from India, he can also be identified with the metamorphosed Amitabha.

hakkō ichi-u. The "whole world under one roof" doctrine implies that the whole world should be ruled by the imperial household. *Hakkō* means four directions (i.e., the world), and *ichi-u* signifies one household. These ancient notions were rehabilitated hand in hand with the official ideology of the Greater East Asia Co-prosperity Sphere.

haniwa. "Unglazed earthenware objects produced primarily in the Kofun period (4th to 6th c.). Used in funeral ceremonies as ornaments, they were placed in rows on top of tumuli or burial mounds.

The forms vary, but they can be divided into two groups: *entō* [cylindrical] *haniwa*, and those which have forms of animals, human figures, houses, etc., attached to the upper part of the *entō*, the latter being termed *keishō* [representational] *haniwa*." (*A Dictionary of Japanese Art Terms* [Tokyo: Tokyo Bijutsu, 1990], p. 519.)

Heijō-kyō. Capital of Japan from 710 to 784, it was located near present-day Nara city. (Nagaoka-kyō nearer to Kyoto was capital from 784 to 794. Heian-kyō marked the beginning of today's Kyoto, imperial capital of Japan from 794 to 1868, when the capital was transferred to Tokyo, the former Edo, following the Meiji Restoration.)

himorogi. Around the boundaries of mountains, forests, and large trees that people held sacred, *tokiwagi* was planted as a fence and demarcator. Later on, this was transformed into a more symbolic altar-like enclosure, where *sakaki* branches were set up, whether outdoors or inside a room—wherever a Shintō ritual is held. Today at building sites four bamboo poles are connected by a rice straw rope hung with white cut paper to delimit a boundary.

Hōnen (1133–1212). Founder of the Jōdo sect of Buddhism, which spread among the masses more widely than any other. Hōnen was exiled at one time, as the increase in the sect's believers threatened older schools.

Hō-o or *jō-kō.* In medieval Japan emperors retired to the priesthood. Although officially relegated to the status of former emperor, they frequently manipulated politics from behind the scenes.

ichioku gyokusai. Last-ditch slogan that appeared near the end of World War II, when Japan's defeat had become inevitable. The words encouraged the nation to fight until the entire population was decimated.

ishi-gumi. Manner of arranging two or more rocks from an aesthetic viewpoint. Despite various famous rock arrangements, there are no particular fixed formulas, other than in reference to *jiwari*, or "how the land is divided."

Itsukushima Jinja. Shrine located at Itsukushima, near Hiroshima. The main pavilion with its broad outdoor platforms and the huge *torii* gate that stands in the waters of the Inland Sea are famous. The Heike clan cherished the shrine.

Izumo. Izumo's legend concerns powerful gods of the Izumo region in Shimane prefecture, some of whose stories also appear in *Kojiki* and *Nihongi*. In one, entitled "Land Pulling" (*Kuni-biki*), for instance, a god (Yatsukamizuomitsu-no-mikoto) cut off a part of the Silla kingdom in the Korean peninsula and pulled it closer to make his land larger. Other stories purvey the creation myth that giant gods made everything.

Jōchō (d.1057). A sculptor of Buddhist (Jōdo sect) statues whose style is known as a revival of the ancient culture of the Tenpyō era (729–749) of Emperor Tenmu. The basic character of his work expresses a rounded, soft, and affectionate image of the Buddhist deity. Jōchō also developed a new technique of wooden sculpture, *yosegi-zukuri*, that involves carving and assembly of many pieces of wood rather than use of a single solid piece.

Jōmon (see **Yayoi**).

Jōruri-ji. Located in present-day Kyoto city, the temple is said to have been built in the Tenpyō era (729–749).

Kan-name-sai. The yearly festival in Ise that celebrates the new harvest through a ritual of offering food to the Sun Goddess. In the Outer Shrine (*gekū*), it takes place from October 15 to 16, in the Inner Shrine (*naikū*), from October 16 to 17. Also at the Imperial Palace, Ise Jingū is recalled through worship on the 17th.

kasa-buchi. A type of ceiling where long boards are arranged in the same direction, supported by frames placed some 30 to 40 centimeters apart.

Kasuga Jinja. Important shrine located in present-day Nara city.

kawara-mono. In medieval Japan, those bound to occupations considered sinful—animal slaughter, tanning, prostitution, burlesque, etc.—were condemned to live along riverbanks, where they mingled with other social outcasts. The term *kawara-mono* (riverbank dwellers) was discriminatory. However, important forms of performing art, such as Noh and Kabuki, are said to have been created by the *kawara-mono*, as well as the arrangement of the famous rock gardens at Ryōan-ji and other temples.

Kei-ha. A school of sculptors who made Buddhist images. It arose in the tenth century and continued to be productive through the seventeenth. In the twelfth century, three masters appeared: Kōkei, Unkei, and Kaikei, all of whom assumed the suffix Kei in their names.

kenmen hō or ***kenmen kihō.*** Interstitial system of measurement in Japanese carpentry, developed from the eighth to fourteenth centuries.

kiwari. The system used to determine general proportion and the scale of details in relationship to the whole in Japanese traditional building. It is said to have been already in partial use by the Nara period (710–784).

kodenchi. The (unused) "old building site" in the context of Ise Jingū's *shikinen-zōkan* (the dismantling and rebuilding that takes place at twenty-year intervals), it is one of two sites occupied in alternation. While the site is empty, it is covered with an expanse of pebbles.

Kōfuku-ji. Located within present-day Nara city, it is considered one of the seven great temples there. It was relocated from Heijō-kyō (the old capital to the south of Nara) in the early eighth century.

kokugaku. National(ist) scholarship. With the growth of modernity and national consciousness in the Edo period, a scholarly movement came into existence in an attempt to clarify the domain proper to Japanese culture, as opposed to the then dominant Chinese trend. Motoori Norinaga was one of its four main adherents and promoters, in addition to Kada-no Azumamaro, Kamo-no Mabuchi, and Hirata Atsutane.

kotodama. Belief among ancient Japanese that spiritual power was inherent in the sound and meaning of a certain set of words, repeated in an incantation. Sometimes considered an extension of animism.

Kumano Jinja. Branch shrine in Yakumo village, Shimane prefecture, of main shrine in Kinki region.

machiai. Area for greeting and light conversation before entering the tearoom (*chashitsu*) for ceremonial tea.

machiya. The generic term for usually humble houses of urban dwellers such as merchants and craftsmen after the Muromachi period (roughly fifteenth to sixteenth centuries). Not subject to sumptuary laws, the basic form of plan derives from the farmhouse vernacular, where the entrance area had a floor of packed earth. The form underwent development over time, from a thatched or wooden roof to tile, and from a one-storied construction to two.

makura kotoba. Stock epithet used in tradtional Japanese poetry. Literally "pillow word(s)," this is a kind of idiomatic device found in Japanese verse. *Makura kotoba*—usually consisting of fewer than five syllables—come before certain words and phrases to contextualize them.

Matsudaira Fumai (1751–1818). Having studied tea ceremony and the doctrines of Zen Buddhism in his youth, he became the seventh head of the feudal domain of Matsue at age 17. In later years, he gave all his time to the tea ceremony, performing notably at Kohō-an at Daitoku-ji in Kyoto.

Matsuya Kaiki. This rare record of tea ceremonies was kept by three generations of lacquerware merchants, the Matsuya of Nara— Hisamasa, Hisayoshi, and Hisashige. Their documentation, which covers more than one hundred years (1533–1650), is one of the most important records concerning the development of the tea ceremony. The notes by Matsuya Hisashige include detailed descriptions of tea ceremonies by such masters as Furuta Oribe, Hosokawa Sansai, and Kobori Enshū.

Meiji Restoration (1867). Under provocation by Western nations, the Tokugawa shōgunate, which had pursued a policy of *sakoku*—or isolation—was defeated by a coalition of *daimyō* (feudal lords), who proposed to support the emperor as nominal head of state. This event, Japan's form of modern revolution, restored sovereignty from the Tokugawa shōgunate to the emperor (*osei fukko*). It entailed rapid modernization and the advent of Japan's subsequent statist mercantilism.

minka. A generic term for vernacular housing in premodern times. Rural dwellings built in the twentieth century may be included in this category, as the form generally refers to farmhouses. *Minka* is defined over against the styles of the ruling class: *shinden-zukuri* and later *shoin-zukuri*.

Munetada (1421–1502). A poet of the Muromachi period who specialized in the linked-verse *renga* form of *waka*, in which syllables are articulated in the order of 5, 7, 5 (first stanza) and 7, 7 (second stanza).

nageshi. Structurally and by extension decoratively, the horizontal member surrounding the inside of a room at the level of the upper rail of its sliding doors. However, one Japanese architectural historian has suggested that *nageshi* be understood as a kind of molding, since it also helps determine the "class" of the room.

nihonga. A term used to differentiate modern Japanese-style painting from oil painting influenced by nineteenth-century European realism and impressionism. The importation of Western styles provoked a revival of Japan-ness on the part of native painters, and the elements of traditional Japanese style were recontextualized in a new quasi-realist framework. Tenshin Okakura led the latter movement.

Nihon Intānashonaru Kenchikukai (Japan International Architectural Association). Established in Kyoto in 1927, its founding and invited members included Seigō Honda, Isaburō Ueno, Walter Gropius, Bruno Taut, Erich Mendelsohn, and Gerrit Rietveld, among others. The manifesto begins: "An architectural style should be based upon true locality, without dependence on traditional form or obsession with nationality."

Norinaga, Motoori (1730–1801). Famed scholar of *kokugaku* (q.v.) in the mid-Edo period. Aside from medical research, he studied the national literature of Japan, including *The Tale of Genji*, and spent thirty years elaborating a textual critique of *kojiki*—the mythical account of Japan's birth as a nation.

Okakura, Tenshin (art name of **Okakura, Kakuzō**) (1862–1913). Leader of the modern visual arts movement in Japan, Okakura established what was to become the Tokyo University of Fine Arts. He later became curator of the East Asian Department, Museum of Fine Arts, Boston. His *The Book of Tea* (1906) was published in New York City.

Ō-name-sai. The first ritual after a *tennō* is enthroned, in which he offers the year's new crops to the Sun Goddess (Amaterasu Ōmikami) and the Gods of Heaven and Earth (Tenshin-chigi). This ritual occurs only once during the lifetime of the sovereign.

ōya-ishi. A type of stone from Tochigi prefecture that is easily shaped because of its softness, yet very durable. It was used widely in Japan for constructing walls, moats, and storehouses—and subsequently as a material for decorative sculpture by Frank Lloyd Wright in the Imperial Hotel, Tokyo.

Ryōkai-mandala. The mandala of the Shingon sect has two domains: *kongō kai* (conceiving Mahavairocana from the standpoint of wisdom) and *taizō kai* (based, instead, on mercy or truth).

sakaki. A portmanteau botanical word for broadleaf nondeciduous trees used in Shintō ritual and related to the tea family.

samurai. The warrior class that ruled Japan from the late twelfth century up until the Meiji Restoration of 1867. The final manifestation of *samurai* strength was the Tokugawa shōgunate. The stratum of *samurai* originally included clans of militia working for aristocrats and the imperial court. They were empowered near the end of the Heian period, and in the twelfth century the Genji clan established a national government in Kamakura.

shikinen-zōkan (Ise Jingū). Each important building in the shrine has an identical "twin," one of which is in use while the other is being rebuilt. The period of rebuilding is predetermined at 20 years and the ritual rebuilding has lasted, it is believed, since the fourteenth year of the reign of Emperor Tenmu (685 C.E.). It is thought that the determination of the period for rebuilding was founded on the perceived life span of the architecture, whose pillars are sunk directly into the ground, without foundations, or on the time needed for passing down the carpentry techniques. The completion of the next rebuilding will be the year 2013.

shinden-zukuri. The style of architecture reserved for aristocrats' residences, which flourished in the Heian period (roughly the ninth to the twelfth centuries). The main living area always faces south and parallel wings extend in front of and behind the main structure, with everything connected by open corridors. In the south garden was a pond, usually with a fishing pavilion.

shoin-zukuri. Building manner that derives from ancient *shinden-zukuri* and developed from the Kamakura through the Muromachi periods (roughly the thirteenth to sixteenth centuries)—brought to fruition in the Momoyama period (roughly the sixteenth to seventeenth centuries). As distinct from *shinden-zukuri*, there is no articulation between *omoya* (main structure) and *hisashi* (peripheral area under the eaves). Square columns are used, and *tatami* eventually came to cover enclosed floor areas. Decoration comprised *tokonoma* (alcoves), *chigai-dana* (decorative shelves), and *tsuke-shoin* (built-in writing niches)—and, above all, raised platforms for seating by rank.

Shōmei. Secret book of carpentry techniques written by Hirauchi Masanobu in 1608 (Keichō 13). It consists of five volumes, divided by building type: palace, gate, temple, tower, and shrine.

Shōsō-in. Located northwest of Tōdai-ji in present-day Nara city, Japan's oldest storage building, housing ancient Buddhist scriptures as well as Emperor Shōmu's treasures, and various rare items from all over Asia. It is a massive log-cabin construction with raised floor.

sōan. *Sōan* originally signified a humble hut with a thatched roof, but later the term came to refer to a purist and reductive style of building. It now defines an important tearoom style originated by Sen no Rikyū (1522–1591).

Sorai, Ogyū (1666–1728). Confucianist philosopher of the mid-Edo period, who rejected the thought of the Chu Hsi School (q.v.).

sukiya-zukuri. A rustically inspired approach to construction based largely on methods of tearoom design and used mainly in buildings consecrated to leisure or informal pursuits. Asymmetry, restraint in décor, and exposed materials are its main characteristics. *Sukiya* first appeared in the late sixteenth century and immediately became popular for aristocratic villas; it later appeared in restaurants and urban pleasure districts.

taisha-zukuri (contrasted with **Sumiyoshi-zukuri**). The main feature of this style of shrine architecture is that, with gable entry (*tsuma-iri*) and a central column that supports its roof ridge (*mune-mochi-bashira*), entrance and stairs are decentered to the right. In addition, the altar is placed immediately behind a wall next to the central column. *Sumiyoshi-zukuri* is another prototype, modeled on the Sumiyoshi Jinja in present-day Osaka. It has gabled roof with gable entry, but, in contrast to *taisha-zukuri*, the entry is placed in the center, and the roof has no curve. The interior is divided into two rooms (front and back).

takafuda. A placard posted by the government announcing laws and regulations, placed in busy areas where people frequently gathered, such as *tsuji* (intersections) of main roads in feudal Japan.

takayuka-shiki jūkyo. A type of housing of the Yayoi period. The roof is usually thatched, the structure is gabled, and the floor is raised. A ladder carved from one solid log (*ganki-bashigo*) is used for access.

tamagaki. Generic term for fences around shrines constructed in any form or material. Cf. also *mizugaki* (sacred hedge).

tateana jūkyo. A type of primitive housing in which the roof is placed over either a sunken floor or a low bank of earth. Size varied as a class-based society developed, though the form lasted up until the early Edo period (seventeenth century).

teikan-heigō-shiki. Translated as "imperial crown style." In the context of the growing nationalism of the 1930s, it was promoted by conservative architects and politicians to counter the international modernist style. The basic structure was of reinforced concrete with pseudo-historicist detailing in brick or tile, the whole surmounted by a pronounced traditional tiled roof.

Tōdai-ji. Located just beyond Nara city, it was first built in 745 by Emperor Shōmu. Jōdo-ji, which Chōgen conceived as one of the seven branches of Tōdai-ji, is located in Ono city in present-day Hyōgo prefecture.

Tōshō-dai-ji. Built in 759 by a monk from Tang, Ganjin, it is located in present-day Nara city.

tsunashiro. A type of ceiling where natural materials, such as bamboo husk, reed, cedar, or Sawara cypress, are braided.

wago. The Japanese language consists of elements of Chinese (especially in the writing system, as well as the substantial terminology of abstract learning) in addition to a lexical core that originated in Japan. *Wago* indicates both these surviving Japanese elements and the language as it is thought to have existed before the importation of Chinese culture from the continent.

waka. A fixed-form verse of 31 syllables, originating in eighth-century Japan, as distinct from influential imported Chinese poetic forms.

wayō. In contrast with later styles of construction introduced to Japan from China in the twelfth to thirteenth centuries (Kamakura period), building styles introduced in the eighth century (Nara period) and transformed in accordance with local taste are called *wayō* (Japanesque) style.

wayō-ka. Heian court culture epitomizes *wayō-ka*, known for a refinement and splendor of detail (in building, music, and literature, as well as in the overall lifestyle of an aristocratic class). It stands in opposition to the spartan and powerful aesthetic of *samurai* culture that arose beginning in the eleventh century, partly under the influence of Zen Buddhism.

yamagoe Amida.　The Buddhist notion of the soul entering heaven, as represented by the invitation of Sanzon (the three Sacred Ones): Amitabha, Avalokitesvara, and Bodhisattva. These three deities of the Amitabha triad are depicted rising from behind a mountain to receive the ascetic into the realm of Paradise.

Yayoi and **Jōmon.**　Terms used for styles of artifacts once thought to have been produced in quite different eras of Japanese prehistory. Yayoi was considered to be an early agricultural society, while Jōmon identifies a hunting, nomadic society. Yayoi style was thought to date from the third century C.E., Jōmon style from a much earlier time—about 10,000 years ago. Yayoi artifacts include bronze bells, swords, and symbolic objects, while Jōmon culture produced mainly various shapes of pottery vessels decorated with a stylized rope design. The sophistication of the former is believed to relate to the imperial lineage. Today doubt has been cast on this cultural categorization, since there is speculation that the two cultures in fact coexisted.

yuniwa.　A place purified in preparation for setting up an altar to enshrine gods and customarily demarcated by sand or pebbles.

Zen-gaku-ren.　An abbreviation of Zen Nihon Gakusei Jichikai Sōrengō (National Federation of Students Self-Government Associations), organized in 1948. Around 1960, it split into different factions that composed the main body of the (anti–Japan Communist Party) new left movement.

Preface

1. *Katsura Villa: Space and Form*, photographs by Yasuhiro Ishimoto, text by Arata Isozaki, translated from the Japanese by John D. Lamb (New York: Rizzoli, 1983).

2. The essay was serialized in the quarterly magazine *Hihyō Kūkan* (Critical Space) (Tokyo: Ōta Shuppan), nos. 21–25 (1999–2000). Also the essay on Tōdai-ji, "The Problematic Called Chōgen," was published in the same magazine, nos. 15–17 (1997–1998).

1 Japanese Taste and Its Recent Historical Construction

1. Under pressure from major Western states, the Tokugawa shōgunate, which had pursued a policy of *sakoku* (closing the nation), was toppled by a coalition of *daimyō* (feudal lords) maintaining *tennō* (the emperor) as a figurehead; this so-called Meiji Restoration (1867) was Japan's form of modern revolution, though referred to as a revival of imperial sovereignty. It was, above all, the beginning of Japan's statist mercantilism and thoroughgoing modernization. [*Trans.*]

2. Tenshin (aka Kakuzō) Okakura led the modern visual art movement in Japan and established what was to become the Tokyo University of Fine Arts. Among his best-known books is Okakura Kakuzō, *The Book of Tea* (New York, 1906; reprinted Rutland, Vermont, and Tokyo: Charles E. Tuttle Company, 1956). [*Trans.*]

3. Ernest Fenollosa came to Japan in 1876 to lecture at Tokyo Imperial University. While teaching philosophy at the university, he researched Japanese art and also helped his disciple Kakuzō Okakura establish an art school there. He was later director of the East Asia Department of the Museum of Fine Arts in Boston. [*Trans.*]

4. Wright's lecture "The Destruction of the Box" was delivered to the Junior Chapter of the AIA in New York in 1952; it is reprinted in Edgar Kaufmann, ed., *An American Architecture: Frank Lloyd Wright* (New York: Horizon Press, 1955), pp. 75–78.

5. Okakura, *The Book of Tea*, p. 45. Note that the attribution itself is no longer considered to be historical. [*Ed.*]

6. Nihon Intānashonaru Kenchikukai was established in Kyoto in 1927. The initial members included Seigō Honda, Isaburō Ueno, and ex officio, as it were, Walter Gropius, Bruno Taut, Erich Mendelsohn, Gerrit Rietveld, and others. The general platform began: "Architectural style should be based upon true locality, without dependence on traditional form or obsession with nationality." [*Trans.*]

7. Different currents of Chinese influence swept Japan throughout history and were assimilated in various ways. For instance, in contrast with styles of architecture introduced in the twelfth to thirteenth centuries (Kamakura period), those introduced in the eighth century (Nara period) were modified according to local taste and are consequently known as *wayō* (Japanesque). [*Trans.*]

8. Bruno Taut, *Nihon—Taut no Nikki* (Japan—Taut's Diaries), trans. Hideo Shinoda (Tokyo: Iwanami Shoten, 1975); entry dated November 4, 1935.

9. Taut, ibid.

10. The Greater East Asia Co-prosperity Sphere was a slogan used during World War II to justify Japan's annexation of parts of Asia, advocating a Japanese-led liberation from colonization by Western forces. The phrase originated in a statement by the then Minister of Foreign Affairs, Hiroaki Matsuoka. [*Trans.*]

11. Hideto Kishida, *Kako no Kōsei* (Composition of the Past) (Tokyo: Kōseisha Shobō, 1929; reprinted Tokyo: Sagami Shobō, 1938, 1951).

12. From Kunio Maekawa's review of the Hiroshima competition, published in *Kenchiku Zasshi* (Architecture Journal), December 1942.

13. For a discussion of "Overcoming Modernity," see Masao Miyoshi and H. D. Harootunian, *Postmodernism and Japan* (Durham: Duke University Press, 1989), especially Harootunian, "Visible Discourses/Invisible Ideologies," p. 67: "In July of 1942, a group of distinguished intellectuals, academics, and critics were summoned to Kyoto by the Literary Society [*Bungaku-kai*] to discuss the theme of 'overcoming the modern.' All of the participants believed that the debate, convened six months after the outbreak of the Pacific War, would mark the end of 'modern civilization'

in Japan and would reveal the outline of a 'glorious new age.' ... Among the better-known participants were figures like Kobayashi Hideo, Nishitani Keiji, Kamei Katsuichirō, Hayashi Fusao, Miyoshi Tatsuji, Kawakami Tetsutarō, and Nakamura Mitsuo." [*Trans.*] More recently, see the chapter "Overcoming Modernity" in Harry Harootunian, *Overcome by Modernity: History, Culture, and Community in Interwar Japan* (Princeton: Princeton University Press, 2000), pp. 34–94. [*Ed.*]

2 Western Structure versus Japanese Space

1. Masao Maruyama, *Studies in the Intellectual History of Tokugawa Japan* (trans. of *Nihon Seiji Shisō-shi Kenkyū*), trans. Mikiso Hane (Tokyo: University of Tokyo Press; Princeton: Princeton University Press, 1974).

2. Ryūichi Hamaguchi, *Nihon Kokumin Kenchiku Yōshiki-no-Kenkyū* (The Problem of Style in Japan's National Architecture), serialized in *Shin Kenchiku*, January, April, July/August, and October 1944. The text was later collected in *Hamaguchi Ryūichi Hyōron Shū—Shimin Shakai-no Design* (Criticism by Ryūichi Hamaguchi—Design in Civil Society) (Tokyo: Jiritsu Shobō, 1998).

3. Bruno Taut, *Nihon—Taut no Nikki*, trans. Hideo Shinoda (Tokyo: Iwanami Shoten, 1975), entry dated May 4, 1933.

4. *Kunstwollen*—"urge to form" or "artistic impulse"—appears in Alois Riegl, *Stilfragen* (1893), Eng. trans. as *Problems of Style* (Princeton: Princeton University Press, 1992). Also see *The Vienna School Reader: Politics and Art Historical Method in the 1930s*, ed. Christopher S. Wood (New York: Zone Books, 2000). [*Trans.*]

5. Banister Fletcher, *A History of Architecture on the Comparative Method, for Students, Craftsmen, and Amateurs* (1896 and subsequent reprintings, now enlarged).

6. See Hamaguchi, *Hamaguchi Ryūichi Hyōron Shū*, p. 53.

7. For instance, he designed such public works as Kyushu Meteorological Observatory (1931), the Central Meteorological Observatory at Shinagawa in Tokyo (1933), Mito Meteorological Station (1935), Osaka Scientific Disaster Research Center (1936), and Ōshima Meteorological Station (1938).

8. "Finally, we have the court architecture developed in the Heian period, with its simple and pure design which is truly Japanese. It is also the expression typically seen in the buildings of the Kyoto Palace. I believe that those who are right-minded might recall this, more than anything else, on the occasion of designing this facility." Hideto Kishida, "On the

Occasion of the Competition for a Japan Cultural Center in Bangkok," in *Shin Kenchiku*, January 1944.

9. Chūta Itō, *Nihon Kenchiku no Jissō* (The Facts of Japanese Architecture) (Tokyo: Shin-Taiyōsha, 1944), p. 194.

10. Kenzō Tange, in *Kenchiku Zasshi*, September 1942, n.p.

11. Kenzō Tange, *Katsura: Tradition and Creation in Japanese Architecture*, with a preface by Walter Gropius (New Haven: Yale University Press, 1960).

12. Hamaguchi, *Hamaguchi Ryūichi Hyōron Shū*, p. 144.

3 Yayoi and Jōmon

1. The name of the building was Shōfū-sō (House of Pine Breezes). When Arthur Drexler visited Japan for the preparation of the project, it was Ryūichi Hamaguchi who gave him a tour of historic architecture throughout Japan. During this trip, Drexler learned that the Kōjō-in structure represented the *shoin* style of residential architecture before having undergone the transforming influence of the *sukiya* style in later centuries.

2. *Sakuteiki* (Treatise on Garden Making) by Toshitsuna Tachibana (1028–1094) is the oldest book on garden design, a compilation of the techniques used to create the *shinden-zukuri* garden. A supplement appeared in 1289, and it is now considered a work in two volumes.

3. *Nageshi* is, structurally, a horizontal member surrounding the inside of a room at the level of the upper rail of its sliding doors. However, one Japanese architectural historian has suggested a similarity to certain types of applied molding, insomuch as this feature helps express the social status of the room.

4. Tetsurō Watsuji was a philosopher who contributed to the development of a conservative theory of culture. His *Koji Junrei* (A Pilgrimage to Ancient Temples) was first published in 1919 (Tokyo: Iwanami Shoten). Another influential work was *Fūdo* (Climate) (1935), which scrutinized the relationship between climate and the characteristics of traditional cultures in East, South, and West Asia and Europe. In the postwar period, Watsuji insisted that the spirit of the new constitution and the *tennō* system could be reconciled. [*Trans.*]

5. Yayoi and Jōmon are terms used for styles of artifacts once thought to have been produced in different periods of the remote Japanese past. Yayoi has been taken to represent an early agricultural society of the third century C.E., while Jōmon signifies a hunting, nomadic society dating

from a prehistorical era about 10,000 years ago. Yayoi artifacts include bronze bells, swords, and other symbolic objects, while Jōmon comprises pottery vessels of various shapes usually decorated with a stylized rope design. The former are sophisticated and thought possibly to have been related to the imperial lineage, while the latter are rough and primitive. Today this periodization has come into question, and there is speculation that these two cultures may even have coexisted.

Okamoto wrote of his national "rediscovery" in *The Rediscovery of Japan—Records of Art of the Land* (Tokyo: Shinchōsha, 1958). [*Trans.*]

6. The house planned by Yoshimura was selected as a gift from Japan to the Museum of Modern Art, where it was exhibited from 1954 to 1955. It was moved to its present location in Philadelphia in 1958. The whole event was meant as a symbolic act of Japan/US friendship following the war. See ⟨http://www.shofuso.com⟩ for a complete account [*Ed.*]

7. Hirotarō Ōta, *Zusetsu Nihon Jutaku-shi* (Illustrated History of Japanese Housing) (Tokyo: Shōkokusha, 1948).

8. Kenzō Tange, *Katsura: Tradition and Creation in Japanese Architecture* (New Haven: Yale University Press, 1960), p. 35.

9. Walter Gropius, preface to Tange, *Katsura*, p. 10.

10. Kobori Enshū (1579–1647), a celebrated tea specialist of the early Edo period, is the subject of part IV of the present book.

11. Tange, *Katsura*, p. v.

12. Zen-gaku-ren, first organized in 1948, is an abridgement of Zen Nihon Gakusei Jichikai Sō-rengō (Union of All Student Self-Government Organizations of Japan). Around 1960, it split into various factions that then coalesced as the "new left movement," in opposition to the Japan Communist Party.

4 Nature and Artifice

1. Regarding the *shikinen zōkan* of Ise Jingū, each building in the shrine complex has an identical double, one of which is in use while the other is disassembled, then rebuilt. The period of rebuilding is officialy set at 20 years. This ritualistic and performative rebuilding has persisted, it is said, since 685 C.E. (i.e., the fourteenth year of the reign of Emperor Tenmu). It is believed that the period of 20 years is predicated on the life span of buildings whose pillars are sunk directly into the ground, without foundation; or it may be the time needed for passing down the necessary carpentry techniques; or there may be another, more mysterious reason. Completion of the next rebuilding is scheduled for the year 2013.

2. Bruno Taut, *Houses and People of Japan* (Tokyo: Sanseidō, 1937), p. 139.

3. Sutemi Horiguchi, *Kenchiku ni okeru Nihontekina-mono* (Japan-ness in Architecture) (1934), now included in *Horiguchi Sutemi Chosaku-shū* (Collected Works of Sutemi Horiguchi) (Tokyo: Kajima Shuppan Kai, 1978), vol. 3.

4. Ibid., p. 239.

5. Sutemi Horiguchi, "Gendai Kenchiku to Sukiya ni tsuite" (On Contemporary Architecture and Sukiya), included in *Horiguchi Sutemi Chosaku-shu*, vol. 5, p. 21.

6. Hirotarō Ōta, *Nihon no Kenchiku, Rekishi to Dento* (Japanese Architecture, Its History and Tradition) (Tokyo: Chikuma Shobō, 1968), p. 50.

7. Kenzō Tange, "Gendai Kenchiku no Sōzō to Nihon Kenchiku no Dentō" (Contemporary Architectural Creation and the Japanese Architectural Tradition), *Shin-kenchiku*, June 1956.

8. Ibid.

9. Chu Hsi (or Tzu) was a philosopher of the Southern Sung dynasty in China. Based upon an earlier cosmology developed in the Northern Sung period, he dualistically grasped the cosmos as comprising *ki* (pneuma), that is being (Nature), and *ri* (reason) or the law of existence. His goal was to present *ri* as a synthesis of nature and reason. During the later Ming and Qing dynasties, Tzu's philosophy was propounded as ideology to solidify and sustain the feudal system. It was subsequently introduced, thus modified, into Edo-period Japan.

10. Masao Maruyama, *Studies in the Intellectual History of Tokugawa Japan*, trans. Mikiso Hane (Tokyo: University of Tokyo Press; Princeton: Princeton University Press, 1974), p. 269.

11. Kenzō Tange and Noboru Kawazoe, *Ise, Prototypes of Japanese Architecture* (Cambridge, Mass.: MIT Press, 1965), pp. 18–19.

12. Ibid., p. 52.

5 *Ka* (Hypothesis) and *Hi* (Spirit)

1. David Riesman, *The Lonely Crowd: A Study of the Changing American Character* (New Haven: Yale University Press, 1950).

2. *Nihon no Toshi Kūkan* (Urban Space in Japan) (Tokyo: Shōkokusha, 1968).

3. *The Manifesto of Metabolism* (Tokyo: Bijutsu Shuppansha, 1960).

4. Christopher Alexander, "A City Is Not a Tree," *Architectural Forum* 122, no. 1 (April 1965).

5. See Kiyonori Kikutake, *Taisha Kenchiku Ron—Ka, Kata, Katachi* (The Metabolic Theory of Architecture—Ka, Kata, Katachi) (Tokyo: Shōko-kusha, 1969).

6. The Japanese language comprises elements of Chinese (notably in the writing system) as well as a core of meanings considered to have originated in Japan. The term *wago* refers to both the Japanese core component and the language itself as it is believed to have existed before the absorption of Chinese influence. [*Trans.*]

7. The power and fascination of the work of the folklorist, novelist, and poet Shinobu Origuchi (1887–1953) epitomizes this Japanese language-power. In his novel *Shisha no Sho* (The Book of the Dead), for instance, he poetically reconstructs a part of Japanese ancient mythology. His use of language returns to the original telling of the myth, rather than supplying an analytic interpretation. Concerning this, see Hisaki Matsuura, *Origuchi Shinobu Ron* (On Shinobu Origuchi) (Tokyo: Ōta Shuppan, 1995). [*Trans.*]

8. Masao Maruyama's concept of *kosō* (the ancient layer) of Japan speaks to this fundamental dimension of cultural consciousness. See "Rekishi Ishiki Ni Okeru Kosō" (The Ancient Layer in the Historical Consciousness) (1972), in *Chūsei to Hangyaku* (Loyalty and Rebellion) (Tokyo: Chikuma Shobō, 1992). [*Trans.*]

9. The members included Teiji Itō, Arata Isozaki, Akira Tsuchida, Yasuyoshi Hayashi, Reiko Tomita, Keiichi Ōmura, Jirō Watanabe, Kenji Fukuzawa, Kei Murai, and Kiyoshi Yamagishi, among others.

10. Arata Isozaki, "Method of Urban Design," included in Isozaki, *Kūkan-e* (Toward Space) (Tokyo: Kajima Shuppan Kai, 1997), p. 118.

11. Arata Isozaki, "Invisible City," ibid., p. 391.

12. Uzō Nishiyama, "Jyūtaku Kūkan no Yō-to/Ko-sei ni okeru Shoku-shin-bunri-ron" (Separation between Eating and Sleeping in Residential Space), in *Collection of Essays for the Assembly of the Architectural Association*, April 1942.

13. *Hakkō ichi-u* (the whole world under one roof) implies that the whole world should be ruled by the imperial house. *Hakkō* means four directions (i.e., the world), and *ichi-u* signifies one household. Such ancient terms

were freely resorted to in the context of official policy implementing the Greater East Asia Co-prosperity Sphere.

14. Arata Isozaki, "The Place of the King as an Absentee," *SD*, January 1984, and later included in *Shuhō ga* (On Method) (Tokyo: Kajima Shuppan Kai, 1997), p. 324.

15. Ibid., p. 326.

16. Roland Barthes, *The Empire of Signs*, trans. Richard Howard (New York: Hill and Wang, 1982).

17. Akira Asada, "Itsu Postmodern wa Kūkyo na Kigō kara Nukedasuka?" (When Will Postmodernity Get Away from the Empty Sign?), *Kōkoku Hihyō*, no. 7/8 (1985).

6 *Ma* (Interstice) and Rubble

1. Arata Isozaki, *Kenchiku no Kaitai* (The Dissolution of Architecture) (Tokyo: Kajima Shuppan Kai, 1977), pp. i–ii.

2. Recently, the piece was reconstructed in full for the Zentrum für Kunst und Medientechnologie at Karlsruhe in 2002, and subsequently began a world tour.

3. Arata Isozaki, "Fuka-katei," text accompanying *Incubation Process*, later published in Isozaki, *Kūkan-e* (Tokyo: Kajima Shuppan Kai, 1997), p. 40.

4. Ibid., p. 39.

5. Kamo-no-Chōmei, *Hōjōki, Visions of a Torn World*, trans. Yasuhiko Moriguchi and David Jenkins (Berkeley, Calif.: Stone Bridge Press, 1996).

6. Bashō, *The Narrow Road to the Far North and Selected Haiku*, trans. Dorothy Britten (Tokyo and New York: Kodansha International, 1974).

7. Munetada (1421–1502) was a poet of the Muromachi period who specialized in the *renga* (linked verse) form of *waka*. [*Trans.*]

8. Dōgen, *Shōbōgenzō, Zen Essays*, trans. Thomas Cleary (Honolulu: University of Hawaii Press, 1986); see the chapter "Being Time" (pp. 104–109). The expression "time comes flying" is however my own translation. [*Trans.*]

9. Arata Isozaki "Yami no kūkan" (The Space of Darkness) (1964), included in *Kūkan-e*, p. 140.

10. Ibid., p. 154.

11. See Motoori Norinaga, *Kojiki-den* (The Ancient Records), trans. and annotated by Ann Wehmeyer (Ithaca, N.Y.: Cornell University Press, 1997).

12. *Ma*, like virtually all ideograms employed in Japanese, is pronounced differently depending on whether it forms part of a compound or is used alone. [*Trans.*]

13. I refer to Roland Barthes, *The Empire of Signs*, trans. Richard Howard (New York: Hill and Wang, 1982).

14. Arata Isozaki, "What Can Be Sold from Japan" (1977), included in Isozaki, *Image Game* (Tokyo: Kajima Shuppan Kai, 1990), p. 166; translation modified.

15. Translation based on entry in Susumu Ōno, *Iwanami Kogo Jiten* (Iwanami Dictionary of Old Japanese) (Tokyo: Iwanami Shoten, 1982).

16. The nine aspects of *ma* selected are as follows:

In *himorogi*, *ma* is a way of indicating the space where the gods' advent occurs: examples are *shinkyō* (mirror to invite gods), *rissa* (mound of sand), and *himorogi* (gods' fence).

In *hashi*, *ma* articulates the world: *en* (periphery), *hashi* (bridge), *fudara-tokai* (Buddhist monks' setting sail on coffin-shaped ships in the quest of becoming living Buddhas), the *kakari-bashi* (a bridge from the earth to the realm of the divine) in Izumo Shrine.

In *yami* (darkness), *ma* is supported through absolute darkness: *yōgō-zu* (painting depicting the unrepresentable: gods as indicated by their shadows), *nigatsu-dō* (where the festival to invite gods, actually a shadow of a priest on a gauze curtain, takes place), and also the conventional Noh stage.

In *suki* (aperture), *ma* is a constructive element of living space: *sōan* (thatched-roof cottage), *katsura-dana* (type of alcove for the exhibition of art), and *okoshi-ezu* (folding paper model for a teahouse, assimilating elevation and plan).

In *utsuroi* (transience), *ma* is a breath sensing the moment of transition: *akigusa* (image of autumn grasses that symbolizes the changing seasons), *gankō* (the flight pattern of wild geese depicted in paintings or used as a compositional device in building), and *tagasode-byōbu* (screen depicting kimono).

In *utsushimi* (projection of the body), *ma* is a topos in which life is being lived: *kura-zashiki* (hybrid storage/living space), *kamado* (cooking stove with embedded kettles), and *shinbutsu-haichi-zu* (the emplacement of Buddha or other gods in a traditional domestic setting).

In *sabi* (an aesthetic analogy with corrosion, or rust), *ma* is filled with an awareness of extinction: *gaki-zōshi* (depiction of the invasion of fate, as grotesque ogres, into a noble family), *kusō-zu* (depiction of inevitable extinction and decay), and *sekitei* (stone garden).

In *susabi* (to play), *ma* is a feature of the arrangement of signs: Tokyo *mura* (Tokyo, that great village where *ma* is filled/eaten up), *sentaku* (divine message), and *Nikkō Karamon* (an extremely decorative gate in Nikkō, which Bruno Taut regarded as kitsch).

In *michiyuki* (the path to go), *ma* organizes the process of transposition: *shinjū-ko* (lovers' suicide journey), *kaiyū-shiki-teien* (large garden designed for strolling), and *gojūsan-tsugi* (53 checkpoints along the Tokaido route in Tokugawa Japan, often depicted or written about).

The following artists originally participated in the "Ma" exhibition: Shirō Kuramata (1934–1991), Kishin Shinoyama (1940–), Kōhei Sugiura (1932–), Jirō Takamatsu (1936–1998), Sotoji Nakamuta (1906–1997), Yukio Futagawa (1932–), Seigō Matsuoka (1944–), Issei Miyake (1938–), Aiko Miyawaki (1929–), Shūji Yamada (1939–), Shimon Yotsuya (1944–), Tatsumi Hijikata (1928–1986), Yōko Ashigawa, Min Tanaka (1945–), Tadashi Suzuki (1939–), Kayoko Shiraishi (1941–), Takehisa Kosugi (1938–), Akio Suzuki (1941–), Tōru Takemitsu (1930–1996), Toshio Kidō (Tendai sect ritual performer) (1930–), Katsuya Yokoyama (1934–), and Seikin Tomiyama.

17. See Arata Isozaki, "On Ruins—The Exhibition of the Japanese Pavilion in the Venice Biennale," *Lotus International* 93 (1997).

18. I several times made presentations concerning the similarities between Platonic *chora* and Japanese *ma* at the ANY conferences that began in 1990. I tried to show how *ma* pointed to a state where time and space were undifferentiated, while *chora* acted as the sieve that articulates the world. It is my contention that "rubble" links the two phenomena. *Chora* as the sieve is shaking the four elements, while rubble is the remaining state of having been shaken out. *Ma* fills the chasm between things with rubble. Thus, in the pebbles of *yuniwa*, or the white sand in stone gardens, I cannot help hearing the vibrations caused by Demiurgos or the wave of voices inviting *kami*.

At the origin of all this were Greece and Japan. But, standing on the border that has now disappeared, I sense both as equidistant. At last the old problematic of Japan-ness is no longer an issue.

7 Fall and Mimicry: A Case Study of the Year 1942 in Japan

1. "What the future architectural style of our nation should be" refers to the title of the first official debate of the Japan Architectural Society. There were four main opinions: Shirō Mishima advocated eclecticism (Japanese/Western); Sada Sekino favored creation of a new style by

learning from all styles of human history; Uheiji Nagano was Eurocentric; and Chūta Itō stressed Japanese tradition since antiquity.

2. See, for example, Benedict Anderson, *Imagined Communities* (London: Verso, 1983).

3. Ryūichi Hamaguchi, "Nihon Kokumin Kenchiku Yōshiki no Sho-mondai" (final part of *The Problem of Style in Japan's National Architecture*), in *Shin Kenchiku*, October 1944 (see ch. 2, note 2).

4. In *Kenchiku Zasshi* (Architecture Journal), no. 690 (September 1942).

5. Shōichi Inoue, *Senjiki Nihon-no Kenchikuka* (Japanese Architects during the War) (Tokyo: Asahi Shinbunsha, 1995), p. 230.

6. Ango Sakaguchi, "Nihon Bunka Shikan" (A Personal View of Japanese Culture), included in *Nihon Ron* (On Japan) (Tokyo: Kawade Shobō Shinsha, 1989), pp. 138–139.

7. Ibid., pp. 115–116.

8. Ango Sakaguchi, "Daraku Ron" (Essay on the Fall) (1946) and "Kokuhō Shobō Kekkō Ron" (Never Mind if National Treasures are Burned Down) (1951), collected in *Nihon Ron*.

9. Sutemi Horiguchi, "Yōshiki naki Yōshiki" (Style without Style) (1939), included in Horiguchi, *Ie to Niwa no Kūkan-kōsei* (The Spatial Composition of Home and Garden) (Tokyo: Kajima Shuppan Kai, 1974).

10. Sutemi Horiguchi, *Rikyū no Chashitsu* (The Teahouse of Rikyū), first published serially in the April, July, and August issues of the journal *Sadō Geppō* in 1940 and republished in book form (Tokyo: Iwanami Shoten, 1949).

11. Sakaguchi, "Nihon Bunka Shikan," p. 140.

12. Sakaguchi, "Kokuhō Shobō Kekkō Ron," p. 296.

13. Hideo Kobayashi, *Mujō to iu Koto* (A Thing Called Transience) (Tokyo: Shinchō Bunko, 1942), p. 74.

14. Hideo Kobayashi, *Motoori Norinaga* (Tokyo: Shinchōsha, 1977).

8 The Problematic Called "Ise"

1. Shunichi Amanuma, *Nihon Kenchikushi-yō* (Summary of Japanese Architectural History) (Nara: Asuka-en, 1927).

2. Chūta Itō, "Nihon Jinja Kenchiku no Hattatsu" (The Development of Japanese Shrine Architecture), *Kenchiku Zasshi* (Architecture Journal), January 1901.

3. Taisha (literally, big shrine), Jinja (shrine), and Jingū (shrine palace) are all slightly differently weighted generic terms for shrine. [*Trans.*]

4. Chūta Itō, "Hōryū-ji Kenchiku Ron" (On the Architecture of Hōryū-ji), in *Kenchiku Zasshi* (Architecture Journal), November 1893.

5. Chūta Itō, "Kodai Kenchiku Ron" (On Ancient Architecture), in *Kōkogaku Kōza* (A Course in Archaeology), August 1930.

6. Bruno Taut, *Nihon-bi no Sai-hakken* (Rediscovery of Japanese Beauty), trans. from the German by Hideo Shinoda (Tokyo: Iwanami Shinsho, 1939), and Bruno Taut, *Nippon* (Japan), trans. from the German by Toshirō Mori (Tokyo: Kōdansha, 1933).

7. Chūta Itō, "Nihon Kenchiku no Hensen" (The Transformation of Japanese Architecture), public lecture of 1934 available in Chūta Itō, *Nihon Kenchiku no Kenkyū* (Studies in Japanese Architecture) (Tokyo: Hara Shobō, 1982), vol. 1, p. 489.

8. Chūta Itō, "Mei-kenchiku Ron" (On Masterpieces of Architecture), published in the literary monthly *Bungei Shunjū*, July 1935; later in *Itō Chūta Chosaku-shū* (Collected Works of Chūta Itō) (Tokyo: Hara Shobō, 1982), vol. 6, p. 107.

9. Sutemi Horiguchi, *Kenchiku ni okeru Nihonteki-na-mono* (Japan-ness in Architecture), in *Horiguchi Sutemi Chosaku-shū* (Collected Works of Sutemi Horiguchi) (Tokyo: Kajima Shuppan Kai, 1978), vol. 3, p. 235.

10. Ibid., p. 230. Taut's essay "Wie ich die japanische Architektur Ansehe?" (How Do I View Japanese Architecture?) was published in the New Year's issue of a prominent new monthly *Kokusai Kenchiku* (International Architecture), January 1934.

11. Bruno Taut, *Houses and People of Japan* (Tokyo: Sanseidō, 1937), p. 139.

12. Chūta Itō, "'Architektur' no Hongi o Ronjite Sono Yakuji o Senteishi, Waga 'Zōka Gakkai' no kaimei o Nozomu" (Discussing the Essence of ARCHITECTURE, in Hopes of Avoiding the Conventional Term *Zōka-gakkai* [Building-House Society] in Its Translation), *Kenchiku Zasshi* (Architecture Journal), June 1894.

13. Hirotarō Ōta, *Nihon no Kenchiku, Rekishi to Dentō* (Japanese Architecture: History and Tradition) (Tokyo: Chikuma Shobō, 1968), p. 50.

14. Noboru Kawazoe, "Shin-iki to Sen-gu" (The Sacred Domain and the Installation of the Shrine), included in *Ise no Ōkami* (The Great God of Ise), ed. Masaaki Ueda (Tokyo: Chikuma Shobō, 1988), p. 29.

15. Ibid., p. 32.

16. Kenzō Tange and Noboru Kawazoe, *Ise, Prototype of Japanese Architecture* (Cambridge, Mass.: MIT Press, 1965), pp. 18–19.

17. See "Form and Design," in Vincent Scully, Jr., *Louis I. Kahn* (New York: George Braziller, 1962).

18. Tange, *Ise*, p. 52.

19. See Taku Tanaka, "Ise Jingū no Sōki to Hatten" (The Inception and Development of Ise Shrine), included in *Tanaka Taku Chosaku-shū* (Collected Works of Taku Tanaka) (Tokyo: Kokusho Kankō Kai, 1985), vol. 4, p. 178.

20. Heijō-kyō was located near Nara city and lasted from 710 to 784. Nagaoka-kyō was located in Mukō city near Kyoto and lasted from 784 to 794. Heian-kyō is essentially today's city of Kyoto, which as capital lasted from 794 to 1868, when it was removed to Tokyo at the Meiji Restoration. [*Trans.*]

21. The first ritual after a *tennō* is enthroned, in which he, unassisted, offers up the year's first crops to the Sun Goddess (Amaterasu Ōmikami) and the Gods of Heaven and Earth (Tenshinchigi). This ritual only occurs once during the lifetime of each emperor. [*Trans.*]

9 Identity over Time

1. Yoshio Watanabe (photographer) and Sutemi Horiguchi, *Ise Jingū* (Tokyo: Heibonsha, 1973); quoting from Horiguchi's essay "Ise Jingū," p. 14.

2. For architectural details of Ise Jingū, see Kenzō Tange and Noboru Kawazoe, *Ise, Prototype of Japanese Architecture*, with photographs by Yoshio Watanabe (Cambridge, Mass.: MIT Press, 1965).

3. Toshio Fukuyama, *Ise Jingū no Kenchiku to Rekishi* (Architecture and History of Ise Jingū) (Tokyo: Nihon Shiryō Kankō Kai, 1976).

4. Toshio Fukuyama, *Jinja Kenchiku no Kenkyū* (Studies in Shrine Architecture) (Tokyo: Chūō Kōron Bijutsu Shuppan, 1984), p. 94.

5. Toshio Fukuyama, *Nihon Kenchiku Shi Kenkyu* (Studies in Japanese Architectural History) (Tokyo: Kokusui Shobō, 1968). Note that the Muromachi period is a broader modern designation for the Ashikaga reign. [*Ed.*]

6. Fukuyama, *Jinja Kenchiku no Kenkyū*, p. 172.

7. The Shōsōin is located just northwest of Tōdai-ji in Nara city. It is the country's oldest storage structure, housing Buddhist texts as well as Emperor Shōmu's art treasures, which include various artifacts, such as musical instruments, from all over Asia. The building is a large-scale log-cabin-style structure raised on posts. [*Trans.*]

8. Yuko Yoshino, *Kakusareta Kamigami—Kodai Shinkō to Inyō-gogyō Setsu* (Hidden Gods—Ancient Worship and Yin-Yang) (Tokyo: Jinbun Shoin, 1992).

9. Fukuyama, *Nihon Kenchiku Shi Kenkyu*, p. 41.

10. Shunpei Kamiyama, *Zoku-Kamigami no Taikei, Kiki Shinwa no Seijiteki Haikei* (*A Sequel-System of Gods: The Political Background of Japanese Mythologies*) (Tokyo: Chukō Shinsho, 1975), p. 157.

11. Teiji Itō, *Chōgen* (Tokyo: Shinchōsha, 1994), p. 196.

12. Eizō Inagaki, "Shikinen Sengū-no Rekishi-teki Kōsatsu" (An Architectural Account of Periodic Relocation), included in *Nihon Kenchiku no Tokushitsu* (Characteristics of Japanese Architecture) (Tokyo: Chūō Kōron, 1976).

13. Martin Heidegger, *Being and Time*, trans. John Macquarrie and Edward Robinson (San Francisco: Harper, 1962), pp. 396ff.

10   Archetype of Veiling

1. *Minashiro* implies ship, receptacle, and femininity—at the same time.

2. *Kan-name-sai* at Ise is the yearly festival ("in which the deities taste [the new rice]") celebrating the new harvest. It accompanies the ritual of offering food to the Sun Goddess (or divine imperial ancestress). In the Outer Shrine (*gekū*), it takes place from October 15 to 16, in the Inner Shrine (*naikū*) from October 16 to 17. Also at the Imperial Palace, Ise Jingū is worshipped on the 17th.

3. See Kazuhiro Tatsumi, *Takadono no Kodai-gaku* (The Ancestry of the Elevated Sanctuary) (Tokyo: Hakusuisha, 1990), p. 148.

4. Ibid., p. 152.

5. Izumo's legend consists of stories concerning the gods of the Izumo region in present-day Shimane prefecture, some of which also appear in *Kojiki* and *Nihongi*. In one of them, entitled "Land Pulling" (*Kuni-biki*), for instance, a god called Yatsukamizuomitsu-no-mikoto cut off a part of the Silla kingdom (located in the Korean peninsula) and pulled it closer

to Japan to enlarge his own territory. Some of these stories also propose the idea that giant gods made everything.

6. In fact there is another exception in Japan—namely, the ancient middle gate at Hōryū-ji. This is said to be owing to the asymmetrical arrangement of the Kondo (Golden Pavilion) and Pagoda (*gojyū-no-tō*) on either side of an imaginary north-south axis; in the center is a lecture hall (*kōdo*). This layout required closing the view through the center by opting for an even number of bays in the gate.

11 A Fabricated Origin: Ise and the Jinshin Disturbance

1. *Nihongi*, trans. W. G. Aston (Rutland, Vermont, and Tokyo: Charles E. Tuttle, 1972), p. 151. The translation is slightly modified and some parenthetical material added. [*Trans.*]

2. Ibid., p. 176.

3. *The Ten Thousand Leaves*, trans. Ian Hideo Levy (Princeton: Princeton University Press, 1981), pp. 128–129.

4. See the section on Empress Jitō in *Nihongi*, pp. 405–406.

5. Ibid., p. 112. Translation slightly modified.

6. Yuko Yoshino, *Jitō Tennō—Nihon Kodai Teiō no Jujutsu* (The Empress Jitō: The Magic of the Ancient Japanese Emperors) (Tokyo: Jinbun Shoin, 1987).

7. Isezō Umezawa, *Kojiki to Nihonshoki no Seiritsu* (The Establishment of *Kojiki* and *Nihongi*) (Tokyo: Yoshikawa Kōbun-kan, 1988), p. 168.

8. Much later on, this caused many Japanese readers to prefer *Kojiki* to *Nihongi*—from a nationalistic point of view. [*Trans.*]

9. Nobukuni Koyasu, "Norinaga Sai-ron" (Norinaga Revisited), in *Hihyō Kūkan*, no. 11 (Tokyo: Fukutake Shoten, 1993), p. 60.

12 The Modern Fate of Pure Geometric Form

1. Adolf Max Vogt, *Russische und französische Revolutions-Architektur 1917/ 1789* (Cologne: M. DuMont Schauberg, 1974).

2. Manfredo Tafuri, *Theories and History of Architecture*, trans. Giorgio Verrecchia (New York: Harper and Row, 1980) pp. 26–28. This esoteric remodeling project for the church in Rome was widely discussed by Tafuri and is now best illustrated in John Wilton-Ely, *Piranesi as Architect*

and Designer (New York: Pierpont Morgan Library and New Haven: Yale University Press, 1993). [*Ed.*].

3. Karl Marx, *The Eighteenth Brumaire of Louis Bonaparte* (New York: International Publishers, 1898), p. 5; quoted in Tafuri, *Theories and History of Architecture*, p. 26.

4. See Emil Kaufmann, *Von Ledoux bis Le Corbusier: Ursprung und Entwicklung der autonomen Architektur* (Vienna: Passer, 1933).

13 Chōgen's Constructivism

1. Tōdai-ji was originally built in 745 by Emperor Shōmu. Jōdo-ji at Ono was founded by Chōgen as a branch establishment of Tōdai-ji. Japanese temples as well as shrines, such as Ise, incorporate various halls consecrated to the different gods of their respective cosmologies. Jōdo-dō is a type of hall for Amitabha as worshipped by the Pure Land sect (Jōdo-shū); in this section we refer to the Jōdo-dō at Jōdo-ji, but the term may also indicate this type of hall, more generally, as found at Pure Land temples throughout Japan. [*Trans.*]

2. This particular book of secret carpentry techniques, *Shōmei*, written by Hirauchi Masanobu in 1608 (Keichō 13), consists of five volumes, divided by building type: palace, gate, temple, tower, and shrine.

14 The Five-Ring Pagoda in Historical Turmoil

1. Kōfuku-ji is considered one of the "seven great temples" of Nara and was relocated from Heijō-kyō (an ancient former capital to the south of Nara) to its present site in the early eighth century.

2. See *Tale of the Heike*, trans., with an introduction, by Helen Craig McCullough (Stanford, California: Stanford University Press, 1988).

3. See Kamo no Chōmei, *Hōjō-ki, Visions of a Torn World*, trans. Yasuhiko Moriguchi and David Jenkins (Berkeley, California: Stone Bridge Press, 1996). Translation modified.

4. Kei-ha is the name of a school of sculptors who supplied Buddhist statues. It arose in the tenth century and continued to be productive through the seventeenth. By the twelfth century, three masters had appeared: Kōkei, Unkei, and Kaikei. All made use of the name Kei. The suffix *ha* indicates "school of."

5. Heian court culture was the epitome of *wayō-ka*. It is known for its refinement and its gorgeousness of detail (in building, music, literature,

and general aristocratic accoutrements), as opposed to the simpler, more powerful aesthetic of *samurai* culture that took hold everywhere after the eleventh century. [*Trans.*]

6. Itsukushima Jinja is located at Itsukushima in present-day Hiroshima prefecture. Its pierlike main pavilion and the *torii* gate standing in the sea are famous. The Heike clan cherished the shrine. [*Trans.*]

7. See Johann Wolfgang von Goethe, *Italian Journey*, ed. Thomas P. Saine and Jeffrey L. Sammons, trans. Robert R. Heitner (New York: Suhrkamp, 1989).

15 Mandala and Site Plan at Jōdo-ji

1. Hachiman is a native Japanese god, but according to the traditional interpretation that all Japanese gods originated in India, he is Amitabha metamorphosed. [*Trans.*]

2. The mandala of Shingon sect Buddhism has two separate domains: *kongō kai* said to approach Mahavairocana from the standpoint of wisdom, and *taizō kai* that approaches the deity via mercy or truth. [*Trans.*]

3. Kasuga Jinja is located in metropolitan Nara, while the more remote Kumano Jinja stands in Yakumo village, Yatsuka county, in Shimane prefecture.

16 The Architectonics of the Jōdo-dō (Pure Land Pavilion) at Jōdo-ji

1. See Hirotarō Ōta, *Nihon Kenchiku no Tokushitsu* (The Nature of Japanese Architecture), Nihon Kenchikushi Ron-shu Series (Tokyo: Iwanami Shoten, 1983).

2. *Gasshō-zukuri* (principal-rafter style) is a type of folk housing preserved in certain areas in central Japan, i.e., Hida and Shirakawa. The roof has a precipitous slope, and the roof truss is massive to accommodate two or three attic stories devoted to silkworm culture.

3. This Jōchō was a sculptor of Jōdo sect Buddhist images. His style was known as a revival of the ancient culture of the Tenpyō era (729–749) of Emperor Tenmu. Their chief characteristic is the soft, rounded style of representation. Jōchō's Buddha statues all share this aspect, thus creating a particularly affectionate image of the Buddhist deity. He also promoted a new technique of wooden sculpture, *yosegi-zukuri*, by means of which an image could be assembled out of several pieces of wood, rather than a single trunk.

4. "In Buddhism, ornament [*sōshoku*] is referred to as *shōgon*. The Buddhist scripture says that Shaka decorated himself gorgeously before he entered ascetic practice. He wore a crown on his head, a *yōraku* [a kind of string] of seven kinds of jewels, and bracelets. The fact that Bosatsu (Bodhisattva) images are decorated with ornaments may be linked to this practice of the historical Buddha before he renounced the world." Quoted with slight changes from *Wa-ei Taisho Nihon Bijitsu Yōgo Jiten* (A Comparative Dictionary of Japanese Art Terms) (Tokyo: Tokyo Bijutsu, 1990).

17 Big Buddha Pavilion (Daibutsu-den) at Tōdai-ji

1. These reconstructions were made by Tadashi Sekino and Minoru Ō-oka. See Tadashi Sekino, "Tenpyo sōritsu no Tōdai-ji Daibutsu-den oyobi sono Butsu-zō" (On the Big Buddha and the Pavilion of Tōdai-ji Built in the Tenpyo Era), *Kenchiku Zasshi* (Architecture Journal), nos. 182 and 183 (1902); and Minoru Ō-oka, *Nanto Nara-dai-ji no Kenkyū* (Studies of Seven Temples in Nara) (Tokyo: Chūō Kōron, 1966).

2. Eisai (1141–1215) founded one of the major Zen sects, Rinzai-shū. He went to Sung twice, in 1168 and 1178, and brought back the seeds to grow tea. The sect is one among those that nurtured the culture of tea in Japan at this time. [*Trans.*]

3. Gyōyū (1163–1241) studied doctrines of both orthodox and esoteric Buddhism (*ken mitsu*). He became priest in residence of Hachiman-gu in Kamakura. But he subsequently moved to Jufuku-ji, where Eisai presided, and made himself the latter's disciple.

18 Chōgen's Archi-vision

1. Hōnen (1133–1212) had founded the Jōdo sect, which more than any other permeated the masses. He was exiled at one time, when the mighty increase in his followers threatened the stability of the older Buddhist sects.

20 Brunelleschi versus Chōgen

1. Antonio Manetti, *De dignitate et excellentia hominis [Vita di Filippo Brunelleschi]*, ms. ca. 1452, first printed in Basel, 1532. (Critical ed., Ann Arbor Microfilms, 1965.)

2. Giorgio Vasari, *Le vite de' più eccellenti pittori, scultori e architettori*, 1568.

21 Chōgen/*Daibutsu-yō* and Eisai/*Zenshu-yō*

1. See Fumihiko Gomi, *Daibutsu Saiken* (Reconstruction of the Big Buddha Pavilion) (Tokyo: Kōdansha Sensho, 1995).

2. Nobuzō Sugiyama, "Chōgen no Kenchiku Giho to Kayano-mori Iseki" (Chōgen's Architectural Engineering and the Ruins of Kayano-mori), *Bukkyō Geijutsu* (Buddhist Art Magazine), no. 105 (1976), p. 57.

23 *Raigō* Materialized

1. Hitotarō Ōta, *Nihon no Kenchiku* (On Japanese Architecture) (Tokyo: Chikuma Shobō, 1968), p. 114.

25 Katsura and Its Space of Ambiguity

1. This chapter and chapter 26 were originally written in 1983; together they formed an essay "Katsura and Its Space of Ambiguity," included in Arata Isozaki, *Mitate-no-shuhō* (Method of Diagnosis) (Tokyo: Kajima Shuppan Kai, 1983). The essay with photographs by Yasuhiro Ishimoto was published in English as *Katsura Villa: Space and Form*, trans. John D. Lamb (New York: Rizzoli, 1983) and also in Japanese (Tokyo: Iwanami Shoten, 1983). The material is retranslated and edited for the present volume, with acknowledgments to the earlier translation. Chapter 27 was written in 2000 and is first translated here. [*Trans.*]

2. The ex-emperor's ninth son Yasuhito (1643–1665) became the third head of the Hachijō Imperial Family.

3. See Akira Naitō, *Shin Katsura Rikyū Ron* (A New Account of Katsura Villa) (Tokyo: Kajima Shuppan Kai, 1967).

4. Prince Yakahito's poetry includes the themes *Katsura san kei* (three sceneries of Katsura) and *Katsura san sō* (three windows of Katsura).

5. In Japanese, the term *konomi* (taste) alters to *[g]onomi* when preceded by a modifier, as in the phrase *Enshū-gonomi*, affording phonetic transition. [*Trans.*]

6. Kenzō Tange, *Katsura: Tradition and Creation in Japanese Architecture* (New Haven: Yale University Press, 1960).

7. See note 1.

8. Osamu Mori, *Katsura Rikyū no Kenkyū* (The Study of Katsura Villa) (Tokyo: Tōto Bunka Shuppan Kai, 1955).

9. Takaho Itagaki and Sutemi Horiguchi, *Kenchiku Yoshiki Ron-sō* (Anthology of Architectural Styles) (Tokyo: Tokyo Rokubun Kan, 1932).

10. Bruno Taut, *Houses and People of Japan* (Tokyo: Sanseidō, 1937), p. 291.

11. Sutemi Horiguchi, *Kenchiku ni okeru Nihonteki-na-mono* (Japan-ness in Architecture), included in *Horiguchi Sutemi Chosaku-shū* (Collected Works of Sutemi Horiguchi) (Tokyo: Kajima Shuppan Kai, 1978), vol. 3. (One should emphasize the eponymous title of the present volume as in large sense a tribute to Horiguchi's taste, courage, and scholarship. [*Ed.*])

12. Sutemi Horiguchi, "Yōshiki naki Yōshiki" (Style without Style), first published in *Kokusai Kenchiku*, February 1939; later included in Horiguchi, *Ie to Niwa no Kūkan-kōsei* (The Spatial Composition of Home and Garden) (Tokyo: Kajima Shuppan Kai, 1974).

13. Sutemi Horiguchi, *Katsura Rikyū* (Tokyo: Mainichi Shinbunsha, 1952).

14. Ibid.

15. Taut, *Houses and People of Japan*, p. 274.

16. Horiguchi, *Katsura Rikyū*.

17. Ibid.

18. This, and the following discussion of Enshū, refer to the mid-1980s, the time of writing of the original essay from which the present chapter is taken. [*Ed.*]

26 Architectonic Polysemy

1. See Teiji Itō, *Chusei Jūtaku Shi* (History of Medieval Residences) (Tokyo: Tokyo University Press, 1958).

2. Tatsusaburō Hayashiya, *Chusei Bunka no Kichō* (The Ethos of Medieval Culture) (Tokyo: Tokyo University Press, 1953). Sumiya is the only extant building of its kind and is today a museum. [*Ed.*]

3. Hirotarō Ōta, *Shoin-zukuri* (Tokyo: Tokyo University Press, 1966).

4. See Akira Naitō, *Shin Katsura Rikyū Ron* (A New Account of Katsura) (Tokyo: Kajima Shuppan Kai, 1967).

5. For a more nuanced discussion, see Hidetoshi Saitō, *Meihō Nihon no Bijutsu, Katsura Rikyū* (Treasures of Japanese Art, Katsura Imperial Villa) (Tokyo: Shōgaku Kan, 1982).

6. The word *kake* has a number of different meanings, including pattern of vocalization, method of drapery, or even buying something on credit. Most suited to Katsura is probably the instance of *kake-kotoba*, where *kake* means word *shift*, or a play on words (paronomasia). [*Trans.*]

7. See Atsushi Mori, *Kobori Enshū* (Tokyo: Sōgensha, 1974).

8. In 1643, Enshū transported the Kyakuden (guest room) of Urin-in to the abbot's quarters at Kohō-an (his own family temple), and then moved the Bōsen tearoom from Ryūkō-in there as well. Subsequently, Enshū attached the Jikinyū-ken Shoin to the northwest side of the Bōsen tearoom, so that the two structures created a corner backdrop to the garden.

9. In his *Katsura Rikyū no Kenkyū* (Tokyo: Tōto Bunka Shuppan Kai, 1955), Osamu Mori confirms the compass bearing of the rise of the mid-autumn moon in Kyoto in 1624 (Kanei 1) at 20 degrees southeast.

10. This refers to the mid-1980s, when this chapter was written in its original form.

11. This was the diary kept between 1635 and 1668 by Hōrin Joshō, chief priest of Kaen-ji in Kyoto, entitled *Kakumei Ki*.

12. Two examples are extant: teahouses at Inari Taisha in Fushimi, Kyoto, and at Minase Jingū, Osaka.

13. We can imagine the older layer of ancient garden design from modern excavations at Mōtsu-ji (built 850) in Hiraizumi, in remote Iwate prefecture. These record the appearance of a Jōdo-style garden from the Heian period—a Buddhist representation of the Pure Land arranged in a mandala-based composition.

14. Cf. note 11. Hōrin Joshō, *Kakumei-ki* (Kyoto: Rokuon-ji, 1964), pp. 366–367.

15. See Imperial Prince Yakahito, *Katsura Betsugyō ni Asobu no Ki* (Record of a Visit to Katsura Villa).

16. *The Ten Thousand Leaves* (Man'yōshu), trans. Ian Hideo Levy (Princeton: Princeton University Press, 1981), p. 294.

17. See Sutemi Horiguchi, *Katsura Rikyū* (Tokyo: Mainichi Shinbunsha, 1952).

27   Authorship of Katsura: The Diagonal Line

1. Matsudaira Fumai (1751–1818) rose to seventh head of the feudal domain of Matsue at the age of 17. He became familiar with the tea ceremony while also studying the doctrines of Zen Buddhism. In the later

years of his life he devoted all his time to tea pursuits and is earlier recorded as having performed the tea ceremony at Kohō-an in Kyoto.

2. The comment comes from the diary of the priest Ishin Sūden of the Konchi-in, dated August 28, 1627.

3. The record of these tea ceremonies was kept by three generations of lacquerware merchants: the Matsuya family of Nara—Hisamasa, Hisayoshi, and Hisashige. Their documentation, of more than a hundred years (1533–1650), is one of the greatest sources for scholarship regarding the development of the tea ceremony in Japan. Documents written by Matsuya Hisashige include detailed descriptions of tea ceremonies conducted by Furuta Oribe, Hosokawa Sansai, and Kobori Enshū, among others.

4. Osamu Mori, "Kobori Enshū no Shigoto" (The Work of Kobori Enshū), in *Pamphlet of the National Treasures Research Center in Nara Prefecture*, 1966, p. 133.

5. Ibid.

6. The accounts by Isao Kumakura and Toshinori Nakamura are taken from their remarks in the symposium "Kinsei, Mitsutan-seki, Enshū" (Modernity, Mitsutan Tearoom, Enshū), held at the Faculty of Architecture, Tokyo University, March 2, 2000. I apologize for any oversimplification I may have interposed.

7. *Shaku* is a unit of measure, about 30.3 cm, used widely in premodern Japan.

8. Moreover, in later years, a legend was put about to the effect that this space had been created exclusively to display calligraphy by the Southern Sung Zen master Mitsutan Kanketsu, an important influence on the Rinzai sect of Japanese Buddhism.

Mitsu-tan (Mittan no Seki)
Tearoom, 301–303, 305

Saigyō, 48–50, 55, 56, 125–127,
129, 185
Saihō-ji, 232
Saito, Hidetoshi, 271, 278, 280, 296
Sakaguchi, Ango, 109–110, 112,
113–114
Sakuteiki (The Record of Garden
Making), 36
samurai class, xiii, 180, 184–187, 202,
218, 220, 243, 265, 269, 270–271,
274, 275–276, 280–281, 297,
304–305, 314. *See also* Tokugawa
shōgunate
San-un-shō Tearoom, 305
San Vitale, Ravenna, 236
Scenery in and around Kyoto (folding
screen), 247, 248
secchu-yō, 179–180
Semper, Gottfried, 145
Sendō Palace, 279, 283
Senpuku-ji, 213
Sert, José Luis, 264
shamanism, 159–160, 163, 165
Shien-sō (House of Purple Haze),
11, 38
Shigehira, Taira, 185
Shimoda, Kikutaro, 8–9
Shimomura, Shōtarō, 257, 258
shinden-zukuri, 30, 31, 41, 47, 49, 51,
193, 237, 263, 282, 312, 314
Shinjuku Station (Tokyo), West
Plaza, 73, 78
Shintōism, 12, 15, 31, 66, 86, 119,
126, 128, 130, 139, 142–144, 151,
219, 232–233, 314
Shitennō-ji, 165
Shōbō Genzō, 89
Shōfū-sō (House of Pine Breezes),
34, 39
shōgunate. *See* Kamakura shōgunate;
samurai class; Tokugawa shōgunate
shoin-zukuri, 35, 41, 49, 241, 269–
271, 278–281, 303, 305, 312, 314
Shōsō-in, 139, 315

shrines and temples, typology of, 12,
119–121, 128, 133–140, 147–158,
165–167, 189–193, 315
Silla. *See* Korea
Sitte, Camillo, 59
Smithson, Alison and Peter, 43, 63,
72
Sōgan, Kōgetsu, 301, 304
Sorai, Ogyū, 52, 55, 313
space, 5–8, 24, 27–31, 51, 89–91,
94–95, 198–199
Japanese, 134–135, 264, 273–274,
277–281
Stalin, Joseph, 14, 61, 175
Sūden, Ishin, 292, 297, 304
Sugiura, Kōhei, 81
Sugiyama, Nobuzō, 227
Suiko, Empress, 164
Sujin, Emperor, 159
sukiya-zukuri, 28, 49, 254, 260, 269–
271, 278–281, 303, 305, 315
Sumiyoshi Jinja, 136, 140
Sung dynasty. *See* China
Sunin, Emperor, 159
Superstudio, 83

Tafuri, Manfredo, 174, 175
Tai-an Teahouse, Myōki-an, 298,
301
Taima-ji, 191, 192
Takasago, 287
Takemitsu, Tōru, 90–91
Taketani, Mitsuo, 65
Takizawa, Mayumi, 307
Tale of Genji, x, xix, 282, 287, 288,
289
Talmud, xii
Tang dynasty. *See* China
Tange, Kenzō, 15–19, 24, 25, 29,
30, 31, 37, 38, 39, 40–43, 45,
50–51, 52–57, 59, 63, 71, 78, 83,
86, 87, 105, 106, 108–109, 128,
129, 252–254, 255, 259, 263–267,
295
Tanizaki, Junichirō, 90
Taoism, 5, 140–142, 144
Tatsumi, Kazuhiro, 155